Beyond the Twelve Bens

A History of Clifden and District 1860-1923

BEYOND the Twelve Bens tells the story of the land that lies between the Twelve Bens and the Atlantic Ocean, and of the people who inhabited it during the years 1860 to 1923.

Having lived through the Famine, the tenant farmers of Connemara in the 1860's were fully aware of the vulnerability of their position and the possibility of crop failure recurring was high; for them the future held no promise or hope. If they stayed, there was a good chance they would watch their children die of starvation, fever or disease resulting from malnutrition. So they emigrated in their thousands, hoping for the promise of work and grasping any chance of enjoying a better life. Their passage was paid by well-meaning English and Irish Gentlemen, who believed this was the only solution to Connemara's problems of poverty and want. But those who remained would, in the years that followed, find other solutions to these problems.

However, before freedom, came fame. The turn of the century found Connemara somewhat more prosperous. A railway line, linking Clifden with Galway, was opened in 1895 at a cost of £9,000 per mile. In October 1907, from the Marconi Station at Derrygimla, the first commercial wireless messages were transmitted and received across the Atlantic. It was at the Station also that the first transatlantic flight landed on June 15, 1919, on board were Captain John Alcock and Lieut Arthur Whitton Brown. These events were to ensure Clifden's place in the history of world communications.

Above all else this book tells of the people of Connemara. For be they rich or poor, their lives and their personalities went into the making of Connemara as we find it today.

Beyond The Twelve Bens is a continuation of the author's first book, *History of Clifden 1810-1860*.

Beyond
The Twelve Bens

A History of Clifden and District 1860 — 1923

Kathleen Villiers-Tuthill

To
JOHN
with love.

First Published: 1986
Second Edition: 1990

By the same author:
HISTORY OF CLIFDEN 1810 — 1860

Cover Courtesy of Bord Fáilte
Published by the Author and Printed by The Connacht Tribune

Contents

Illustrations

ABBREVIATIONS

C.T.	Connaught Telegraph.
Conn. Trib.	Connacht Tribune.
G.V.	Galway Vindicator.
SPO	State Papers Office.

Acknowledgements

The staff of the National Library of Ireland; State Papers Office, Dublin Castle; Commissioners of Land; The Institute of Engineers of Ireland; Minnesota Historical Society; Wyoming State Archives, Museums and Historical Department; J.P. Cusack, Connacht Tribune Galway; Sr. M Consilio, Convent of Mercy Clifden; Richard Collis Johnson, The Newberry Library, Chicago and Stewart Clark, Dublin, for cartography. A special word of thanks to Eoin Lavelle for simplifying the J.H. Ryan Paper on the Galway to Clifden Railway; Paddy Clarke for his assistance in my research on the Marconi Wireless Station, Derrygimla.

My thanks also to the many decendants of the families dealt with in this work, for their reminiscences and their patient co-operation in answering my many questions, and for allowing me carry off precious family photographs. To Mrs Alice Coneys for making available to me documents and papers and allowing me to reproduce billheads pertaining to local business houses.

For writing the Foreword, my sincere thanks to Pat Lindsay: who's friendship and advice I have been fortunate to receive, and for proof-reading the manuscript he has my eternal gratitude. My thanks also to Jean Curtin for a superb job typing the manuscript. To my sisters, Barbara Clark and Mary Broderick, for baby-sitting my two sons while I set about interviewing, what at times felt like the entire population of Connemara. To my mother Mrs Teresa Broderick whose criticism was often sought and always appreciated. Most of all, I am deeply grateful to my sponsors, for their generous contribution towards the publication of this work. Extracts from the following publications by permission of their publishers.

From *Memories; Wise and Otherwise* by Rt. Hon. Sir Henry Robinson with permission of Macmillian Publishing Company. From *Isaac Butt and Home Rule* by David Thornley with permission of Grafton Books. From *The Splendid Pauper* by Allen Andrews with permission of Harrap.

Foreword

During the first half of the nineteenth century Samuel Ferguson wrote prolifically in both prose and poetry. In relation to history he made one fascinating exhortation. He urged historians not to concentrate on history in the broad spectrum of the national scene. Such treatment would necessarily be short on detail. He would prefer accounts of local communities. Thus, he argued, would people take pride in their origins and traditions; and, although he did not specifically say so, they might benefit from the experience of a degree of catharsis emanating from an hitherto unknown cause of shame or at least regret. Kathleen Villiers-Tuthill's efforts are, consciously or unconsciously, a response to Ferguson's advice.

In the latter half of this century histories of parishes and baronies multiply year by year. The painstaking research involved is considerable; indeed the careless and often wanton destruction of the sources makes such research more difficult still. Nevertheless these difficulties have been commendably overcome. The author of this book has in this respect, shown extraordinary perseverance and tenacity of purpose.

Her History of Clifden is the result. It is her tribute to her native town, its people, and those of the surrounding district. And their appreciation shall, one hopes, manifest itself in the book's success.

Following the precept of Stephen Gwynn she writes truthfully and charitably. In these pages the industry of the landed people is properly highlighted; the employment they gave is demonstrated in its real importance; their interest in the people's welfare, responsible though it was, does not end merely with the provision of employment.

Recognising hardship they successfully directed their energies to the areas of necessary charitable activities. Up to this very day their achievements have been submerged in a continuous spate of pseudo-patriotic verbiage.

Not alone in Clifden and its surrounds but all over our country stand grim reminders of purposeless acts. Gaunt chimney stacks, rising from roofless wall, ochroid by futile flames mar the beauty of skylines. How useful such buildings now would be in this era of a return to community services! How different might life in Clifden be today if a Marconi Radio Station with the inevitable modern extensions still existed!

The Author poses the question: was the fight for the land qualified by its subsequent use? Potatoes and other crops from overseas! No! Fallow fields truthfully testify! Putting the record straight shall always be the monument to Mrs. Villiers-Tuthill's great literary effort.

Patrick Lindsay
Annaghvaan Island

Chapter I

Clifden - Its foundation and development

Ironically it was the famine of 1822 and the state of distress it created in the west of Ireland that contributed most to the foundation of the town of Clifden. The idea of building a market town and seaport on his estates on the western seaboard was first voiced by John D'Arcy in 1812, but it was ten years before the fruits of his determined efforts began to show signs of success.

When John D'Arcy inherited his Connemara estates in 1804 they were thinly inhabited by fishermen and mountain farmers. The stark landscape of mountain, rock and bog yielded little by way of income to its occupants or landlord. Perhaps this is why the tradition of smuggling became so prevalent along its western coast.

The D'Arcy estates were Kylemore, Sillery and Ardbear. Access was by sea or along the many bridle ways through central Connemara, which were difficult to travel. It was against this background and, it would appear, little private capital, that John embarked on a scheme to establish a new town and seaport at Ardbear. He encouraged merchants into the district,

'offering leases, for ever, of a plot of ground for building, together with four acres of mountain land at a short distance from the proposed site of the town, at 25/- per acre. The earliest agreements between Mr D'Arcy and his tenants were verbal; later when the tenant had built his house and attempts were made to reclaim the land, a written agreement was drawn up'.[1]

However, the venture did not develop as fast as its promoter would have wished. When the potato crop failed in 1821-22, John seized upon the opportunity and canvassed Dublin Castle to contribute Government funds towards the betterment of the population. He wrote a number of letters explaining their poor conditions and pointed out his efforts to establish a town and bring law and order to Connemara. He suggested ways aid could be distributed. Alexander Nimmo, engineer to the western district, was sent to Clifden in 1822. He drew up plans for a quay at the town and various Government bodies contributed financially to its construction. Mr Nimmo was also responsible for the laying down of roads through central Connemara and along the coast, linking Clifden with Galway and Westport.

The following years were to see the town prosper and develop. Contributing factors were; high prices stimulated by exports, local brewing and distilling and the growing population.

'Vessels came to the port from as far away as London and Liverpool. Salt, iron, pitch, tar, hemp, groceries and manufactured goods were imported; corn was taken in return; and for a short time timber was imported from America'.[2]

1. Kathleen Villiers-Tuthill. History of Clifden 1810-1860. P.15.
2. ibid P.17.

11

Lisdoonvarna
10 July 1857

Having seen an article in some of
the papers, stating, that religious persecution
existed in Lisdoon, and that the lives, and
properties of the protestant inhabitants of that
Town, were in danger from the repeated attacks
of the Roman Catholics, I deem it my duty
as the proprietor, and resident Magistrate, to
state to you, for his Excellency's information,
that a more unfounded calumny. never
disgraced the columns of a Publick Journal,
I feel gratified in being able to assure his
Excellency, that in no part of Ireland. do
persons differing in their religious creeds,
live on kinder, or better terms, notwithstanding
the attempts, which have been lately!
to sow the seeds of religious dissension
among them, by two Persons. totally
unconnected with the country, the Revd
Ellis, Curate of some parish in the
county of Mayo, and a young Man of the
name of Campbell. Who was a Tutor in
family, but whom I was obliged to part with
in consequence of his intermeddling, and consta

habit, of abusing the People of the Country these two persons having done every thing in power to irritate, and excite the feelings, of Roman Catholics of the Country, by Abusing themselves, their Religion, and their pastor in the hope of inducing a retaliation, on a they might fasten the name of persecution a having failed in their attempt, now endeavour to make a portion of the Publick believe (for their own sinister motives) that the dislike contempt, and disgust, which their conduct has elicited, is levelled at Protestantism, and that they are Martyrs to the cause — as a Magistrate anxious to preserve the peace, and happiness, which I am happy to say has always existed in this Country I have felt it my duty, to give no countenance to their proceedings, for which they have not been very sparing, in their attacks, on my Magisterial bis — this however, give me but very little concern; Satisfied that my Character as a Magistrate for the last thirty years, during which I held the Commission of the peace can suffer but little by the indecent attacks of such persons, And I feel assured that had his Excellency a doubt of the rectitude of my decisions he would at once communicate it and thereby afford me the means of clearing it up —

I have the Honor to be
Sir your obt St
John D'Arcy

13

John D'Arcy's letter to Dublin Castle July 10, 1837. See. Kathleen Villiers-Tuthill: History of Clifden 1810-1860. p.30.

At one time it was said some of the best corn in the country was grown in the district.

The shopkeepers thrived, 'several of which had risen, from a property of less than £50, to one of from £500 to £1,000, in a space of three years'. [3] In the midst of this prosperity on October 10 1839, John D'Arcy died. At fifty-four he had seen his dream take shape and develop into reality. He had, what in 1812 had seemed impossible, created a prosperous modern town in the backward wilderness of Connemara. His position was now taken over by his oldest son Hyacinth who 'differed greatly from his father, appearing to lack the latter's insight and leadership. His complete neglect or failure to understand his tenants led to many clashes between them, and instead of preventing trouble, as his father had always done, Hyacinth tended to be the cause of it'. [4]

Famine

The rapid development of the town and the prosperity of its occupants were suddenly to come to an end when, in 1845, it was announced that blight had swept the country and total crop failure was imminent. The five years that followed were perhaps the most horrific in the history of the town up to the present day. What began with hunger, due to the failure of the potato crop in 1845, had developed by 1846 into starvation, accompanied by famine fever; dysentery and scurvy went on to kill large numbers of the entire population.

Government aid proved inadequate to deal with the situation. A Government food depot was set up in the town with strict instructions to 'sell very small quantities at low cost, or to give it away free to the very poor'. [5] Hyacinth D'Arcy continued to complain 'of the inability of Government to keep up supplies of food in the area, stating that as Government supplies went down, cost on the open market went up beyond all reasonable prices'. 'On 21st

3. ibid P.22.
4. ibid P.34.
5. ibid P.47.

of September (1846) a large number of men came down to the (Clifden) Castle lawn to complain of their distress,'[6]

Public works were established, the Society of Friends set up soup kitchens; the Clifden Relief Committee continued to collect contributions and purchase supplies. However no amount of effort seemed to reduce the numbers turning out each day begging for food.

Late in 1847 Jame Hack Tuke, a member of the Quaker family from York, visited the town and reported 'many of these poor creatures had taken up their abode in some holes or cavities in the hillside where gravel appeared to have been dug'. A poor lad of about fourteen begged for 'a little meal to keep the life in me', he was 'a breathing skeleton, wasted with hunger and sores'.[7]

By 1848 nine tenths of the population were on relief. The exact number of dead will never be known as records were not kept. They were buried 'often without Church services and sometimes whole families were buried together in one grave'.[8] 'To both landlord and tenant alike it would appear that God had deserted them!' The west had suffered perhaps more than any other part of the country. In Connemara 'the population thinned out to a handful; some areas were almost completely deserted. Starvation, fever and emigration cleared the countryside leaving behind bleak deserted cabins, orphaned children and a memory which was to remain with the people of Ireland up to the present day'.[9]

A town for sale

The famine changed the face of Clifden, as it did equally dramatically the entire country. The landlords for the most part were bankrupt, their estates being on sale in the Encumbered Estates Court. Their tenants, now reduced in number, strove to come to terms with the deterioration in their living conditions. The shopkeepers, because they depended on the farming classes for business, were themselves, if not bankrupt, then almost certainly close to that situation.

Clifden, Kylemore and Sillery estates were put on sale on November 18, 1850 by Hyacinth D'Arcy. Clifden Castle, the greater portion of the town and surrounding townlands, were purchased by Thomas and Charles Eyre, Pulteny Street Bath, Somerset, for the sum of £21,245. Thomas later bought up Charles's share and on July 16, 1864 gave the estates, as a gift, to his nephew, Charles's son, John Joseph Eyre of Saint John's Wood, London. Hyacinth D'Arcy then renewed his life as a clergyman and became Rector of Omey and Clifden.

South and east of the town the old Martin Estate was almost all, in 1860, the property of the Law Life Assurance Company London. Mr George J. Robinson, the Company Land Agent, lived at Ballinahinch Castle. North of the town, as far as Kylemore, became the property of a number of English and Irish gentlemen; among them were Mitchell Henry, who built the magnificent Castle of Kylemore, Robert Graham of Ballinakill Lodge, Rev. A. Magee, a retired Catholic priest who came from London and lived at Doon Park, F. Twining of Cleggan House and A.E. Acheson who resided at Shanboolard Hall.

6. ibid P.48.
7. ibid P.51-52.
8. ibid P. 51.
9. ibid P. 53.

15

THE REV. HYACINTH D'ARCY,

WILL PREACH (D.V.) IN

CHRIST CHURCH, CLIFDEN,

ON SUNDAY EVENING, JULY 12, 1857,

SERVICE AT SEVEN O'CLOCK.

SUBJECT:

TRUE BAPTISM & ITS EFFECTS.

EPISTLE, Romans vi. 3-11.

"Know ye not, that so many of us as were baptized into Jesus Christ were baptized into his death? Therefore we are buried with him by baptism into death: that like as Christ was raised up from the dead by the glory of the Father, even so we also should walk in newness of life. For if we have been planted together in the likeness of his death, we shall be also in the likeness of his resurrection: Knowing this, that our old man is crucified with him, that the body of sin might be destroyed, that henceforth we should not serve sin. For he that is dead is freed from sin. Now if we be dead with Christ, we believe that we shall also live with him: Knowing that Christ being raised from the dead dieth no more; death hath no more dominion over him. For in that he died, he died unto sin once: but in that he liveth, he liveth unto God. Likewise reckon ye also yourselves to be dead indeed unto sin, but alive unto God through Jesus Christ our Lord."

GOSPEL, Mark viii. 1-9.

"In those days the multitude being very great, and having nothing to eat, Jesus called his disciples unto him, and saith unto them, I have compassion on the multitude, because they have now been with me three days, and have nothing to eat: And if I send them away fasting to their own houses, they will faint by the way: for divers of them came from far. And his disciples answered him, From whence can a man satisfy these men with bread here in the wilderness? And he asked them, How many loaves have ye? And they said, Seven. And he commanded the people to sit down on the ground: and he took the seven loaves, and gave thanks, and brake, and gave to his disciples to set before them; and they did set them before the people. And they had a few small fishes; and he blessed, and commanded to set them also before them. So they did eat, and were filled: and they took up of the broken meat that was left seven baskets. And they that had eaten were about four thousand: and he sent them away."

MY DEAR ROMAN CATHOLIC FRIENDS,

The epistle to be read in your chapel on Sunday, is St. Paul's answer to the objections raised in his day, and continually

Sermon by Rev. Hyacinth D'Arcy. July 12, 1857.

made in every day since, to the doctrine he taught in the fifth chapter; namely, that the justification of a sinner is a free gift, that it is all of grace; that is, his *free favour*; that it is through the obedience unto death of one man, even Jesus Christ, as fully and completely as was our sin and death, by the sin of one, and even more so, for that was of one sin to the condemnation of all, but in this case the *free gift*, is of many offences unto justification. The Roman objectors of St. Paul's day, who may be said to have been the seed that brought forth the fruit of the present Roman Church, opposed St. Paul with the same answer that all Roman Catholics give now, to those who teach the same doctrine. Shall we continue in sin that grace may abound? Do not the present Roman Church and all Roman Catholics, prove they are followers of the objectors, and not of St. Paul? Those six verses are his answer. Does he not teach that in the true baptism; there is such a uniting to Christ, that there is a participation in his death, so that his death is the sinner's death, and he so shares in all the benefits of it, that he is commanded to reckon himself dead with him, and therefore JUSTIFIED from sin, and as Christ was raised from the dead, so should they also be raised out of their sin, into what he calls newness of life, which will shew itself in a separation from sin, and following the example of Christ. If it be true that He died to sin and died once, that death hath no more dominion over him, can it be true that he is offered for sin in every mass? If it be an offering for sin there must be shedding of blood, if the blood be shed there is death, and which is true? St. Paul says, dieth now no more. The Lord give you wisdom and understanding.

Your sincere friend,

HYACINTH D'ARCY.

HYMN.

Alas! and did my Saviour bleed,
    And did my Sov'reign die?
Did he devote his sacred head,
    For such a wretch as I?

Well might the sun in darkness hide,
    And shut his glories in,
When Christ, the great Creator, died
    For man his creature's sin!

Thus might I hide my blushing face,
    The while his cross appears;
Dissolve my heart in thankfulness,
    And melt my eyes to tears.

But flowing tears can ne'er repay
    The debt of love I owe;
Here, Lord, I give myself away;
    O help me so to do.

Galway: Printed at the EXPRESS Office.

17

THE REV. HYACINTH D'ARCY,

WILL PREACH (D.V.) IN

CHRIST CHURCH, CLIFDEN,

ON SUNDAY EVENING, AUGUST 2, 1857,

SERVICE AT SEVEN O'CLOCK.

SUBJECT:

The Danger of being led by Priests.

Epistle and Gospel to be read in Roman Catholic Chapel —see Roman Missal.

EPISTLE, 1 Cor. x. 6-13.

" Now these things were our examples, to the intent we should not lust after evil things, as they also lusted. Neither be ye idolaters, as were some of them ; as it is written, The people sat down to eat and drink, and rose up to play. Neither let us commit fornication, as some of them committed, and fell in one day three and twenty thousand. Neither let us tempt Christ, as some of them also tempted, and were destroyed of serpents. Neither murmur ye, as some of them also murmured, and were destroyed of the destroyer. Now all these things happened unto them for ensamples : and they are written for our admonition, upon whom the ends of the world are come. Wherefore let him that thinketh he standeth take heed lest he fall. There hath no temptation taken you but such as is common to man : but God is faithful, who will not suffer you to be tempted above that ye are able, but will with the temptation also make a way to escape, that ye may be able to bear it."

GOSPEL, Luke xix. 41-47.

" And when he was come near, he beheld the city, and wept over it, saying, If thou hadst known, even thou, at least in this thy day, the things which belong unto thy peace ! but now they are hid from thine eyes. For the days shall come upon thee, that thine enemies shall cast a trench about thee, and compass thee around, and keep thee in on every side, and shall lay thee even with the ground, and thy children within thee ; and they shall not leave in thee one stone upon another ; because thou knewest not the time of thy visitation. And he went into the temple, and began to cast out them that sold therein, and them that bought ; saying unto them, It is written, My house is the house of prayer : but ye have made it a den of thieves. And he taught daily in the temple. But the chief priests and the scribes and the chief of the people sought to destroy him."

MY DEAR ROMAN CATHOLIC FRIENDS,

The following is the Collect for next Sunday in the Missal :—

" May the ears of thy mercy, O Lord, be open to the prayers of thy suppliants ; and that they may succeed in their desires, make them ask those things that are agreeable to thee. Through Jesus Christ, our Lord."

The men who wrote this Collect believed the passage that is written in the Word of God : " And this is the confidence we have in Him

Sermon by Rev. Hyacinth D'Arcy. August 2, 1857. See Villiers-Tuthill p. 71.

that, if we ask anything according to His will, He heareth us; and if we know that he hear us, whatsoever we ask, we know that we have the petitions that we desired of him."—See even Dr. Cullen's new Bible, 1 John v. 14, 15. Give up, then, crying to dead men and dead women, whom your Priest pleases to call saints, and make the above prayer to God, to whom it is addressed, earnestly and sincerely, with confidence that he hears. May He give His Spirit to bless this tract to your soul. The portion in the Epistle recounts for you some of God's dealings with the Jewish Church. It shows that although great promises were made to the seed of Abraham, and that although they were partakers of all the outward forms, and were thus outwardly identified with the Church, all this did not secure them from sin, from being covetous, from being idolators, fornicators, murmurers, tempters of Christ, &c. Nor where they sinned did it secure them from the consequences of sin, the wrath of God. So that there fell of them in one day even three and twenty thousand. But it teaches you more, it points out that God had more in view than punishing them; it is written, "these things happened unto them for ensamples, and are written for our admonition," for our warning, or, as Dr. Cullen's New Bible has it, correction. If there be therefore, a covetous man, an idolator, a fornicator, a tempter of Christ, a murmurer, let them be warned, let them flee from the wrath to come. If God so dealt with them as a figure, what shall the end be of them who have the example before their eyes? But the Gospel is a further example, and the most fearful of all. It tells us of the Lord Jesus Christ *weeping* over Jerusalem, while he prophesied of its utter destruction. Look now at St Paul's letter to the Roman Church, Romans xi. 20, 21—"Be not highminded, but fear; for if God spared not the natural branches, take heed lest he also *spare not* THEE." What was their sin? While it was their day of grace and privilege, they shut their eyes to him who was their peace, trusting in their sacrifices and righteousnesses of their own, and giving themselves up to the guidance of men. At the instigation of their priests, with wicked hands they crucified and slew the Lord of life and glory, whom God raised from the dead. They rejected the only remedy for all their sins, and crowned them all by so doing, so that seeing He was the son of God himself, there remained no more sacrifice for sin, and they perished in them miserably.

Oh, what have those priests to answer for? Who bribed Judas to betray him?—See Dr. Cullen's Bible, Matt. xxvi. 14—THE CHIEF PRIESTS!! Who sought out false witnesses against him?—Matthew xxvi. 59—THE CHIEF PRIESTS!! Who took counsel to put him to death?—Matt. xxvii. 1—THE CHIEF PRIESTS!! Who "moved the people" when even Pilate was determined to let Him go? Who, I say, PERSUADED THE MULTITUDE THAT THEY SHOULD DESTROY JESUS? The Priests!! THE CHIEF PRIESTS!!!—Matthew xxvii. 20. See Dr. Cullen's Bible, written for our example, and read in the Clifden Chapel. Yet, who persuaded the multitude in Clifden market, on Saturday last, to stone the men that said the Son of God was sent from heaven to make satisfaction for sin, And that God the Father was satisfied with it, and therefore raised him from the dead. Who moved the people? THE PRIESTS!! THE PRIESTS!! Who denounced this doctrine as heresy? THE PRIESTS!! Let Clifden beware. Be no longer deceived by Priests. We preach to you Christ an all-sufficient Saviour, and Him crucified an all-sufficient sacrifice. Nothing more and nothing less. Flee from the Church of Rome, whose doom is as sure as that of Jerusalem, but delayed that you may escape. Were He on earth, he would say with tears, "COME OUT OF HER, MY PEOPLE."

The Lord shew you mercy, is the earnest prayer of your sincere friend,

HYACINTH D'ARCY.

Galway: Printed at the Express Office.

19

Among them, these gentlemen made up the local Magistrates, were the chief employers and Guardians of the Union. Unlike their predecessors, they usually had private incomes. Some of them were the owners of estates in other parts of Ireland and England. Thus they were in a much more secure postion than the D'Arcy's or Martins had been. Although they resided a long distance from Dublin, they appear to have lived a very full and active social life locally.

Tenant Farmers

After the famine, attempts were made to clear the land of tenants and replace them with livestock as the income from rents were unreliable and troublesome to collect. This was done by encouraging the tenants to emigrate with the aid of financial assistance; the peasants did not need much encouragement. Having lived through the famine they were fully aware of the vulnerability of their position and the possibility of crop failure recurring was high; there was a good chance they would watch their children die of starvation, fever or disease resulting from malnutrition. So they emigrated, hoping for that promise of work and grasping any chance of enjoying a better life. They went in their thousands, often whole families together. Sometimes the oldest went first, and he or she would send the passage money for the next, who in turn would do the same.

Connemara was now almost deserted. Some townlands had only one tenth of the population it had before the famine. They landed on the shores of Canada and America, usually speaking nothing but their native Irish and carrying with them memories of starvation, horror and bitterness. These memories would remain with them for the rest of their lives and were passed on to their children and their children's children. This fact is still evident in certain aspects of current U.S.A. politics.

Those who remained looked on hopelessly as cabin after cabin became vacant about them. They watched their new landlords settle into their 'big' houses or build themselves new ones; they watched and they waited, praying the crop would be good this year and given a few good harvests, perhaps the future might brighten. The peasants of Connemara never raised their hopes too high. They had learned to accept that any advances they would make in this world would be made only by hard work and the benevolence of their landlord.

The small numbers remaining in the area made it possible for holdings to be increased and great strides were made by the tenants, usually with the assistance of members of the family then living in America, to purchase cattle, in order to reduce their dependance on crops.

Although other vegetables were added, the potato was still the mainstay of their diet. Since its introduction to this country in 1846, Indian meal was relied upon as a substitute for the potato in time of crop failure and in summer, when it was distributed to the very poor through the Workhouse administration.

The Shopkeepers and Merchants

As the land was acquired by new owners, so too were some business premises in the town. Shopkeepers sold their businesses and left the area, perhaps in the belief the town would never recover or that the steady stream of emigrants would continue, thus leaving the town deserted and non-profitable.

However, some families did remain, a good number of whom were sons of small farmers from the locality. They had come into town in the early years of its conception, attracted by John D'Arcy's offer of sites and the future promise of a thriving business. It was not very difficult to open up a business at that time. Some began with little or nothing; others used wooden crates for counters and old boxes to display their goods. The story of some of these families are known to us; the fate of the remainder became lost in the years that followed. As these families will be referred to several times in the pages to follow, it will be necessary to elaborate somewhat on their background and places of origin. Intermarriage was common amongst the families but I have tried to simplify this with cross-references.

Casey

In the late 1820s, during the construction of the main Galway to Clifden road, several men came into the district seeking employment, many of whom remained in the area. Among these was a man named Casey. When the road was completed, young Casey leased land at Derrlea and married a Miss King, daughter of a member of the Coastguard stationed at Ross. Several children were born and the family moved to Streamstown. Two sons, James (1851-1924) and William (1853-1906), married the daughters of shopkeepers in the town and, through them, inherited the family business. James married Honoria Malloy and after selling the Malloy business, they moved to a premises on the main street. This premises is today occupied by James's grandson, also named James.

William, known as Bill, ran a drapery store on market street. His son Joseph became a doctor and practiced, first as Dispensery Doctor for Carna, and then in 1914 replaced Dr Pitt Gorham at Clifden. Dr Casey lived with his wife May Lee[a] and family at Stella Maris on Sea View until his death in 1948.

William's daughter Lena married John King, Clerk of the Petty Sessions, and they had two sons Leo and Jack[b] and three daughters. Another daughter, Mary Beatrice, known as Bay, inherited the family business and married her next door neighbour E.J. King.[c]

Connolly (Conneely)

Originally farmers from Errislannan, the Conneelys anglicised their name to Connolly — as was the custom of the time — when they first took up residence in Clifden about 1815. John Connolly took a building lease from John D'Arcy, and built a premises near the entrance to Market Hill Lane on Market Street. From here he ran a drapery and general provision store.

John married Mary, daughter of Redmond Joyce; originally from Recess but at this time a shopkeeper in the town and Vice Chairman of the Board of Guardians. They had two sons, Redmond Joyce Connolly and John J. Connolly. John Senior died of cholera and his wife Mary re-married a Customs officer named O'Keeffe.

The O'Keeffe's had one son, Thomas J. and a daughter Helena. Mary continued to run the family shop until her death, when it passed on to her

a. see Lee p. 32.
b. see p. 187.
c. see King p. 32.

21

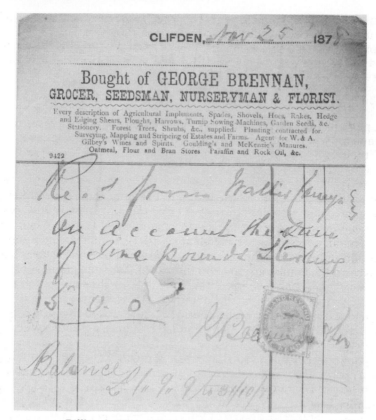

CLIFDEN, _Nov 25_ 187_8_

Bought of GEORGE BRENNAN,
GROCER, SEEDSMAN, NURSERYMAN & FLORIST.

Every description of Agricultural Implements, Spades, Shovels, Hoes, Rakes, Hedge and Edging Shears, Ploughs, Harrows, Turnip Sowing Machines, Garden Seeds, &c. Stationery. Forest Trees, Shrubs, &c., supplied. Planting contracted for. Surveying, Mapping and Striping of Estates and Farms. Agent for W. & A. Gilbey's Wines and Spirits. Goulding's and McKenzie's Manures. Oatmeal, Flour and Bran Stores Paraffin and Rock Oil, &c.

Billhead. George Brennan November 25, 1878.

daughter who never married but instead cared for her half-brother John J. Connolly. The other brother, Redmond J. opened a law practice in Ballinrobe, but after some years came back to Clifden. Here he practised under his own name as a solicitor and went on to achieve great success during the years of the land war, 1879-1880. He also farmed land on the outskirts of the town.

Thomas J. O'Keeffe, Redmond's half-brother, also qualified as a solicitor. He emigrated to America but retired to Clifden later in life where he died.

Redmond married a Miss Johnson from Kanturk, Co. Cork. They had two sons and seven daughters. Three daughters died at an early age. The others, Elizabeth married a Dr O'Beirne of Galway and Marguerite, Florrie and one other died unmarried. The sons were John Francis, known as Frank, who inherited land from his father and Henry Grattan who inherited the law practice.

Frank married Mary King, daughter of Con King and sister of E.J. King of The Square. He trained racehorses in a small way locally, then moved with his wife to Dublin where his two children were born. (Frank, his son, became a solicitor and worked at the General Post Office in Dublin. His daughter May married and emigrated with her husband to England, but later returned to reside in Bray, Co. Wicklow). Frank Senior later moved to England and died there, his family remaining in Dublin. Henry Grattan never married. He educated his nephew Frank with the intention that he should carry on the family practice. However, on Henry's death, October 16, 1952, the practice was sold to Mac Dermot and Allen, Solicitors, of Galway, who still own and conduct a thriving business there.

Martin Connolly

Martin, perhaps a brother of John, came to Clifden about the same year, 1815. He opened a drapery store on Market Street and married Honoria Gorham. Two of their children, Andrew and Hanoria, married a sister and brother named Joyce[d] from the same street.

Andrew (b. 1820) married Catherine Joyce and together they had six children. Catherine died in 1861 and in 1872 Andrew emigrated to Pittsburgh where he opened a store. He took four of his children with him, leaving the youngest two in the care of their aunt, Hanoria Joyce, these joined the family a few years later. Andrew prospered in Pittsburgh and his decendants still maintain strong links with their cousins in Ireland today. Honoria married Peter Joyce and they too emigrated to Pittsburgh.

D'Arcy

Although the early history of the town tends to concentrate on the D'Arcys of Clifden Castle, there was at the same time living in the district another branch of the D'Arcy Tribe — the D'Arcys at Coolacly on Kingstown Bay. The exact relationship between these two men, John D'Arcy of Clifden Castle and John D'Arcy of Coolacly, is difficult to ascertain, but it is believed they were cousins.

John D'Arcy of Coolacly was a Roman Catholic. His house, a long one-storey building, was situated on a winding stretch of road known as D'Arcy Street, which ran along the shore of Kingstown Bay. His lands were poor and rocky with few tenants. On September 10, 1840 he married Winifred King (—1881) and they are believed to have had three daughters and three sons. Stories of John are still told by the older inhabitants of Coolacly today. It is said he was first revered and respected by his tenants; he strove to educate them by reading aloud extracts from the Freeman's Journal, while they laboured in his fields, as part payment of rent. He pointed out to them the injusticies of the landlord system and the advantages of the Land League. However, in time, with emigration and the benevolence of sons and daughters in America and England, the tenants were becoming wealthier than their landlord.

Forced to sell his property, John moved to a small cottage on the main Galway road, opposite the workhouse, and there lived out his life until his death in 1898.

One son, also named John, (b. 1845) after retiring from the Royal Navy, returned to Clifden and opened a public house and grocery store on Main Street. He never married and after his death in 1915 his property went to his niece Mamie Cloherty.

Little is known of the second son William (b. August 8, 1853) but it is believed he married in England and had a family there.

The third son, Patrick, lived a clandestine life in London; as a young man he

d. see Joyce p. 32.

23

joined the Royal Navy, but while at sea fell foul of his captain. While on remand his ship anchored somewhere in the West Indies. Here Patrick escaped, jumped ship and swam ashore. Once ashore he changed his name to Boland and lived a clandestine existence there for many years. Still using the name Boland he returned to London, married and had one daughter. For the rest of his life he continued to call himself by his false name as did his daughter, although she was aware of her true family name and visited Coolacly regularly before World War Two. She died unmarried in the late 1960s.

John's daughter Winifred, named after her mother, emigrated to America and married a man named Cloherty, originally from Roundstone. Together they had three children, Winifred, Eddie[e] and Mary. Mary, known as Mamie, came to Clifden at the request of her uncle John and lived with him and his widowed sister Mrs Anne Clancy over John's business on Main Street, which she inherited after John's death in 1915.

In 1922 Mamie married Lieutenant Michael Lavelle,[f] M.C. Master of the Clifden Workhouse and son of Michael Lavelle D.C. Streamstown. In 1932 Michael and Mamie inherited Echo Point House on the outskirts of the town and sold the business on Main Street to Bernard Ludden. Michael became Rate Inspector for the district and was an active member in all community groups. Mamie died childless on May 15, 1945.[g]

John J. D'Arcy

Another cousin, also named John (1847-1931) was a timber merchant and seed dealer. He also owned hookers which were used for transporting goods along the coast.

In his early years, John J. worked hard to acquire a considerable nest egg and after his marriage to Bridget King he built a comfortable home on the beach road and named it Echo Point. No expense was spared on the materials used in the construction of Echo Point. To prove that the house would have a golden foundation, a half-sovereign was set into each cornerstone. A garden and orchard were laid down and a boathouse built on the shore; just outside the high garden wall. He grew his own tobacco in his greenhouse and liked to experiment with rare fruits in his garden.

The house, protected from the road by a high wall, can be reached by ascending the wide steps to the front door; often on returning from lavish entertainment, usually at the home of Monsignor McAlpine, John J. negotiated these steps on his posterior, cursing his wisdom on ever having them laid.

A Magistrate and member of the Board of Guardians, John J. was a small round man who always dressed in plus-fours. He invested heavily abroad and often attended board meetings both in Dublin and London. While in Dublin he stayed at the Gresham Hotel, in O'Connell Street, and, in order to ensure his

e. In America the Clohertys became Claritys. Eddie's son Ed Clarity (d. Sept. 7, 1985) became a well known photographer on the New York Daily News and his son Captain Michael Clarity was, until recent retirement. C.O. of the Naval Station at Pearl Harbour.

f. see Michael Lavelle p. 189.

g. Michael later married Teresa Joyce from Coolacly and together they had one son, Michael Joyce, and two daughters, Barbara and Kathleen, (the author). Michael died November 19, 1951. Teresa married again, 1957, Frank Broderick and they had one daughter, Mary. Teresa died June 13, 1989.

identity be known, he had letters addressed to him at the hotel sent from Clifden before his departure. Mrs D'Arcy died childless and after John J's death on December 14, 1931, as mentioned previously, Echo Point became the property of his cousin Mamie and her husband Michael Lavelle.

At this point I feel compelled to elaborate a little more on the private life of John J. D'Arcy. Shortly after returning from their honeymoon, the D'Arcys were visited by the mother of one of John J's former housemaids. She placed on the shop counter, before the young bride, a small baby; John J's illegitimate son. The woman vented her anger on the couple and informed them her daughter had emigrated to America, leaving the boy with her. Offers of assistance from the D'Arcys were refused. However the old woman moved house when an old enemy of John J's made a house available on the Sky Road,

Echo Point home of John J. D'Arcy and birthplace of the author.

in order that the boy be reared in close proximity to its father. The child was named John D'Arcy and at times, as he grew older, his grandmother would stand him on a wall overlooking Echo Point and called out: 'There is your father now' as John J. mounted the steps to the street.

Although he showed him no recognition on the street, each Saturday night the boy would knock on the door of Echo Point and the housekeeper would hand him out money received from his father.

Attempts to have the boy educated were refused, and it was not until his deathbed that John J formally recognised his illegitimate son. All his money and investments were left to him in his will.

The boy grew to manhood, never marrying, he tended his small farm until his death in the early 1960s. In his will he left the residue of John J's money to the Catholic Church and this was used to convert an old schoolhouse at Kingstown into a small church.

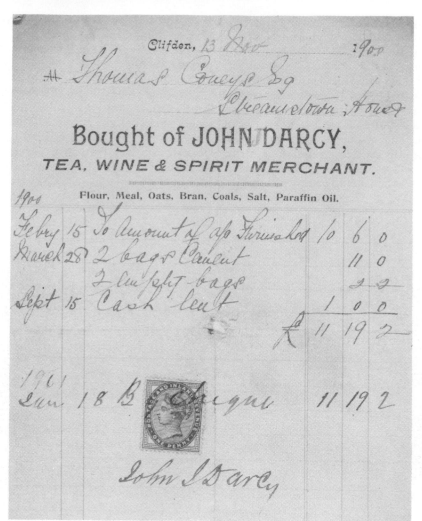

Clifden, 13 Dec 1900

M Thomas Coneys Esq
Streamstown House

Bought of JOHN DARCY,
TEA, WINE & SPIRIT MERCHANT.

Flour, Meal, Oats, Bran, Coals, Salt, Paraffin Oil.

1900			£	s	d
Febry	15	To Amount of a/c Furnished	10	6	0
March	28	2 bags Cement		11	0
		2 empty bags		2	2
Sept	15	Cash lent	1	0	0
		£	11	19	2
1901					
Jan	18	By Cheque	11	19	2

John J Darcy

Billhead. John J. D'Arcy.

Gorham

Anthony Gorham was the son of a tenant sheep farmer from Salrock, high in the mountains at Killary Harbour. A native Irish speaker, he was sent to Galway at an early age to learn English. He later began to operate a hooker, transporting goods from Galway to the many villages along the coast. Anthony married Margaret O'Higgins and they had two children, Joseph born in 1830 and Teresa. After Margaret's death Anthony married again, in 1843, Mary Hanoria Coneys from Aughrus. In this marriage he had five sons and four daughters.

Sometime before 1855 — the exact year is unknown — Anthony opened a shop at 97 Market Street, a property that was to remain in the family for the next hundred years. From this premises he managed to educate his family, the

386

THE
CLIFDEN CHEAP WAREHOUSE

IMPORTER of HARDWARE, IRONMONGERY,   BRUSHES, POWDER, CHINA and DELPH,
OILS, PAINTS and WINDOW GLASS,   ROOM-PAPER, DYE-STUFFS, &c.,
LATHS & TILES of EVERY DESCRIPTION,   PLAIN AND FANCY STATIONERY,
BAR IRON and STEEL.   GUN POWDER & DYNAMITE.

MARKET SQUARE, CLIFDEN 19 Nov? 1903

Thomas Coneys Esq J.P.

Bo.^t of William Gorham

1901

			£		
Oct 4	To Amt of a/c furnished		4	13	9
	To 4 Boards 12×9×½ at 10			3	4
1902	1 D.º ×¾ .. 4			1	0
March 14	To ½ Bag of Cement 3/6			4	7
19	1 Eve shoot putty Eve Bolts 2d			2	2
	1 Eve shoot Holdfast				8
Oct 6	To 1 Bag of Cement 5/3			6	4
8	1 Stone Mastic 4lb 1Pt Linseed oil 6			2	0
	Lampblack 2 14 lb of glue 5 6				8
23	To 12 Packets coopers dip 4d			13	0
			6	7	6
Cr By Cheque on acct			5	0	0
	Nov 28 1903			1	7	6

W.G.

The Cheap Clifden Warehouse

27

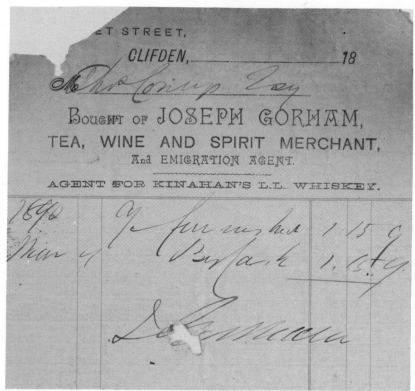

Billhead. Joseph Gorham.

boys having the distinction of being among the first Roman Catholics to enter Queens College Galway. He became firmly established in the rising middle classes of the town.

Anthony died in 1871 and was buried in the old graveyard in the town centre. Joseph, the son by his first marriage, went on to open his own business on the main street, a public house and general grocery store. He became a very active member in the community and a Magistrate; he owned land on the outskirts of the town and dealt a good deal in cattle. Joseph died unmarried. His sister Teresa married Mr King and lived first at South Hill Ardbear and later in their newly built house, Stella Maris at Sea View.

The daughters of the second marriage were Harriet, Mariah, Margaret and Delia. All, apart from Harriet who died young, lived out their lives in and about the town, none of them ever marrying.

Of the five sons from that marriage, four of whom became doctors, Patrick Charles born 1849, better known as Pit, was perhaps the best known member of the family. Pit became medical officer for Roundstone in 1873 and remained there until he succeeded Dr Payne in Clifden in 1884. A renowned sportsman, he possessed many trophies for fishing and shooting. He retired in 1914 and died a few years later at his home Sea View, unmarried.

The newspapers recorded his death with the following words:

28

'As a recanteur he had few equals', he was 'associated with all movements for Clifden's good and was foremost in performing acts of kindness. He assisted Lady Aberdeen in the campaign against TB and earned the everlasting gratitude of the poor of whom he was particularly fond'. He 'met nearly all the celebrities of Great Britain, including George Wyndham, Arthur Balfour, Lord Dudley and was prominent in Connemara in welcoming Edward VII and Alexandra in 1903'.

Pit Gorham will always be remembered in Clifden and to this day stories are told of his quick wit and sometimes bizarre behaviour while resident at Sea View.

The three other doctors were Anthony, John and James. Anthony, born 1843, a surgeon with the Royal Navy, retired to Glen Irene at Clifden and died unmarried. John practised with the Merchant Navy and died in Africa. James was born in 1851, he practised first in Letterfrack and later in London. He married in 1899 Mary Smith, sister of the Liberal M.P. William Smith. They had two children, Maurice[h] and Honoria.

James' wife died in London and after his retirement he returned to Clifden, where he lived out the remainder of his life with his sister at Glen Irene on the beach road. The fourth brother William, born 1846, took over the family business at Market Street; he married and had one daughter Mary. Mary married Anthony Morris (p. 148), and continued to run the business for many years. The children of Anthony and Mary still reside in Clifden today.

Griffin and Stanley

The Griffins, originally from Limerick, came to Clifden in 1821. That year, James Griffin opened a drapery store on the corner of Market street; this property remains in the family to this day. Through James's sons Roger, born 1841 and John, born 1847, a thriving business was established. John also acted as Clerk of the Union for many years.

The business was passed on by John to his daughter Margaret. Margaret married in 1884 Samuel Stanley, a bank official serving with the Clifden branch of the National Bank. After their marriage, Margaret continued to run her business and raise their family while Samuel, whose greatest passions in life were shooting and fishing, stayed with the Bank, transferring on marriage to Athy and again to New Ross until retirement. Of their three children only one, Gerald, survived. Their only daughter died very young and their eldest son Percy died at the early age of twenty-one. Gerald, after his marriage in 1908 to Sabina Loftus, took over the business.

Down through the generations, the family remained prominent in the social life and activities of the town. They were most respected in business; they had the reputation among the tenants and small farmers as being a decent and honest house with which to do business. Through the years, adjoining shops were purchased and the business expanded, making it the largest drapery store in the town.

Gerald was one of the early members of the Sinn Fein club and down through the years took an active interest in politics. He was also a member of the Town

h. Maurice, educated at Sandhurst and Oxford, after a distinguished career at the BBC from 1926 to 1947, became Director of Broadcasting at RTE from 1953 until 1960.

John Griffin.   *Mrs John Griffin.*

Margaret Ann Griffin.

Samuel Robert Stanley and wife,
Margaret Griffin.

Gerald and Sabina Stanley.

Development Committee. The Stanleys had five sons, Percy, Robert, Paddy, Albert and Kevin and three daughters, Rita, Ina and Martha. Gerald purchased South Hill in Fall in 1921 and the children spent their early childhood there.

At a time when there was little employment to be had, they employed on average ten people. Four women employed as dressmakers occupied the top of the shop; two girls and two men were employed as assistants and a further two girls were employed as maids to the family.

After Gerald's retirement the business was taken over by his son Percy, thereby continuing the unbroken tradition of over one hundred and sixty years of business at the corner of Market Street.

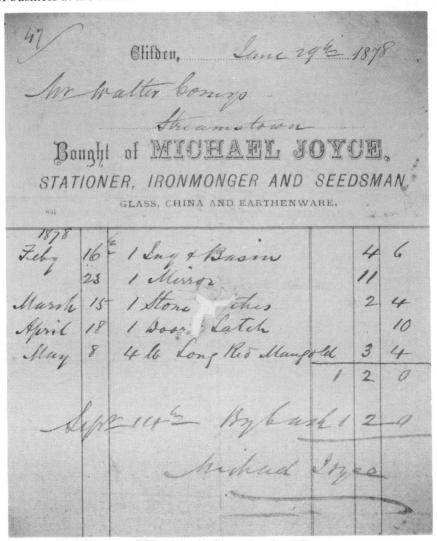

Billhead. Michael Joyce June 29, 1878.

Joyce

The Joyces of Market Street were, in 1855 and perhaps before, the owners of a hardware shop and public house situated on either side of the arch and entrance to Market Hill Lane. The family originally came from Garramon, Recess.

Michael Joyce, known as 'Long Michael' had seven children and ran the public house. One daughter, Catherine, married Andrew Connolly, a draper from the same street, a son Peter married Andrew's sister Honoria. Another son Michael, known as 'Short Michael', to distinguish him from his father, ran the hardware business. He never married but lived instead with his maiden sister Nora.

The eldest daughter Mary married her next door neighbour Michael Lydon, and it is their children who went on to represent this family up to the present day.[i]

King

The King family came originally from the Roundstone district. John King owned a public house and general merchant store on the corner of Market and Main Street. His son Cornelius, known as Con, was Relieving Officer with the Union. Con inherited the family business from his father, he married and had two sons and a daughter. One son, Edward Joseph, known as EJ, married his next door neighbour Bea Casey and they had one daughter Rita. He, in turn, took over the family business and became a well known figure in the town. His brother, whose name is not known, emigrated to Boston and was never heard of again. Their sister Mary married Frank Connolly.[j]

Lee

James Lee, originally from the Roundstone district, purchased a grocery store on the corner of Market and Bridge Street. He and his wife Bridget had two sons, Michael J who qualified as a doctor; it is not known if he practised in Clifden, he died December 22, 1888.

The second son Bernard J (—1915) a prominent figure in community life, took over the business and like many of his contemporaries purchased grazing land outside the town. Bernard and his wife Margaret had four sons and four daughters. One son Bernard A. better known as Ambrose, became a solicitor and practised in Clifden from May 1921 until his death on March 30, 1933. Two other sons became doctors, Michael who practiced in Newport, Co. Mayo, and Alfred who practised in England. The oldest son, James, took over the family business. He married and had two daughters, but following his death on August 19, 1950 the corner shop was sold to Kevin Stanley. Bernard's four daughters were educated in England. Rita married Dr Paddy Muldoon, May married the local dispensary doctor, Michael Casey.[k] Imelda married Thomas O'Flaherty of Ballyconneely and Delia married Commandant O'Malley.[l]

i see Lydon p. 34.
j see Connolly p. 21.
k. see Casey p. 21.
l. see Commandent O'Malley p. 224.

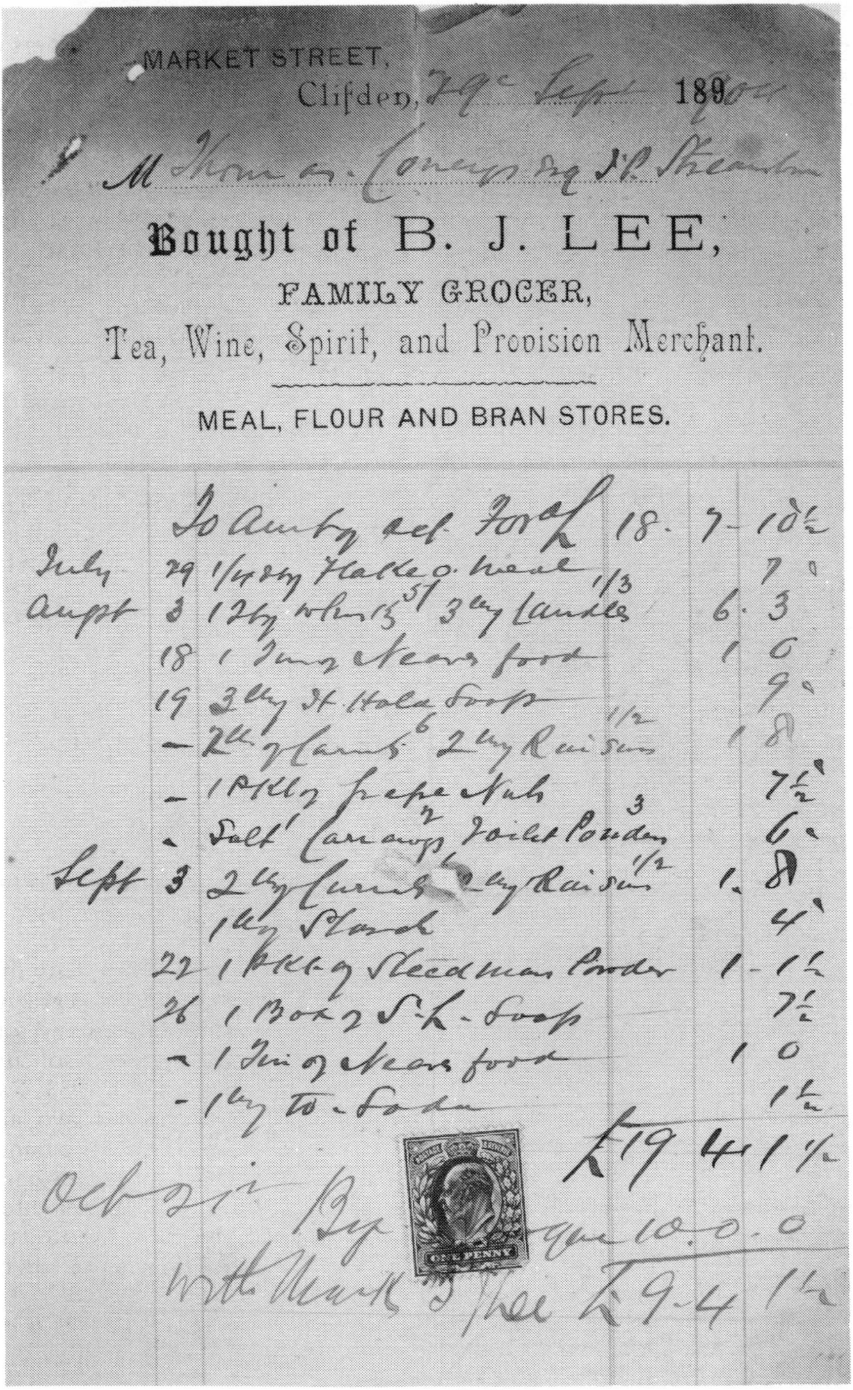

MARKET STREET,

Clifden, 29th Sept 1904

M Thomas Conneys Esq

Bought of B. J. LEE,

FAMILY GROCER,

Tea, Wine, Spirit, and Provision Merchant.

MEAL, FLOUR AND BRAN STORES.

		To Amt of acct forwd	18 - 7 -	10½
July	29	1/4 cwt Flake O. Meal		7 0
Augst	3	12 lbs Whiting 3 lbs Candles	6	3
	18	1 Tin of Neaves food	1	6
	19	3 lbs St. Hala Soap		9
	–	2 lbs of Currants 2 lbs Raisins	1	8
	–	1 Pkt of Grape Nuts		7½
	–	Salt Carraways Toilet Powder		6
Sept	3	2 lbs Currants 2 lbs Raisins	1	8
		1 lb Starch		4
	22	1 Pkt of Steedmans Powder	1 -	1½
	26	1 Box of S.L. Soap		7½
	–	1 Tin of Neaves food	1	0
	–	1 lb W. Soda		1½
			£19 4	1½

Oct 21 By cheque 10.0.0

With thanks B. Lee £9-4-1½

ONE PENNY

B.J. Lee Sept. 29, 1904.

Lyden

The Lyden family came from South Connemara. The exact year they opened their business in the town is not known. However, by 1855 their public house and family grocery were well established.

Michael Lyden married his next door neighbour Mary Joyce and together they had eight children. The most prominent of these was Father Patrick, Fanny, his sister, and John M.

Father Patrick, attached to the Diocese of Tuam, was a close friend of Archbishop J. MacHale. He was one of the promoters of St. Joseph's Church and travelled extensively fund raising for its construction. He suffered from poor health and while abroad recuperating, he died at Queenstown South Africa on August 30, 1880. Fanny joined the local Sisters in the Convent of Mercy and became Mother Magdalene.

John M. took over the family business and went on to establish his own public house, grocery and bakery further along the same street. In 1907 he married Eileen O'Malley of Kilmilkin, Maam. Eileen, who trained in London, was a Domestic Science instructress in Ballyconneely. Her brothers were well-known surgeons and doctors in Galway and London and her cousin Padraig O'Maille[m] was a well-known political figure in Connemara.

John M. and Eileen Lyden, June 1907.

Back Row L to R.: Michael Lyden, Michael Joyce, James Lyden. Front Row L to R: Nora Connolly (cousin home from America), Kate Lyden, Hanoria Joyce, Margaret Lyden.

Both Eileen and John M were prominent members of Sinn Fein. Eileen was the leader of the local Cumann na mBan, while John M. was an official of the Sinn Fein courts. Their political activities and sympathies caused their home to be burned down by the Black and Tans on March 17 1921, as were a number of

m. See Padric O'Maille. p. 191.

others in the town. John M. contacted pneumonia while 'on the run' following this episode and died within the year. Also during that year Eileen spent a short term in Galway Jail for membership of Cumann na mBan. After John M's death, Eileen carried on the running of the business with her six young children.

An incident which occurred during the Civil War will give an insight into Eileen's business sense and ability to capitalise on opportune circumstances. During the occupation of Clifden by the Republicans, communications between the town and the outside world were cut. The railway was out of operation, roads were impassable and phone links were down. Guinness stocks were running low in the locality. Eileen contacted the other publicans in the area and arranged for an order to be sent by Marconi Wireless Station at Derrygimla to Guinness's in London. Guinness's confirmed through Marconi station that the consignment would arrive by ship at Roundstone Harbour. As all petrol was commandeered by the Republicans, horses and carts were the only transport available and these converged on Roundstone on the scheduled day of arrival. However things did not go without a hitch; as the craft reached Roundstone Bay it anchored off from the harbour and for days the sounds of the crew enjoying the cargo could be heard plainly across the bay. Not to be outwitted, Eileen contacted her friend, local Republican, Gerald Bartley, who, along with some of his men, 'persuaded' the crew to dock and unload the cargo.

Following this display of business ability, Eileen was offered the Guinness Agency for Connemara but declined. Eileen later married Michael O'Neill and continued to run her business until 1950 when she retired and went to live with her daughter Mrs Kathleen Lavelle in Main Street. Her grandchildren, the Lavelles in Clifden and the Joyces in Recess, are the representatives of this family in the area today.

Guiness Cheque.

Blight — The Recurring Problem

The first half of the 1860s saw a steady improvement in the conditions of the town and adjoining tenant farmers. As always however in Connemara, good times would not last for long. In 1866 it was reported that two thirds of the potato crop was a total loss and the remainder was almost unfit for human use. Owing to continuous rain during the harvest, the corn crop was slow to ripen, was inferior in quality and far under the average yield. After harvesting, the weather deteriorated and most of the crop remained in the fields and was so badly damaged that it had to be sent to market and sold at reduced prices. This was a severe blow to the poor whose reliance on the potato crop to support them throughout the coming winter would in consequence force them to purchase Indian meal at high prices on the Clifden market as a substitute.

Recognising all the signs and remembering past experiences of crop failure, prompt action was taken. On October 24 1866 a meeting was held in the town, from which a Memorial was sent by the Clergy and Gentry of Connemara to Dublin Castle, informing them of conditions in the area and requesting assistance for the poor. The Memorial was signed by Martin R. Hart, secretary, and George J. Robinson, Chairman of Union.[10]

All requests were, however, referred to the Workhouse who, as always, pleaded their inability to cope with the situation. The Poor Rate in the Clifden Electoral Division was four shillings and seven pence in the pound and always proved difficult to collect and was considered insufficient to meet the needs.

The winter that followed was extremely severe and a great effort was made to keep the cattle alive. Cattle were now considered the principal capital and wealth of the district. When the fodder had been consumed, the oats and potatoes which would normally have been reserved for human consumption, were given to the cattle to keep them from perishing. As the bad weather contnued through February and March of 1867 and stores diminished a large proportion of the potato left for seed was fed to the cattle.

The sacrifices were to a great degree ineffective. The following returns from the books of dealers in hides and skins in the town show that cattle in large numbers died between December 1, 1866 and April 30, 1867

Mr Gorham	purchased	385 hides of cows and calves
Mr Lydon	purchased	350 hides of cows and calves
Mr Flaherty	purchased	283 hides of cows and calves
Mr Connelly (sic)	purchased	335 hides of cows and calves
Redmond Connelly (sic)	do	250 hides of cows and calves

Total 1603[11]

Coming into the summer of 1867 the remaining cattle were said to be in a wretched condition due to cold and hunger. Many of them were said to be able only to crawl along.

During the bad weather, boats with provisions from Galway were unable to make the journey to Clifden and this resulted in great scarcity. Large numbers of people travelled daily along the Roundstone road making their way to Clifden to buy Indian Meal. By May 1867 prices were very high, higher than they had been for years; while they always rose for the summer, it was unusual for them to rise so early and so high. Hay was now almost impossible to be had and the price, when it did at last appear on the market, was £7 and £8 per ton. Potatoes, when available, were selling at 8d and 9d per stone. Indian meal

10. SPO.
11. SPO.

which was now the principal food, was 1s 10d per stone. It was thought that unless families had some money in reserve, they would be unable to maintain themselves without aid from some source or other. The pawnbroker's office in the town had every space filled with beds, bedclothes, fishing gear etc. Having spent all his own capital, the proprietor was offering to any available investors, money at 12% to enable him to meet the demand for loans on pledges. The demand for cash was brought about by the shopkeepers of the town refusing to give credit, something they had always been willing to do in the past.

Tenants of the Law Life Assurance Company in the Cleggan area were evicted and their houses pulled down, not for non-payment of rent but for sub-dividing. The original tenants had sub-divided their holdings, something that was not allowed on the property of the Assurance Company. Sub-division was a practice frowned on by many as it usually resulted in high rents and profiteering by the middle man. Some of those evicted left for Scotland, while others remained living in miserable mud huts. Further south, in the Roundstone area, among tenants of the Assurance Company, fuel was said to be in very short supply. Normally there would be no great demand for fuel this early in the year (May 1867) but now the population were eating Indian meal which required a great deal more cooking than potatoes and there were fears that it would not be cooked sufficiently, which could result in widespread sickness.

Employment

Although conditions of the tenants along the coast were bad, rents had been paid. This was done with money received in advance from a Mr Hazell, agent for the firm of Patterson & Company of Glasgow, for kelp due to be harvested throughout the summer. That year alone, £3,000 had been advanced to small farmers along the coast. Apart from that, there was little employment to be had.

At Kylemore, Mitchell Henry was building his Castle and gave employment to about one hundred persons at wages ranging from seven shillings to ten shillings per week. To earn that, labourers walked to Kylemore from as far away as Renvyle, and further.

Following a visit made to the area by the Poor Law Inspector, Dr Brodie, in May 1867 and his subsequent report, the Government offered some employment on the unfinished roads begun during the famine. After repeated requests by the local farmers and fishermen of Errislannan, plans were made for a pier to be built at Boat Harbour. The estimated cost was between £590.8s0d and £600.0s.0d. It was hoped that three quarters, or £450 of this sum would be given in a grant under the Fishery Piers and Harbour Act and that the remaining £150 would be provided by local contributions or by means of a Government loan. Work was carried out by the Board of Works immediately funds were made available.

The Poor Law Commission Office at Dublin informed the Board of Guardians at Clifden on May 17, 1867, that they were aware of the existing distress and advised them to collect all outstanding rates. The Master of the Workhouse was instructed to submit a report on the bedding and clothing and to estimate further requirements.

They were reminded that they were responsible for all relief in the area and that if what remained in the Treasury and the arrears, when collected, were insufficient in aggregate to meet all the requirements of the extraordinary distress, then further funds must be obtained.

The Clerk of the Union was directed to prepare and submit to the Guardians an estimate for a supplementary rate according to the circumstances of each electoral division.[12]

Fenian Activity

In 1858 the Fenian Brotherhood was founded in New York by John O'Mahony. In Ireland the same year James Stephens founded the Irish Republican Brotherhood. Members of both organisations were known as Fenians whose aim was the creation of an independent, democratic republic.

By 1866 Fenianism was said to be widespread throughout Connemara. Reports of large numbers of strangers coming into the area without any apparent employment and yet appeared to have plenty of means at their disposal, greatly alarmed the police. Frightened men complained of the danger inherent in the isolation of the district which had only a 'Sub-Inspector of Constabulary and twenty four men of all ranks to protect them'.[13] By early March the 'strangers' were reported to have left without having caused any disturbance.

However, in March 1867 an anonymous letter was received by the Chief of Police entitled 'Fore Warned is Fore Armed',[14] informing them that on the eve of St. Patrick's Day, the Fenians of Ballinafad, Letterece, (the fishery) and Clifden planned to render all bridges between Clifden and Oughterard and Clifden and Westport impassable, and a simultaneous attack was to be made on all police stations and coastguard stations in the district.

The letter also pointed out that a Martin D'Arcy had an Irish-American living with him and that this man had gone to Linkelirnagh (sic) regularly for the past two months, taking two or four men with him on the pretext of hunting.

On receipt of this information the following action was taken. The entire constabulary for the Clifden and Roundstone area were collected together in their respective headquarter stations and the same was done with the coastguard. They remained there from March 16 until March 20 but again no disturbance took place.[n]

Police Station for Cleggan and Tully

Later that year (1867) it was decided to open police stations at Cleggan and Tully. This met with opposition from the County Inspector who informed Clifden and Dublin Castle that he could not spare five men for a station at Cleggan due to 'shortage all over the county'.[15] However, the new station was justified by the fact that whenever an offence was committed in the Cleggan area, the offenders left for Boffin Island before the police could arrive from

12. SPO.
13. ibid.
14. SPO.
15. ibid.
n. On the night of 5-6 March 1867, armed revolts did take place in Dublin, Cork, Tipperary and Limerick, but these failed and were quickly crushed.

38

Clifden. There among the population they hid and should the police conduct a search they hid in the numerous caves on the island. To search the caves properly usually took weeks and as often as not, the offenders were never found.

In 1868 a house was rented for the Cleggan station for £20 per annum and the force consisted of one constable and five sub-constables. This was to be a permanent station.

The one at Tully was to be a temporary station and a house was rented from Mr Bake for £14 per annum. This was situated in the village; one reason given for its establishment was to prevent any further annoyance of Protestant Clergy and Scripture Readers.

Guardians of the Union and Magistrates of the District 1868

Chairman of the Union George J. Robinson, J.P. Ballinahinch Castle.
Vice Chairman John C. Jones, J.P., Ballinconneely Lodge.
Deputy Vice Chairman Walter S. Wall, Errislannan
Treasurer Provincial Bank of Ireland, Galway
Clerk and Returning Officer John Burke
Master and Matron John Heanue and Margaret Concannon
ChaplainsEstablished Church, Rev. C.B. Campbell
   Roman Catholic, Very Rev. C.B. McManus
Medical Officer William H. Suffield, M.D.
Relieving Officers Cornelius King, Clifden, Joseph Mangan, Roundstone

Medical Officers of Dispensary Districts and Registrars of Births, Deaths and Marriages

- **Clifden** Dr Suffield and M.G. Painter
- **Roundstone** C.J. Payne, M.D.
- **Renvyle** Alex Speer Keer, M.R.C.S.E.
Stamp Distributor John Griffin, Clifden

Magistrates

Edgar Henry Blake Renvyle
Capt. Maurice C.J. Blake, Bunowen Castle
Valentine Blake, Towerhill and Bunowen Castle
Edward Browne, Rosleague, Letterfrack.
Rev. Hyacinth D'Arcy, Clifden Rectory
Alex Dickson, South Hill, Clifden
J.J. Eyre, Clifden Castle
Francis J. Graham, Ballinakill Lodge
Mitchell Henry, Kylemore
John Campbell Jones, Ballyconneely Lodge
Resident Magistrate: Garrett Parkinson, Clifden. [16]

16. Thom's Directory.

CHAPTER II

1879 — That Troubled Year

The People and the Courts

A sitting of the Petty Session Court at Clifden, reported fully in the county newspapers of the day, gives perhaps the clearest insight into the lives of the people. Not in the least perturbed by the surroundings or the consequences of their language, the witnesses in these courts described circumstances and events, usually with such clarity and wit, that having read the newspaper reports, one comes away with a deeper knowledge of their lives than any history book can convey.

One such case appeared before the courts on July 26, 1879. It reveals the actions of the sharp businessmen of the town who, always on the lookout for a good deal, never wished to lose an opportunity to outwit those considered to be their betters.

The Reverend's Horses

The case was brought by Rev. James A. Magee against J.J. D'Arcy, P.J. King, Canavan and Murray for illegal seizure of, and selling by auction, ten horses, the property of Rev. Magee, and for damages for assault.[1]

Rev. Magee, a retired Catholic Priest, had come from London in 1848 and lived outside Clifden at Doon Park. His father was said to have been a General in the British Army and his mother 'a wealthy lady — a convert to the Catholic faith'.[2] 'The father earnestly desired that the son should join the army; the mother desired that he should study for the priesthood. To the surprise of both parents, the boy took up the law as a profession and became a Barrister of Law'.[3] He went on to become a Medical Doctor before eventually becoming a priest and a Doctor of Divinity.

After the death of his mother, his father married again and from the estates of his mother and step-mother Rev. Magee inherited a large fortune. He retired due to ill-health and came to live in Connemara where he purchased the townlands of Doon, Cushtrough, part of Knockbrack and the Islands of Crow, High and Friar. The Reverend 'was not remembered as the kindest of landlords, indeed, it is said he once had to be visited by the parish priest of Clifden to be reminded of his duties to his tenants.'[4]

The following incident gives the impression the Reverend Father was not entirely held in very high regard by his tenants or townspeople.

The events which led up to the case began, when Rev. Magee had an informal notice service on one of his tenants, Michael Coyne, who owed him

1. C.T. July 26 1879.
2. Rev. Fr. M. O'Donnell, Ecclesiastical and Secular History of Connemara (1942) unpublished manuscript.
3. O'Donnell.
4. Villiers-Tuthill P.64.

Main Street. c1880. Courtesy National Library.

the sum of £81 for a mare and half-year's rent. A solicitor informed Mr Coyne that the notice was defective, and he then brought a Civil Bill action against Rev. Magee. A decree was obtained but on appeal the amount was reduced. The costs of the action were such that Rev. Magee now became debtor to Coyne for £31.[5]

The decree was handed to Mr Redington, Sub-Sheriff of Galway, but Rev. Magee refused to pay, saying he would put the £31 against the amount owed to him by Coyne, after the Sheriff had collected it. Coyne, described by the police sergeant as a 'clever fellow' knowing the money would be stopped, appointed his own special bailiff. When on Monday April 21, James Joyce, the special bailiff, went to Rev. Magee asking for the amount of £31.1.4d owed to Coyne, Magee began to laugh and humbugged Joyce. Coyne, who had accompanied Joyce, then pointed out ten horses belonging to Magee and they proceeded to drive the horses off Magee's land and into town. The horses were placed in the pound, awaiting an auction set for Friday April 25.

The following day, Rev. Magee sent Mr. Connolly, solicitor, to Galway. He gave the Sheriff's man £37 to cover all costs; the Sheriff was out of town and did not return until the 25th. A telegram was sent to Mullarkey, the auctioneer, telling him to withdraw the sale, stating that the money had been paid. Later there was some controversy over the exact time the telegram was received. A notice was posted on the pound door warning the public not to buy; Mr Connolly having announced the facts cautioned against purchase of the horses. All advice was ignored and excitement grew in the town as Friday morning approached. A bellman was sent out by Coyne and Joyce announcing the sale was to be held at twelve noon in the market square with Joyce acting as

5. C.T. July 26 1879.

auctioneer. George Brennan, Rev. Magee's agent, sent out another bellman to say the amount was lodged in Galway.

Mr Connolly and Brennan then went to the pound and told the people repeatedly that the money had been paid and it would be a dangerous thing to buy. To this Coyne replied that he would get 'men of straw' to bid for the horses. Brennan then paid thirteen shillings, pound-keeper's fees, but the horses were not given up. He then agreed with the pound-keeper that he and some other of the Reverend's tenants, who were with him, would grab the horses as soon as the pound door was opened, thinking that the horses would be released one at a time and sold individually. But plans were afoot and the sale went ahead despite warnings.

The horses were kept in the pound and were put up in one lot. No one bid on them at first. John J. D'Arcy bid £5.0.0d while the horses were estimated to be worth £79.10s.0d., a man named McDonagh bid and then Henry Murray bid £21.10s.0d and the horses were sold. Joyce then went through the town saying the horses had been sold. Murray apparently had £50 in the National Bank, money it was said he received from Mr Eyre when put off his land. On his way to the bank, Murray called into Joseph Gorham's public house for a glass of brandy. Among the men at the bar was John J. D'Arcy, P.J. King, son of the postmaster, and Joseph Gorham. Gorham asked Murray if he would like to sell the horses and offered him £1.10s.0d. profit. Murray agreed. Then Gorham, D'Arcy and King went to the Bank with Murray and although he received the money from Gorham, D'Arcy and King contributed their share.

The crowd then moved to the entrance of the pound; the keeper let out one of the horses and then told two of Magee's men to go and take the rest. One of Joyce's sons took charge of the horse that was released and the crowd held back Devane, one of Magee's men, while Conneely, another of Magee's men, attempted to take the horse from young Joyce. The crowd then moved towards Conneely and J.J. D'Arcy took Conneely's stick and began to kick him in the legs.

Amidst great confusion the horses were taken away by D'Arcy's men and were next seen in Cashel, South Connemara, in the charge of a man named Canavan. Notices were later served on J.J. D'Arcy, P.J. King, Canavan and Murray and the case came before Judge Harrison on July 26, 1879 and drew a large attendance. Coyne and his family were now believed to be in Scotland. The Judge, after reviewing the evidence at length, advised the jury that the two main points at issue were:- was the sale a 'bona fide' sale or not, and what was the actual value of the horses on the day of sale.

During questioning, Magee's man Conneely admitted to taking a glass of whiskey with his breakfast that morning, but strongly denied that he was the leader of, what was commonly called, 'Magee's irregular forces' or 'Rev. Magee's raiders'. Under questioning, Murray stated he inspected the horses a couple of times while they were in the pound, soon after they arrived and again just before the sale. It was his impression, he said, that the horses were in bad condition and had improved while in the pound! This obvious insult to the quality of Rev. Magee's lands was met with great laughter in court.

The jury, after some deliberation found that the sale was 'bona fide' and for the plaintiff that the value of the horses was £60. In the assault case Mr D'Arcy was fined £15 damages and costs.[6]

Religious Violence

1879 saw another outburst of religious conflict and violence. The Irish Church Mission, already over twenty years established in the West, still persisted in their vigorous proselytizing of Connemara. The Society 'Persuaded that the religion of the majority is idolatory, certain clergymen and their lay backers deliberately set themselves to the task of demoralising and undermining it'.[7]

Their orphanages, mission schools and church services were usually not interfered with but open-air meetings, circulars and placards denouncing the teachings of the Roman Catholic Church stirred up emotions among the Catholic population, often resulting in violence.

As a result of a number of attacks on scripture readers and their property in early 1879, the number of police had to be increased and the cost of supporting these was levied on the 'people already suffering from a series of bad harvests.'[8]

Another expense levied on the taxpayer, as a result of these outbursts, was the settlement of malicious injury claims which came before a Special Session of the Courts at Clifden on June 10, 1879. On the bench were, George J. Robinson, J.P. in the Chair, John Hall, Walter S. Wall, Gillman Browne, John Armstrong and Captain Blake.[9]

The assorted cesspayers in attendance were Messrs Coleman R. Broughton, Richard Kearney and Charles Stewart. The Secretary of the Grand Jury, Walter Seymour was also present.

One of the first cases to be considered was the claim for the breakage of forty panes of glass, a door etc. in the school at Barnahalla, which was attacked and wrecked on March 23, and the scripture reader Mr MacNeice was said to have been assaulted.

The solicitor engaged on behalf of the ratepayers was Mr W. Ffrench Henderson, and on behalf of the Irish Church Mission, Mr Edward Concannon. During cross-examination Mr Ffrench Henderson showed that the door must have been in use twenty years or so as part of the rotting timber was produced in court. Mr James Guilfoyle, carpenter, stated he would repair the door for a few pounds, and would give his word that he would do the job, 'providing that the Irish Church Mission would not bind him to put in such rotten timber as was there before, for the like of which would not be had in Connemara.'

Mr Cranston, glazier for Kylemore Castle, said he would glaze the windows at 4d per pane and would walk four or five miles each day to do the job. For this claim the magistrates allowed £4.10s.0d.

The next claim was for the burning of Belleck (Belleek) school for which £120 was claimed. Witness for the Irish Church Mission Mrs Young, the occupant, claimed the fire was malicious and broke out in the early hours of the

6. C.T. July 26, 1879. Reported in full.
7. ibid. July 6 1879.
8. ibid.
9. ibid. July 14 1879.

morning. Mr Ffrench Henderson however called a number of witnesses and attempted to prove that the fire commenced around the chimney and was caused either accidently by the occupants or by some of their followers: one of whom referred to as a "jumper"[a] who 'in one of his fits of Biblical piety some two months before' swore he would burn the house over Mrs Young because she would not give clothes to his childern."[10]

While cross-examining one of Mr Ffrench Henderson's witnesses, Mr Concannon said he did not see the use in examining 'such fools' at which a terrible uproar was caused in court at the insult. Mr Concannon then denied using the words and if he did he did not mean them. The people shouted at him and said he was a liar and should withdraw them. Mr Concannon was making matters worse by explanation so that the people continued to protest. One man, face to face with him, said 'You have always a dirty mouth and cannot examine the witness as a gentleman'. Others called after him 'Badger'. The people still insisted that he should withdraw the offensive language and after some time Mr Concannon apologized.

The court continued in this atmosphere with banter and insult thrown at the solicitor and Magistrates by the public. When the vote was taken and the majority of the Magistrates voted for malice and awarded the sum of £50, a great uproar followed. More insults followed, one of the associated cesspayers Mr C. Broughton then stood up and said he felt himself bound to protest in the strongest manner against the conduct of the bench who voted for malice when the evidence before them clearly showed the opposite. He was about to leave but the people prevailed upon him to see it out to the end.

A voice from the crowd complained there were Magistrates on the Bench who paid neither rates nor tax. 'Yes', another called, 'we have to pay poor rate to support their bastards in the workhouse'. 'This was beyond endurance', the newspaper reported, 'yet, there was no contradiction.'. Another man stood up and said 'We have some magistrates on the bench whose mothers and sisters are engaged in the proselytising system, that bone of discord among the peaceable people of Connemara. How can an impartial judgement be got from a bench composed of such men?'. One voice from the crowd threatened, 'We shall pay it (the claim) and more and will afterwards get rid of the souper schools.'

The Irish Church Mission then instructed their solicitor to withdraw further claims due to be heard on that day.[11]

Following more clashes the newspapers of the day asked the question:- 'Over most of Ireland handfuls of Protestants live in peace surrounded by Catholics: why not so in Connemara?' They then went on to attempt to answer it. 'The Mission people have the law on their side but it is easy to use one's legal liberty so as to become an intolerable nuisance to one's neighbours.'[12] It went on to state a real missionary has no policeman at his back and that their attitude provoked hostility. The Chief Secretary at Dublin Castle was called upon to help dampen down aroused emotions in the area and he requested Canon

10. C.T. June 14, 1879.
11. ibid.
12. ibid.
a. 'Jumper' was the name given to Roman Catholics who regularly 'jumped' from religion to another.

44

Hussey, head of the Irish Church Mission to take control of his members, but was informed by the Canon that the orders to 'restrain the circulation or exhibition of tracts or placards of an offensive character had not been observed.'[13]

The County newspaper stated that 'The Catholics of Connemara respected their Protestant neighbours and desired to live on the most intimate and friendly terms with them. But they would not allow themselves to be insulted with impunity by troops of proselytising vagabonds who forfeit by their blasphemies and misconduct, anything like good neighbourhood from the inhabitants of any district cursed by their presence.'[14]

The Chief Secretary advised the dignitaries of the Protestant Church to abstain from giving offence to the religious feelings of the people and to impress upon those in the employment of the Irish Church Mission the importance of adopting a similar course of action.

Survival

The combination of three bad harvests and extremely severe winters resulted in 1879 in yet another famine, the severeity of which was surpassed only by the Great Famine of 1847. The effects of the 1879 crop failure were felt throughout the country when vast numbers of the population found themselves once again facing starvation.

'That year, 1879, was an appalling one for the small farmers in Ireland. Their livestock was unsaleable, their potatoes a total failure, they were in arrears with their rents, heavily in debot to the shopkeepers, and as they had no fixity of tenure they could not obtain credit for as much as a loaf of bread.'[15]

A descriptive letter written by Mrs Agnes Eyre, Clifden Castle, dated June 27 1879, to the Connaught Telegraph, requesting donations to be sent to the National Bank or Post Office in the town to help alleviate the conditions of the poor, gives a clear picture of the reality of their plight.

'From this remote spot — ever first to feel and last to recover from visitations now so general' describing the weather as 'hardly a summer up to the middle of June.' 'Rains washed out of the earth almost every seed put in'. Sheep and cattle, particularly the young 'starving in the bitter wind'.

'Poverty has long since gone beyond measurements by statistics. Figures for other than arithmetic would be needed to picture the sights that meet us at every turn of the highway; still more poignantly in lonely hovels amongst rocky interstices of the shore, worst of all in the numerous islands scattered for leagues along the bold Atlantic, gaunt hunger in many an eye, a prayer for food on almost every lip. Yet is there no wrath in their eyes; no malice on those lips; no wishes for evil to imaginary evil-doers. The calamity is accepted as beyond human avoidance, not only is there no tendency to exaggerate, there is anxiety to underrate individual suffering. Only in direct extremity, and then chiefly on the part of parents for their famishing and nearly naked children does anguish find its natural utterance. To what is thus mentioned the writer bears the personal testimony of varied experience. It is

13. ibid. June 12 1879.
14. ibid.
15. The Rt Hon. Sir Henry Robinson Bart., K.C.B. Memories: Wise and Otherwise. p.9.

on occasions of this nature that the proverbial qualities of the Irish peasant — and here he is the Irish of the Irish — manifest themselves strikingly, untemptable honesty, patience and even cheerfulness under privations that would be incredible unless witnessed, above all ever-ready sacrifice of self, where domestic and neighbourly affection is concerned; these characteristics were never more prominent than in this most severe trial.'[16]

Along with money, Mrs Eyre requested clothes for children and adults.

Foreign Correspondents

Various English and American correspondents visited the West to see for themselves if conditions were as reported. Their weekly bulletins appeared in newspapers throughout England, Ireland and America and confirmed that conditions were every bit as bad, if not worse, than suspected. Their reports brought home to those who had left this country in 1847 the reality of the situation and, coupled with their own memories, they were prompted to respond generously to all calls for aid.

One correspondent, J.F. Moir Bussy, writing from Clifden in September 1879, posed the question, 'what is in store for them' and then answered with 'they will die of sheer starvation unless the wherewithal to keep body and soul together is brought to them, or they will become desperate with desperation that seizes upon honest men when the weak voices of their little helpless ones are crying out for food. The landlords for the moment will not be able to save them by reduction of rent, for the payment of any rent at all in the vast majority of cases is simply out of the question.'[17]

In November of the same year, James Berry from Carna wrote to the newspaper describing conditions in the parish of Moyrus, South Connemara. 'The parish of Moyrus with a population of eight hundred families, has not today as much potatoes in it as would support one hundred families, until next July, nor will there be found fifty people here in next March who will have or can buy twelve stone of seed potatoes,' 'and what will become of them?' he asks, 'nothing but of course starve.' Some men in the area who in the past had fifteen cows and had perhaps fifteen or twenty horses now had neither cow, sheep nor horse and were in debt up perhaps to £20 for meal, not to mention rent. He blamed the landlords of the area for the reversal in fortune of these people, men, he claimed, who had purchased patches of the great Martin property and who had now set it 'at a pound against the shilling it paid formerly.'

Giving as an example a townland which twenty years ago was rented from the Law Life Assurance Company by his uncle, Edward O'Malley, Parish Priest, for £6, it was raised to £11 and never went higher. It was later purchased by 'the hero of Killalornty' and pays now £110 at least, 'there are twenty tenants upon it with about five cows between them. The same man is the landlord of two islands here, he has these islands set as four to one against the Poor Law Valuation.' The reason the tenants were able to pay these exorbitant rates was the abundance of kelp in the area. Every February, Mr Hazel and Mr Stephens, kelp agents, came 'with bags of money' which they gave to families, to some as

16. C.T. July 5, 1879.
17. C.T. September 27, 1879.

much as £100. This money enabled them to buy seed potatoes and provisions and they had the summer and autumn months to earn and pay back the money by harvesting the kelp. But the kelp market had now collapsed and still the landlord wants the same rent.[18]

Mr Berry wrote of boys having little or no clothes and going about their chores in nothing but calico shirts. Young men who got wet collecting seaweed on the shore had to get into bed, even in midday, while their clothes were drying for they had no others. One honest family who could get no credit sent its youngest member around asking for the loan of an egg in every house and then she exchanged them for a few handfuls of meal. The previous July when the weather was so stormy that boats could not come from Galway to Roundstone or Clifden, meal could not be got at any price and the people were starving, he writes of one 'magnificent woman (who) ran to Galway, a distance of forty two miles to buy a half cwt of Indian Meal, take it on her back, and arrived at home, having saved her children, though she ran a distance of eighty two miles'.[19]

Market Street. c1880. Courtesy National Library.

Government Aid or Private Charity

By January 1880, money began to arrive from France, England and other parts of Ireland and America. Many fathers and husbands crossed to England and Scotland seeking work. In Carna the Sisters of Mercy opened a small convent and during December and January clothed one hundred naked children attending their schools.[20]

While 'the Poor Law Unions were not financially in a position to afford relief on the scale necessary to meet such widespread destitution'[21] the Government continued to reject requests for public works in favour of charitable

18. C.T. December 6, 1879.
19. C.T. December 6, 1879.
20. ibid. January 3, 1880.
21. Robinson.

47

distributions. A number of people were against this method of helping the people, feeling the population should be dignified with work. There was also the growing fear that the people would grow dependent on charity and release the Government of its obligation to provide employment for the region. Mitchell Henry[b] voiced his opinion in a letter to the newspapers dated December 24 1879: 'in my humble opinion, (charity) is the very worst method of assisting people who are anxious to give a return for what they receive.'[22]

On Tuesday January 6 1880, a meeting of about eight hundred people from Clifden and district was held in the old chapel house. The purpose of the meeting was to consider the great distress in the district. Among those present were: Dean McManus, P.P., Rev. W.R. Ring, Rev. B. McAndres, Rev. P.J. Corcoran C.C., E.J. Eyre, Messrs E. Morrissey, Joseph Gorham, John Geraghty, T. Mullarkey, John King, William Gorham, Hubert Mullarkey, J.J. D'Arcy, M.P. Hart, Bernard Bodkin, Thomas O'Neill, P.J. Brennan, John M. Lydon, Charles Mullarkey. T.P. Geraghty, Andrew Lydon, Berard J. Lee and M.J. Lydon.

After hearing speeches by Rev. McManus and Rev. Corcoran, Joseph Gorham said that although 'fully recognising the demoralising effect the administering relief dissociated from exaction of its equivalent in labour' but conditions in Clifden were such that 'charity is necessary'. He went on to beg assistance from the committees for the Irish distressed funds now being collected in England and Ireland.

E.J. Eyre, Clifden Castle, said: 'That as it is most desirable that employment be given to the needy instead of public charity, we urge upon the Government the duty incumbent upon our rulers to start in Connemara some public works of which several, such as the construction of a railway from Galway to Clifden, might be undertaken with public advantage and with prospect of remuneration to the promoters'. Mr Eyre believed few out of Connemara had a knowledge of the capability of the people from the district who were willing to work.

Also present at the meeting was Mr W. Sampson, well-known Liverpool Town Councillor and Mr English of the Liverpool press, they were engaged as a committee sent by the English and Irish in Liverpool to investigate the distress.[23]

Shipwreck

A testament to the bad weather of January was a report of a shipwreck off Slyne Head. The crew of the 1020 ton ship named *Verity* landed safely at Slackport on Monday January 5 after abandoning their ship which later went ashore on the rocks off Slyne Head and broke up.

The ship had left Waterford for New York on December 17 1879 after discharging a cargo of grain at Ferrybank, Waterford. Three young men from Yellow Roads, Waterford, were taken on board working their passage to America in an attempt to escape from the terrible conditions in the country at that time. On December 30 when they were over seven hundred miles from Ireland a terrible storm blew up. The heavy seas and wind carried away the

22. C.T. January 3, 1880.
23. G.V. January 7, 1880.
b. see Mitchell Henry p. 51.

rigging and they lost control of the ship. During the storm two men were drowned and two others seriously injured. The crew cut off the rigging and the vessel began to leak. They then drifted for six days. They signalled to passing vessels but to no avail.

On Saturday evening the sailors saw a lighthouse, Slyne Head. At 9.30 on Sunday morning they lowered two boats and collecting their clothes, boarded them and were in the boats until 11 o'clock on Monday morning when they landed at Slackport and were immediately surrounded by 'Irish-speaking peasants'. The crew were then transported to Clifden where they awaited instructions from their Company.[24]

Islands in Trouble

In January 1880 the inhabitants of the islands off the coast of Galway and Mayo were said to be extremely poor and in need of assistance. The islands were described as being densely populated and extremely difficult to reach due to the bad weather.

Henry A. Robinson, Local Government Board Inspector from Ballinrobe, made two attempts to visit the islands but the weather prevented this. He requested a gunboat or some such vessel to assist him in his efforts. This was obtained in February when the gunboat 'Goshawk' was despatched to Galway along with fifty tons of meal to be distributed to the islands, a gift from 'The Dutchess of Marlborough Relief Fund'.[25] However, the weather was so bad Mr Robinson was prevented from visiting all the islands. Large quantities of flour and meal were expected to be sent by the Mansion House Relief Committee and the Dutchess of Marlborough Relief fund from Galway and Westport for distribution to the islands through Clifden, Roundstone and Letterfrack.

As always, the remoteness of this region created problems as the cost of transport by road was prohibitive and the same trip by special steamer would cost at least £30. The only alternative was the use of Hookers, and these would require protection, as boats of their size were likely to pull into small harbours when weather was bad and were then likely to be attacked and plundered, as they had been at Cashel Bay on the night of February 17.[26] Having explained all this to Dublin Castle, Mr Robinson then requested that the 'Goshawk' be retained to distribute the food and this was granted.

On the February 21, the islands were said to be crying out for food but the weather was still very bad. Another gunboat, the Orwell was sent to assist Goshawk. A third vessel was offered but the Mansion House Relief Committee said it was not required. By March the gunboats had completed their task and left the area.

During the flurry of activity to get food to the islands, a request by a Mr D Seanard, owner of some islands along the coast, for the use of the gunboat after its tour of duty with Mr Robinson was completed, was refused. Mr Seanard wished to visit his islands to serve law papers on the inhabitants and said he would require a large force for the protection of the bailiff.[27] Although his request at that time was refused, it is safe to assume that, at a later date, Mr

24. G.V. January 10, 1880.
25. SPO.
26. SPO.
27. ibid.

49

Seanard would have been given the use of the gunboat and the back-up force he required. The gunboat would then return to the islands and be instrumental in evicting the very people it had worked so hard to save from starvation.

Three Landlords of Credit

A special mention in the newspapers was given to three landlords said to be doing their duty by the people.

Mr. John Kendall, Ardagh Lodge, Clifden, who with his usual liberality selected and purchased twelve tons of best kind of seed potatoes in London, forwarded to his tenants in Errislannan. He also expended a large sum annually on his property. It was hoped that many landlords would follow his example to enable their tenants put down the proper kind of seed potato.

Captain Thomas of Salruck, Killary, applied a loan of £1000 in wages among his tenants who were engaged in reclaiming and draining.

Mitchell Henry, who, it said, resided 'in a rose blooming in the desert' employed not only his tentants but the entire population in his area.[28] .

August 1880, and although the harvest looked promising, the exodus of Irish agricultural labourers had begun. An estimated 'Five thousand passed through Dublin',[29] in the first few days of that month. The people having lived on credit for the past three years were now in debt. Rent would soon be due and perhaps last year's had still to be paid. If the harvest was plentiful there would be no relief and no employment. Part of the crop would be sold to pay their debts, leaving themselves short. Then next summer, faced with no provisions, no work and no money they would once again seek credit and once again be in debt. So crop or no crop, the future offered no improvement. It had taken years of poor harvests to accumulate their debts and it would take years of bountiful harvests to clear them.

28. G.V. February 4, 1880.
29. C.T. August 7, 1880.

CHAPTER III

Home Rule and The Land War

The 1870's saw a growing desire for Home Rule in Ireland. The Irish Party at Westminster under the leadership of Isaac Butt used their increase in numbers to advantage in their campaign. The people of Connemara were represented by Mitchell Henry, a supporter of Butt, and very much in favour of Home Rule.

Mitchell Henry (1816-1910)

Mitchel Henry, a consulting surgeon at Middlesex Hospital inherited a considerable fortune from his father, a Manchester merchant, in 1862. At great expense, he built Kylemore Castle, developed extensive gardens and reclaimed thousands of acres of land, creating employment wherever possible. A former Liberal candidate for Manchester, he first went forward in February 1871 in the Galway by-election and was returned unopposed; he went on to represent Galway until 1884. Henry was known as a moderate politician and an extremely active member of the party, strongly supporting Isaac Butt. When in London he resided at his home Straheden House, but a great deal of the year was spent at Kylemore Castle. He kept in close touch with his constituents and was fully aware of their circumstances and expressed his knowledge of their conditions in his many letters to the press.

As a North of England man, he recognised the extremes between the inhabitants of the industrial towns of the North, and those of Clifden. He appreciated the potential of the area, the possibility of development with the extension of the Galway railway to Clifden, the increase of arable land by reclaiming the wastelands in the district; he must have watched with apprehension the labour force of the future emigrate in their thousands to the cities of England and America. He took it upon himself to educate the English people on the circumstances of the Irish tenant farmer, while at the same time cautioning the Irish not to push too hard and fast in their request for Home Rule and land reform. Like Butt, he believed in the parliamentary process and appealed to the English sense of reason and fair play to achieve their aims. Although a close associate and admirer of Butt, by 1877 he was, like many others in the party, a little weary of Butt's slowness to act and his lack of direction or firmhandedness with the Government. Charles Stewart Parnell had how joined the 'obstructionists' of the party; this small group tried to delay legislation, which they could not hope to defeat, by a series of long speeches and interruptions. Henry never supported obstruction as he believed it wasted the public time and brought Parliament into contempt.

At a Banquet given in January 1877, Henry rose to add his voice to those critical of Butt and called for action. In the next session of Parliament, he told them:

'It would be their duty to follow a very bold course; he was not in favour of shaking hands all round, of thankfulness for small mercies. What they

Kylemore Castle home of Mitchell Henry M.P. — Photograph by B. Holberton.

wanted was their national rights, and they would be friends with those men who would assist them to gain those rights; they would not be friends with those who resisted them.'[1]

As Butt's leadership came more and more into question, Parnell and his followers began to remove themselves from the rest of the party. In August 1877 the Home Rule Association of Great Britain elected Parnell as President for the following year. Henry summed up the situation, the division in the party and the contrasts between the actions of Parnell and Butt when he wrote:

'Some of Parnell's work has been praiseworthy, some wrongheaded, he wrote, but above all he had succeeded in conveying that impression of sincerity which was so lacking in the party as a whole. The party was full of absentees and buffoons, who were more ready to repudiate than to cheer each other; they were taken seriously by no one, and eighty of that type would be no more use than their present number.

For all this, there is in my judgement but one remedy, and that is, as I ventured to say in a former letter a new departure in Irish politics, to be planned at a Conference in Dublin, and then really to be carried out in an orderly, methodical, and businesslike manner. I am not an advocate for a pig-headed course of obstruction". "I am in favour of vigour and reality in our proceedings and I do not hesitate to say that what makes Mr Parnell and

1. David Thornley: Isaac Butt and Home Rule, p. 298 Nation, 10 Feb. 1877.

some others so hateful to the English press and to most of the English members is that they think them formidable, because not likely to be bought by office, or by what is quite as fatal by personal flattery."[2]

He approached the parliamentary session of 1878 fully realising the state of the party, "if anything is done it will be done by the obstructives and by nobody else. But it would be done as in the last session, as a faction, not as a party.'[3] He admitted privately to Butt that: 'I believe our influence as a party is gone'.[4]

Isaac Butt died on May 5, 1879. The contest for Chairman of the party was between Mitchell Henry and William Shaw. Shaw was elected. Joseph Gillis Biggar, one of the obstructionists, 'voted for Henry, as the better man; Parnell voted for Shaw, whom he could oust'.[5] Parnell later succeeded in doing so when in 1880 he was elected Leader of the Party.

Tenants Rights

As the politicians at Westminster fought for Home Rule, an even more intense battle was about to begin at home; the fight for the land. The conditions of the tenant farmers in the West, already mentioned in Chapter II, contributed greatly to establishment of the Land League. This organisation which began in Co. Mayo, soon spread throughout the country and was to achieve more for the tenant farmer than any organisation had before. It began with a series of Tenants Rights meetings organised by Michael Davitt to demand a reduction of rents and to denounce the whole landlord system.

Frowned on by the clergy at first and supported by a number of politicians and middle classes, the tenants rights meetings became the dread of Dublin Castle and the local police force; they feared the crowds would reach the numbers present at the Monster Meetings held by Daniel O'Connell in 1842 and of the outbreak of violence after the meetings. On June 15 1879 it was announced in the Roman Catholic Church in Clifden by Dean McManus that the following Saturday, it being Market Day, a Tenants Rights meeting would be held in the town, for the purpose of inducing the landlords of the country to reduce their rents. The local police informed Dublin Castle, saying they did not expect this to meet the proportions of a 'Monster' meeting but that they would watch the proceedings carefully. Daily reports were sent to Dublin as fears grew that the meeting would be attended by large numbers. However, market day arrived and no meeting was held; the police were baffled.[6]

Later in the month, they obtained information from a 'reliable source' that a big meeting was planned for July 1. A large crowd of upwards of four to five thousand people were expected to attend. Its main promoters were said to be the Catholic Curates and the shopkeepers of Clifden. The speakers were expected to be drawn from the same class. Violent speeches were expected and violent resolutions passed. Thirty men charged with riot and assault on Irish Church Mission scripture readers were due to appear at the Petty Sessions on the same day and this it was feared would add fuel to the fire.

A large force of fifty eight policemen arrived in the town, and it was generally

2. David Thornley p. 337 Freeman's Journal, 11 Sept. 1877.
3. ibid. p. 345.
4. ibid. p. 348.
5. ibid. p. 379.
6. SPO

believed this was because of the cases due to appear before the Courts but they were also there to prevent violence breaking out during the expected meeting. A Mr Johnston was sent by Dublin Castle to report on the meeting; he carried the credentials of a newspaper reporter for the *Daily Express* and turned up in the town as such.[7] Again, no meeting took place. It was not until Wednesday September 6 that the meeting was held. There was said to be about ten thousand persons in attendance and the usual display of extra police was made. Dean McManus presided and several spirited resolutions were passed. The speakers included Rev. B. McAndrew, P.P., Rev. J. Maloney, P.P., Rev. D. Fahy, C.C., Messrs Mitchell Henry M.P., Joseph Gorman and P.J. King. The proceedings were said to be most orderly.[8]

Mitchell Henry identified strongly with the need to improve the position of the tenant farmers. One week later, in a letter sent to a meeting held at Tuam, he regretted he was unable to attend but said he made it a rule not to attend meetings on Sundays as he felt this was the Lord's Day and should be kept as such. He referred to the successful meeting held at Clifden and went on to say, where rents had been raised over the past two years they would have to come down as the tenants cannot pay. 'All tenants must be given security of tenure with fair rents, ascertained if necessary by arbitration and the right of freely selling their interest.'[9]

The desire for tenants rights went hand in hand with the desire for Home Rule for it seemed impossible to obtain the first without backing it up with some form of the second. The majority of M.P.s recognised the fact and called for some form of partial Home Rule. Henry referred to this in his letter. 'We require to have the management of our own land affairs and of all business that is not of an Imperial nature. We pay far and away a larger share of Imperial taxation than rightly falls to our share and in addition the money unjustly taken from us is spent in England where it funds salaries and wages for a countless host. Let us have the spending of some part of this taxation on our own soil and soon Ireland will show reclaimed farms and happy occupiers in plenty, with good roads, railways, tramways and decent dwellings. Irish discontent in a large measure means Irish hunger, and the question of the hour is just now the bread and butter question'. 'I have no doubt whatever that out of the present evils which have fallen so hardly on us, great and permanent good will come to all. A famished and starving people cannot be neglected, and our self-complacent rulers in England will find that nature herself is fighting on our side.'[10]

The Land League

In October 1879 Davitt formed the Irish National Land League at Dublin with Charles Stewart Parnell M.P. as President. Its objectives were to bring about a reduction in rents, to protect the tenant against eviction for non-payment of unfair rent and to enable, by reform in the laws, each tenant to own his holding by paying a fair rent for a number of years.

7. SPO
8. C.T. Sept. 13, 1879.
9. ibid. Sept. 27, 1879.
10. C.T. Sept. 27, 1879.

Following this, Henry appears to have withheld his support and instead criticised the League for encouraging violence. The tenant farmers in and around Clifden, like the rest of the country held their leases very much on the whim of the landlord; they were usually of short duration, about thirty-one years and the rent was revised usually upwards on the expiration of the lease. During the term of the lease the tenant would perhaps build a house, farm buildings and improve their land. Then after thirty one years of hard work, the lease would run out and all that stood before the tenant was now the property of the landlord. They were dependent entirely on the goodwill of the landlord not to raise the rent above their capability to pay. If they were unable to meet this new rent they were turned out. Once evicted the tenant could obtain no work for there was none to be had in the area; he obtained no credit as there was little hope of him repaying it, so it was a choice between living in a ditch or the workhouse.

Landlords scarcely ever made improvements on land to be let to tenants; the greater proportion of those lands let were either bog, mountain or rocky ground, and very little improvement beyond the yearly necessary cultivation was carried out by the tenant, as such improvements would only raise their rents. Tenants in fear of being evicted sowed the most productive crops; these were not always the best suited to the land or the lessees as successive famines had proved. Wasteland was never reclaimed by the tenant as this would raise rents, and apart from Mitchell Henry had not been reclaimed by the landlords either.

Griffiths Valuation was said to be no guide to the rents in the area as in some cases the rents were double, in others treble, while in some places they may be nearly equal, but in general the rents were much higher.

The Winter of 1879 and early 1880 saw a rise in crime and a deepening of the rift that existed between the public and those enforcing the law. Landlords bullocks and sheep were ran off cliffs; the burning of houses, ricks of turf, stacks of hay, straw, farming utensils and stores were carried out. These methods were used as a weapon against unfair eviction and as a warning to landlords or their agents, or to tenants who had paid their rents, or men who took over land where the previous tenants were evicted.

Split in the Party

Following the election in March 1880, the new Parliament reassembled in May, with sixty-five Irish Nationalists. Thirty five backed Parnell; twenty-six moderates were led by William Shaw and there were four uncommitted. The election was won by the Liberals led by Gladstone.

William Shaw and his supports, with Mitchell Henry among them, sat on the Government side of the House, while Parnell and his followers sat on the opposite side. Gladstone set up a Government Committee to advise him on the land question in Ireland, and Henry's attitude was to give the Government time to do the job he felt it would carry out. 'Our attitude towards the Liberal Party,' he said 'should be one of watchful expectation.' Henry was complimented in the Press for his 'able and statesmanlike speeches on the Irish questions.' They reported that one of his favourite ideas was that 'Ireland is a vast underdeveloped estate which could easily be made productive and thus afford

Connemara Women. Courtesy National Library.

sufficient sustenance for the people, and an improved condition of life for all classes in the country.[11]

Although a firm believer in the necessity for a revision of tenants rights and that more attention should be paid to the entire Irish agrarian problems, he did not approve of the aggressive tactics adopted by the Land League; instead he continued to believe that the Parliamentary process and trust in Gladstone was the way to achieve their aims.

Throughout the country more riots took place at evictions and acts of violence were regular occurrences. In November 1880 Parnell was among the Land League leaders prosecuted for conspiring to prevent the payment of rents.

The same month Henry wrote to the papers defending the Government. 'I am convinced Mr Gladstone's Government is determined to deal with the Land Question in a thorough and complete manner. I am also convinced that the best service tenants can render to their own cause will be giving full evidence to the Commissioners who are entirely impartial and most anxious to arrive at the truth', 'and unless the Government does come up to the full measure of justice in this matter, no one will oppose them more earnestly than myself. In the meantime we are bound to give them fair play, and not to render their task impossible by putting forth unreasonable demands and fierce cries.' 'What we have to do is to see that the cultivator of the soil has full justice done to him - in other words, that the poor tenant shall find the law his friend, not his enemy. However, the resources of the country must be opened out and taxation and absentee drain must be abolished.'[12]

11. G.V. July 28, 1880.
12. ibid.

Process Serving at Errismore

On September 19, 1880 at Ennis, Parnell, while addressing a meeting, urged the tenants to resist eviction and to keep a firm grip on their homesteads. Before being evicted the tenants were served with processes of ejectment and decrees would then be obtained against them at the quarter sessions. They would then be visited by the bailiff who was usually accompanied by soldiers to assist him in evicting the tenant.

In 1880 the process servers for this district were: Patrick Kelly, Roundstone; John Browne, Clifden; Martin D'Arcy and Dominick D'Arcy, Clifden; Thomas O'Flaherty, Renvyle and Letterfrack. A visit by these men to a district usually meant trouble and the vivid description of one such visit to Bunowen reported in full in the newspapers gives us some idea of the horror and fear the recipient of these notices felt when the process server called.

On Friday September 17, 1880 a large force of extra policemen, seventy eight in all under Sub-Inspectors Mills and Dunne, arrived in Clifden from Galway.[13] At 10 o'clock the next morning they arrived at Errismore where they began serving processes on the Bunowen estate of Charles J. Blake. The property was said to support a mountain sheep or wiry cattle and consisting of nothing but a rocky landscape running into the Atlantic and ending in Slyne Head. The tenants did not make their living out of the land but only had their houses there 'in a convenient position to enable them to fish and preserve kelp'. These tenants were now victims of the failed kelp market. Sixteen tenants were served that day, many of them were widows and the only place left for them was the workhouse. Most of the ejectments were for a year and a half or two years rent in arrear. Although the rents were small the tenants had been living on relief meal during the winter and were unable to pay. John Brown from Clifden was the process server and he was accompanied by Mr Parkinson R.M.

The first notice to be served was on Val Clogherty, whose house was on the roadside and within sight of Mr Blake's Castle. The local people had got word of the arrival of the police and were gathered together in a boreen, 'great strapping fellows, dressed in yellow flannel trousers and usual vest with flannel sleeves, their faces coloured with the pure air of the Atlantic and their fists bearing big cudgels, which spoke of moral and physical force combined.' Rev. Fr. Flannery, 'The active young curate of the parish' arrived and tried to restrain the people. As the police approached Clogherty's cabin the people threw themselves in a mass in front of them. Mr Parkinson tried to force his way to the door but they prevented him from reaching it; he then read part of the Riot Act to them and ordered the police to fix swords. After doing this, the police made a 'gentle sort of charge', but the people stood firm 'and a riot was imminent.' Rev. Flannery then came forward and urged the people to cease, telling them this was not an ejectment but only a notice and that it was vain to attempt to resist. The people then drew aside and Browne fixed the notice on the door claiming two years rent £15.18s.4d. The police, with Brown in their midst, marched down the road and notices were posted on Mary McDonagh's door for £10.18.8d and Mary Sweeney's for £10.18.8d and Peter Burke's for £10.18.8d. These three were for two years rent. The people did not follow the

13. This description is compiled from a report in the Connaught Telegraph, September 25, 1880.

police but remained grouped opposite Clogherty's. A few minutes later a Mr Thomas Brennan of the Land League arrived by car from Clifden and was loudly cheered.

The police then turned off the road and began to cross a 'vast sandy stretch by the seashore'. The sun was beating down on the sands and to the left the ocean looked beautifully green and broke into 'puffs of snowy clouds over the numberless rocky stripes' on the shore. The people now began to follow the police. The procession made its way across the sandy flats towards some hills in the distance. 'In command of the police walked Mr Parkinson, a stout gentleman with white head and benevolent expression, an aspect which he very soon lost, with a luncheon bag strapped across his shoulder and an umbrella in his hand, his son by his side, he directed operations during the greater part of the day.' 'Behind the commander-in-chief and his personal staff marched the seventy eight policemen with rifles in hand, in the midst of them being Mr Browne, a man dressed like an ordinary peasant, with a pale face and a hunted look. A short distance behind the string of police walked Fr Flannan with a riding whip in his hand, Mr Brennan walking by his side, heading a collection of 500 or 600 men, women and children, who in imitation of the police marched four deep.' There were cries from the people of 'God Save Ireland' and 'Down with Landlordism, no more will be served.'

Mr Brennan then began to address the people. He told them he had come from Dublin at the request of the Errismore Land League to use whatever influence he could over the people and ask them 'not to be guilty of any act that could disgrace Ireland' and to avoid bloodshed. He asked them not to offer physical resistance to the police, who were only doing their duty, a duty that he was sure was to most of them a very disagreeable duty indeed. He asked them today to act prudently as became Irishmen, 'but also to act as became Irishmen determined that the accursed system of Landlordism must go down. (applause).'

The police had now crossed the sands and were marching upon the hillside, 'a wretched dwelling with a door but no window.' The people rushed and surrounded the house with a living wall. The police stopped a few feet away and Mr Parkinson tried to force his way to the door but failed; the order was given to fix swords and march. Cries and yells came from the people surrounding the house while the tenant, an old widow woman, sat a little distance away with her face in her hands, crooning and wailing as if she were already evicted. Other women shouted insults at Browne and the police, and told the men to hold their ground. When Rev. Flannery went to the men and tried to have them stop, the women called after him, 'Look at the priest putting the poor people to death.' The police pressed forward, Mr Brennan, Rev. Flannery and Mr Parkinson were between the two groups and directly in front of the bayonets and in the scuffling that took place were fortunate not to be injured. Rev. Flannery tried to force a passage to the door; Mr Brennan tried to help him at the same time shouting 'We are not able to resist these buckshot warriors.' He then called out 'let those minions of the English law carry out their fell purpose'. In a few seconds the police reached the door. 'A line of bayonets were then formed and out of the main body of police stepped forth Mr Browne and walking through the passage kept for him, posted the process on the door.'

58

Fisherman's Cottage. Courtesy National Library.

Mr Browne was then surrounded by police as he served notices on the next two doors of the cabins of John Coyne and Pat Duane for two years rent at £12.10.0d. Swords were then unfixed and they marched again along the shore line. The people now made a show of resistance at the next two houses. The next house to be visited had no road to it. They had to follow a route which ran up against a hill, crossed over stone walls and empty potato patches on to the house. But Mr Brennan had directed the front and back door of the house be pulled off and the inhabitants turned out. All the people then stood to one side as the police approached. Someone called out to Browne and told him 'he would yet be serving processes in a warmer place and would have a police escort then too.' Browne walked into the house and put the process on the dresser. Word was sent ahead and every door was removed and the remainder of the notices were served in this way.

The rest of the tenants to be served included Mary McNamara a widow, one and a half years rent; Monica King, for two years rent £15.7.0d.; John Roach, two years, £32.10.0d., Matt Gould two years £24.0.0d.; Val Conneely, fisherman, living on the water's edge, two years, £2.0.0d.; Michael King, £13.5.0d. Pat Leahy two years £25.0.0d.

It was four o'clock in the afternoon before the last process was served. 'The police it is fair to say did their duty without the least unkindness, many of them privately made no scruple of stating their dislike for the work they were engaged in.'. Having completed their task the police marched back to the main road where they rested and ate their provisions. Later cars collected them and returned them to Clifden. Mr Brennan then spoke to the people on the sand, expressing his regret at having to restrain them; he wished he could have called them to a more manly battle for their country's national and social regeneration. 'But it is necessary to have education of the mind as well as power of the arm in the struggle which we are now fighting, and we want, through the means of public meetings, to teach you that you were not born to be the slave of any class, that you were born with the same rights as a peer, and that you should assert these rights. This movement should not be confined to the tenants farmers alone, it concerns every man who works for his daily bread.' 'I would ask all to join in one manly struggle, in one great organisation for the destruction of Irish Landlordism'. He then went on to criticise landlords saying they 'regard you as white slaves who have been sent into this world specially to minister to their wants and I ask you today to pledge yourselves here to record a vow never to leave off the work until you destroy their power. (applause)'.

He advised them it is their duty not pay rent this year; if they pay rent and their children die of starvation in the coming winter they will be responsible before God for their murder. Rent, he told them, 'should be paid out of what is left over after feeding, clothing and educating one's family, if you have any left when this is done then pay your rent.' He advised the people to buy the newspaper after Mass on Sundays and gather together to discuss and interchange ideas and go on with the work of education, 'and let the voice of the country go forward demanding the abolition of landlordism', he concluded.[14]

In the same newspaper a letter appeared from Charles J. Blake, landlord of Bunowen. He explained that the custom on Bunowen was to collect half year rent, due on November 1, in the month of July following and the rent due May 1, in the following December. In July 1879 Mr Blake's brother went to Bunowen Castle to collect the November 1878 rents; many of the poorest tenants had not as yet paid the May 1878 rent.

With one or two exceptions, none of the tenants, about seventy in all, paid their rent. In December 1879 he went to Bunowen himself and told the tenants he would forgive the half year to November 1878, which they had failed to pay his brother, if they would pay half year to May 1879. All but one tenant, and he only paid part of his rent, failed to pay.

Before leaving Bunowen he told them as the winter was likely to be a trying one, he would not press until the summer and then he would expect all who were able to pay to do so. In August 1880 his brother again visited the Castle but got nothing. He explained that the tenants held their land at Griffith's Valuation and in some cases it was very low. He then decided to select names of persons from each townland that he considered were able to pay a year's rent and directed ejectment processes to be issued against them, more to discourage the others than to collect the small amount due. He complained that the influence of the Land League had been brought to bear on the tenants as he knew them all his life and always 'exhibited towards me the warmest feelings of regard and affection.' He concluded by saying, 'I shall only say that, so far from driving out any of the poor tenants from their holdings, I shall retain them on my land on any terms as long as circumstances will allow me. I seek to recover rent not from those who are unable to pay but from those who are unwilling to pay it'.[15]

Thanks to the attention of the press, the evictions were averted but only for a short time. In May 1882 evictions were carried out on this estate.

14. This description is compiled from a report in Connaught Telegraph, September 25, 1880.
15. C.T. September 25, 1880.

Mitchell Henry's opposition to Parnell

In a letter to the English Radical League on January 5, 1881, Henry revealed his feelings that the Land League were leading the people into violence and agitation and away from the source of a successful conclusion to their demands. 'Unfortunately this present agitation has unhinged society completely and I doubt whether since the French Revolution there was ever such a reign of terror as now exists in Ireland. The leaders of the movement do not want the Land question settled in a just manner, because they know that if the bulk of the people have a secure hold on their farms, and can feel sure that their improvements will belong to themselves they will become orderly and contented. This would not suit the extreme men who are fattening on the agitation, and secretly urging the poor ignorant people to dangers which they themselves do not share. I receive numerous letters from influential priests and laymen, who have always been the true friends of the Irish tenants and of the Irish people, deploring the present state of things and lamenting that truth and honesty are banished from Ireland. The attitude of the democracy of England has a powerful effect on public opinion. Let us work together for justice to all, and especially for the poor man. And let us sternly set out faces against the outrage on man and beast and the reign of terror which is a disgrace to civilisation.'[16]

Because of his outspoken views regarding Parnell and the leaders of the Land League, it was rumoured that he had to leave his home at Kylemore that Christmas as a result of threats. Denouncing these rumours in the newspaper, Henry explained he had spent Christmas at Kylemore and leaving his family there returned to London to do some work with the Agricultural Commission. He said he was disappointed with his tenants 'but that is owing to the secret agent of the Land League whose doctrine of the "Land for the people" and directions to them to pay no rent are interpreted to mean, as indeed they are told, that every landlord is a robber and intruder. I have only 125 tenants, very few of whom have paid anything, although many would pay if they were not intimidated by a lawless confederation who have succeeded in completely changing the character and behaviour of the people, I trust and believe only temporary. Permit me to say I have a great respect for Mr Davitt who has been abusing me, more than I have for other persons of higher position. Mr Davitt makes no concealment of the fact that the object he has in view are such as must prevent any honest man from taking the oath of allegiance to the Queen at the table of the House of Commons and he has consequently always refused to become a member of Parliament'.[17]

January 1881 saw the trial of Parnell and other leaders ending in acquittal. Verbal attacks on Henry were now frequent. On February 21 1881, Major John Talbot D'Arcy, second son of John D'Arcy, referred to him in his speech at a meeting in Ballinsloe, when he said he never blamed a man for changing his opinions but he did blame the member for the county Mitchell Henry, who was a member of the League, for deserting from their ranks when his services were most required. Henry writing to the newspapers demanded a public retraction and repair of the injury done to him by Major D'Arcy's comments. Stating he

16. G.V. January 5, 1881.
17. G.V. January 19, 1881.

was never a member of the League and that he refused to have anything to do with them. He had, he wrote, on several occasions expressed his dissent from Parnell's policy; on two of those occasions he 'challenged Parnell's opinion on public platforms in his presence, and after his speeches, once at Galway and once at Manchester. That was the time he (Parnell) was groping his way to the land question, for it is notorious that he never took the slightest interest in it during his early time in Parliament and did not adopt land reform as his cry until the policy of obstruction had failed in the House of Commons and Mr Davitt suggested a more telling cry to him.'

Declaring he has always let his views on the Land question and Home Rule be known and they remain the same, 'the stupid, irrational, almost insane policy of the last few months has resulted in crippling the Irish vote in Parliament forever,' 'because once it became plain that the object was to degrade Parliament there was not a cabman or costermonger in England who did not turn against the Irish members.' Directing his remarks to Major D'Arcy he continued, 'You yourself may judge me as you like, but I call on you not to misrepresent me or to pander to the momentary excitement of a Land League meeting by accusing me of a baseness of conduct. I challenge you or anybody else to point out a single instance in which I have concealed my opinions, or failed to stick to them.'[18] The challenge was never taken up and the conflict seemed to end there.

Evictions and the Land Act

During the summer of 1881 there was an increase in the number of Land League meetings throughout the country. Evictions for non-payment of rent became commonplace; the tenants backed by the Land League were refusing to pay rents and the landlords pressed forward with the evictions. Among those were the landlords previously praised for their support and assistance during the famine of 1879.

On June 22 1881 about one hundred Royal Irish Constabulary under the command of Sub-Sheriffs Lennon and Warburton and one hundred military under the command of Major Simpson and Capt. Lynskey of the Brigade Depot, accompanied Sub-Inspector John Reddington and five bailiffs who went to Connemara to evict two families on the property of Mr J.S. Kirwan of Blindwell Tuam, at Carraroe; nine families on the property of Mrs Suffield of Clifden, at Belleck, just outside the town, and two families on the property of John Kendall London at Derrygimlea near Clifden. Also present were Messrs Beckett and Dennepy R.M.'s. The R.I.C. were drafted in from different out-stations and marched to the docks where they boarded a ship named '*Valorous*' and two gunboats, the *Merlin* and the *Imogene*. The military marched from Renmore Barracks and were made up of equal numbers of the 87th and 84th Regiment. They were preceded by the regimental band which attracted a great crowd.

According to the newspaper report, the *Valorous* and gunboats were first to call at Carraroe, where they were to remain for two days, evict the two families and offer protection to process servers who were to serve a large number of ejectment and civil bills in the area. They were then to continue along the coast

18. G.V. March 2, 1881.

to Clifden to carry out the evictions in Belleck and Derrygimlea and afterwards return to Galway.[19] The newspapers carry no further mention of the incident so it is assumed all went according to plan.

A Land Bill was brought before the House based on the recommendations of the Government Commission and it became law in 1881. This Act provided for the setting up of a Land Court to arbitrate between the landlord and the tenant. The Court was empowered to fix a fair rent and while the tenant paid this rent he could not be evicted. The Act also enabled the tenant to sell his interest in the farm on leaving it. This was the first of a series of Land Acts up to 1921 which was to result in the tenant eventually becoming the owner of his holding.

As Mitchell Henry had predicted, once the Land Act became law the Land League found itself beaten. Parnell continued to address meetings and after a challenging speech in Wexford he was arrested, along with other leaders, on October 12, and placed in Kilmainham jail. On the 18th of that month a manifesto calling on tenant farmers to pay no rents was issued by the League but it got little support. The result was that on October 20, the Land League was outlawed. That winter saw an increase in crime and evictions continued along the Connemara coast.

The Law Life Assurance Company, owners of the once Martin Estate of Ballinahinch had sold out to a Mr Berridge of London. George Robinson remained on as agent and was now living at Roundstone. Like the rest of Connemara, the tenants were in arrear with rent, two and a half years up to May 1881. In September of that year they sent a memorial to Mr Berridge in which they laid down what they were prepared to do with a view to having the outstanding rent settled at once. They offered to pay one year's rent up to May 1881 and to join the landlord in procuring from the Land Commission a loan for the payment of the rest of the arrears in accordance with the terms of the new Land Act. Mr Berridge replied immediately, saying, 'The proposals which it (memorial) contains shall receive my best consideration and I hope to be able in a short time to communicate with you further theron.' This letter was written on September 15. The tenants did not hear again from Mr Berridge until Christmas Day; he agreed to accept their proposals under certain conditions but as these conditions were unacceptable to the tenants the result was that in the middle of January 1882, Roundstone Bay was visited by the gunboats and thirty two families were evicted; 'amidst the booming of cannon from Her Majesty's warships in the bay, and the scattering broadcast of Mr Forster's buckshot,' Rev Joseph Malone Parish Priest wrote to the newspapers describing the event. The shots were fired not at the tenants but at their livestock who scattered and were promptly chased by the soliders 'into the sea they rush to render captive the victims of their buckshot; namely the geese which they wantonly killed and which belonged to the honest though poor, industrious evicted tenantry.' On returning to the ships the soldiers were reprimanded and it was said put into cold irons, 'not for wantonly interfering with the property of the poor, but for allowing their ammunition to get damp in their anxiety to seize their ill-gotten prey.'[20] More evictions were expected to take place in the coming days.

19. G.V. June 25, 1881.
20. G.V. January 21, 1882.

Sub-Sheriff Mr Reddington spent the first two weeks in May 1882 carrying out evictions on the property of Mr Berridge, Mrs Kirwan, Mr Eyre, Clifden Castle, Mr Blake and Mrs Wall, Errislannon. The Sub-Sheriff was accompanied by a large force of the 84th Connaught Rangers under the command of Major Pope. They travelled aboard the *Seahorse* which was accompanied by the gunboat *Redwing*. They evicted by day and returned to the ship each night.

The evictions were said to be of the most extensive character, one hundred and fifty families in all having been evicted. Once again Berridge's tenants appeared to make up the greater number. At Carraroe the Sub-Sheriff and his escort had to walk over ten miles inland to carry out their work. There were many emotional scenes as many of the families were very poor but the military were not opposed. On the Eyre estate as elsewhere the evictions were for non-payment of rents and the evicted were the occupiers of small farms with rents generally ranging from £1 to £5. Again no resistance or disturbance took place.

Arrears Bill

In May 1882 Parnell and his colleagues were released from prison after reaching an agreement, known as the 'Kilmainham Treaty' with the Government. Out of this agreement came the Arrears Bill which provided for the paying of one year's rent of the arrears by the tenant, one year's rent by the State and the wiping out of all other arrears. It protected tenants with arrears of rent from eviction and enabled them to approach the Land Court for the fixing of a fair rent. Parnell agreed to use his influence to stop acts of agrarian outrage and reduce tension throughout the country. This addition to the Land Act came a little too late for the evicted tenants of Connemara and their only fate was to join the thousands of other families seeking assisted passages to America.

Henry summed up the political situation as he saw it, in his letter to Board of Guardian of the Glenamaddy Union as follows:

'The frightful waste of time, and the irritation which has arisen from the course taken by a certain number of the Irish representatives has completely poisoned the minds of the English and Scottish members who were our friends, either into declared enemies or indifferent lookers-on. However unpopular such an opinion may make me, I solemnly declare my conviction, that if ordinary commonsense had been used in Parliament and if the policy of Mr Butt had been followed, that is, to convince by argument and not to attempt to exasperate for the mere sake of exasperation, not only would the Land Bill have been passed long before it was passed, but there would have been no coercion, and the material development of Ireland by drainage, reclamation and making of light railways would have been dealth with by Parliament.

As it is, Ireland now lies bound hand and foot for a long term of years, all sympathy for the country has been destroyed and the reputation of the Irish people as a God-fearing, honest, and gallant race has been rudely shaken in the eyes of the world.

So long as I remain in Parliament, I shall pursue the same policy that I have always done, that is to endeavour to promote the practical good of the country and to speak the truth so far as I know it.'[21]

After the election of 1884 Henry no longer represented Galway. From 1885-6 he was M.P. for Glasgow; the Castle was sold to the Duke and Duchess of Manchester in 1903. On his death in 1910 Henry's body was returned to Kylemore and laid to rest beside that of his wife.

21. G.V. August 12, 1882.

CHAPTER IV

Execution and Emigration

The Letterfrack Murders

An example of the heinous murders committed throughout the country at this time in the name of the Land can be seen in what became known as the barbaric and brutal Letterfrack Murders.

This was the murder of John Lydon (a herd of Francis Graham at Letterfrack) and his son Martin. The murders took place on April 24 1881 and were carried out by six or seven men at the still of the night. The reasons were never completely clear; the identity of the murderers never satisfactorily proven. The guilt of Patrick Walsh, executed for perpetrating the act was never accepted by the country at large.

When John Lydon along with his wife and children moved to Bannogaes, Letterfrack, where he became herd for Francis Graham, the local Landlord, the family were accepted in the neighbourhood as very poor, quiet, inoffensive people. The land on which Lydon worked had previously been occupied by Stephen Walsh and his family. In September 1877 after an amicable agreement had been reached between Walsh and Joseph McDonnell, agent for Mr Graham, Walsh was forgiven arrears of rent and costs when he gave up these lands and moved to Letterfrack village, where he took up other lands but still remained a tenant of Mr Graham.

On the night in question, Sunday April 24 1881, the Lydon family were asleep in the only bedroom in the cabin. Mrs Nappy Lydon shared one bed with three of her children, Thomas, aged about twelve, John, aged five or six, and Ellen who was three. The other bed in the room was occupied by her husband and son Martin, aged about twenty. Margaret, their older daughter, was attending the wake of Tom Conroy in Letterfrack village.

Between ten and eleven o'clock the family were awakened by noise outside the cabin. Six or seven men pushed open the cabin door and came up to the bedroom. They first approached Mrs Lydon's bed and she began to scream, 'We're killed',[1] as they ran their hands up along the bedclothes and over her legs. Finding only Mrs Lydon and the children they turned to her husband. He shouted at them to leave him alone that he was sick, but one of the men said he should get out. They then caught hold of him, pulled him out of the bed and, taking him outside, they laid him down on the stones. They came back into the room for Martin who was now crying and screaming. Two of them reached down and caught hold of his legs and pulled him from the room. He held on to the jamb of the kitchen door but one of the men called out to him, 'Out, out, you ...' and kicked him twice in his right side and, shoving him out, threw him down on his side.

Someone then gave the command, 'Fire', five or six shots rang out. Mrs Lydon stood at the window with Thomas and watched them kill her husband

1. G.V. August 19 1882.

and son. The flashes of the shots came in through the kitchen doorway, but the night was too dark for her to recognise the murderers. Throughout the shooting Martin was screaming but his father remained quiet. Martin then pretended he was dead and someone said, 'That will do, they will herd no more'. Another voice said, 'March', and they marched away in a body towards the river and Letterfrack.[2]

When Mrs Lydon was sure they had left, she and Thomas went outside where her husband was lying on the flagstones. She asked him how he was but he did not reply; he was dead. She then went to Martin who appeared to be seriously injured. When he asked how his father was, she answered, 'I think he is dead'.[3] With Thomas to help her, she dragged them both inside. Martin then told her that Patrick Walsh, son of Stephen, was in the party and that he was one of those who had pulled him out of the bed and it was he who kicked him as he held on to the kitchen door and told him to get out.

At about five o'clock in the morning, Margaret returned from the wake to find her father dead and her brother dying. Martin asked her if Patrick Walsh was at the wake. She told him he was. 'If he was, he was here too last night',[4] he said. Then he told her he was going to die and to go for the Priest.

Along with the Priest, Dr. James Gorham arrived. On examining Martin he discovered a wound in his chest where the bullet had entered and lodged in the lung; he also had wounds in the wrist and groin. He felt there was a chance of recovery as Martin was young and strong, but he was still suffering from shock after the experience. Later Dr. Gorham carried out a postmortem on John Lydon. The fatal bullet had entered the body between the fourth and fifth ribs, travelled upwards and inwards, dividing the main blood vessels from the heart artery and causing a fatal haemorrhage; the bullet then entered the lung. There was another wound in the back part of the right side and from this wound he extracted a revolver bullet. There was a further wound on the left side of the chest.

Dying man's accusation

About nine o'clock on Monday morning, Constable Joseph Butler came to the house. Martin heard him in the kitchen talking to his mother and he called him into the bedroom. The body of John Lydon was in the same room. Martin told the constable he was going to die and to sit down and he would tell him all. The Constable advised him to tell the truth and Martin proceeded to tell him that Patrick Walsh was one of the men who came into the room, and that he was one of those who caught him by the legs and pulled him out of the bed. He recognised Patrick Walsh's voice when he said, 'Out, out you ...' and then gave him two kicks on the right side before shoving him out. He continued with a description of the shooting and how, after completing the job, the men marched away in a body.

The Constable then went to Letterfrack to see Mr John Charles Hall, a Royal Magistrate, and then proceeded to arrest Patrick Walsh. Constable Butler was then joined by County Inspector Cullen, Mr Hall and Patrick Walsh. They all

2. ibid.
3. G.V. August 19, 1882.
4. ibid.

Letterfrack Village. Courtesy National Library.

went to Lydon's house and there in the presence of Walsh, Martin Lydon was sworn and his statement was taken down in writng. He repeated the statement made to Constable Butler. Patrick Walsh was then taken to the Clifden Bridewell having been remanded by Mr Hall for a week. Dr Gorham worked diligently for the next month in an attempt to keep Martin alive. On Wednesday May 4, he applied to Dublin Castle for the assistance of a surgeon experienced in treating bullet wounds. Professor Pye of Queens College Galway was sent to examine Martin. The Professor approved of the treatment carried out by Dr Gorham and agreed that Martin was in too precarious a condition to attempt an extraction of the bullet.

The inquest on John Lydon found a verdict that the deceased had been brutally murdered by some persons unknown. Following Patrick Walsh's arrest, it appears no further arrests were made, except a man named Joyce who was arrested on April 29 on board the Steamer, the *Phoenician,* leaving Galway for Boston.[5] Joyce was taken before Mr Hill, R.M., but there was no evidence to warrant his remand. He was set free in time to board the steamer and sail for America.

On Tuesday, May 3 1881, Patrick Walsh, described as aged about twenty, a butcher and car owner, was brought before Clifden Petty Sessions and charged with being concerned in the wilful murder of John Lydon on the night of April 24. The case was heard by Mr Parkinson R.M. and Mr Gorham, J.P. and after a short affidavit by Sub-Inspector Dunne was read, to the effect that Martin

5. G.V. August 30 1881.

Lydon was not sufficiently recovered to attend, the prisoner was remanded for a further week.[6]

On Saturday May 21, Martin Lydon died about four o'clock in the afternoon. A post mortem was carried out by Dr James Gorham assisted by his brother Dr Pit Gorham. At the inquest that followed, the jury found a verdict of wilful and malicious murder, but by whom they had no direct evidence to show.[7]

On the following night, the house of Michael Lydon, herd of Mr McDonnell, agent for Mr Graham, was burnt to the ground. Michael Lydon was the nephew of John Lydon, the murdered man. Since his uncle's murder he and his family (wife and four very young children) were living with relatives. Each morning he and his wife went back to their home, which was situated in a remote mountain glen. There they would attend to the farm business and return each evening to their relatives' house. On the night of the fire, furniture, clothes, bedclothes were burnt; even a sheepdog, tied in the house, was burnt to death. The police visited the scene but made no discoveries.[8]

It would appear that the charge against Walsh for the murder of John Lydon was dropped and the charge of murdering Martin Lydon only, then proceeded.

On June 29 the case came before the investigating Magistrates. Walsh was brought by an armed body of police from the Bridewell to be present at the investigation. The case for the prosecution was based on a deposition made by Martin Lydon, in which he identified Walsh as one of the persons who attacked him. The case for the defence was based on Walsh's alibi that he spent the entire night at Tom Conroy's wake at Letterfrack and therefore could not have been party to the crime.

Margaret Lydon was called to give evidence and swore she spent the night at the wake and did not see Walsh there until twelve o'clock or afterwards. She particularly remembered him entering as she remarked to Bridget Lacey, seated beside her, that Walsh lived so near she wondered why he had not been there earlier.

Constable Kavanagh gave evidence of the distance from the barracks to Lydon's house and also to the wake house. He had walked the distance taking the shortest route through fields, walking at a regular pace, he covered the distance to Lydon's house in twenty-three minutes.

When the case for the prosecution was concluded, Mr. Connolly, Solicitor for the accused, was asked if he had any witnesses to call. He said he had, but did not wish to produce them then or name them in case they would be arrested under the Coercion Act, for coming forward to give evidence and thus deprive his client of their evidence at the coming Assizes. The accused was then sent to trial in the Galway Azzizes.

On Tuesday July 26, 1881 the case came up at the Summer Assizes Crown Court before Lord Justice Fitzgibbon. Patrick (Pat) Walsh pleaded not guilty and Mr Sergeant Robinson who appeared on behalf of the Crown asked the Judge to postpone the trial until the next Assizes. The application was grounded on an affidavit of Sub-Inspector Dunne of Clifden, who said the police recently obtained fresh information regarding the murder which they had not yet had time to investigate and also that he believed further material

6. ibid. May 7 1881.
7. ibid. May 25 1881.
8. G.V. July 1, 1881.

69

evidence would be procured before the next Assizes if the case were to be postponed. Mr Francis Nolan on behalf of the prisoner opposed the application but Lord Justice Fitzgibbon granted the request and postponed the trial until the next Assizes.

The case next appeared one year later July 19, 1882. This time Mr Sergeant Robinson instructed Mr T.D. O'Farrell Crown Solicitor who appeared on behalf of the Attorney General and Mr Charles O'Malley, instructed by Mr R.J. Connolly acted on behalf of the accused. The Judge in the case was Mr Justice O'Reilly.

Mr O'Farrell requested that the case be transferred to Dublin where the accused would be sent immediately to be tried. Mr Chrles O'Malley argued that the case had already come up three or four times and been postponed but the judge agreed to transfer the case to Dublin. Later that day eighteen witnesses entered into their own recognizances to attend the trial in Dublin.

The Trial

Finally the case was tried on Wednesday August 16, 1882 at the Commission Court before Mr Justice Lawson. The prosecution was conducted by Solicitor-General M.P. Mr James Murphy, Q.C., and Mr Edward Sullivan, who were instructed by Mr George Bodkin, Crown Solicitor. Messrs Charles O'Malley Q.C. and Bodkin, instructed by Mr Redmond Connelly defended the prisoner.

The prisoner was described by the newspaper as a 'young man of respectable appearance of the farming class'.[9]

The Solicitor-General stated the case for the Crown and the prisoner at the bar was charged with the murder of Martin Lydon, the crime being described as one of an 'agrarian character'.[10] The court was told that Stephen Walsh, father of the prisoner had held a small farm from Mr Graham, Ballinakill Lodge, but having some disagreement with his Landlord had yielded up possession of the land on being forgiven costs and arrears of rent then due. John Lydon was then put onto the land as herdsman and on the night of April 24 between ten and eleven o'clock he along with his son Martin were taken from their bed by a group of men and shot. The Solicitor-General recommended that the Jury find Pat Walsh guilty as the evidence would show.

A number of witnesses were then called. Mr Somerville, Civil Engineer, was called and produced a plan giving detailed measurements showing the distance between the wake house, Lydon's house and Walsh's house. Joseph McDonnell, agent for Mr Graham, was examined on the circumstances regarding Stephen Walsh vacating his holding. He mentioned that the Walshes were prosecuted several times for trespassing and that he had received money from them for same.

Nappy Lydon, the widow of John, was then called upon to give evidence and described the events of the night. On cross-examination by Mr O'Malley, she said she told her story to the Magistrates in English and gave her evidence at the inquest in English but admitted she did not have a good understanding of the language. She was now being questioned in Irish through an interpreter and caused some amusements by answering one of the questions in 'capital

9. G.V. August 19, 1882.
10. G.V. August 19, 1882.

70

English'.[11] The Judge instructed the interpreter to stand aside and the questions continued in English but Mrs Lydon replied in Irish and refused to answer directly. As she continued to answer in Irish, cross-examination was discontinued.

Among the witnesses then called was Margaret Lydon, sister of the dead man. She repeated her evidence given at the inquest; that she attended the wake of Tom Conroy on the night in question and did not see Pat Walsh there until he entered the door at about 12.15 am. She mentioned Walsh's big dark great-coat and that she had never seen the coat before. A youth named Free was called and gave evidence that Walsh did not arrive at the wake until twelve-fifteen and remarks were passed among those present about a great coat he was wearing. Constable Edward Colligan, R.I.C., while examined by Mr Murphy, stated that on March 7, 1882 he made a thorough search of the house of Honor Walsh, the prisoner's mother, and found concealed in the thatch a rifle. The house had been re-thatched since the rifle was placed there. It was later stated that the house had been re-thatched in December 1881 or January 1882.

The rifle was then displayed and James Faherty was called and he stated that he sold the gun to Pat Walsh in February or beginning of March 1881 for £1, half in cash down and half in fishing nets. Faherty had bought it seven years previously from a coastguard official. A Michael Faherty identified the gun also; he made his living fixing guns and had done some work on this particular one; he recognised it because it was a 'peculiar' style of gun.

Mr John Harris, gunsmith from the Dublin firm of Trulock and Harris, said the gun was what they called a Russian gun, made in England for the Russian market. It had an irregular bore that was between the bore of English guns twelve and thirteen. The bullet given to him by Dr Gorham taken from the body of John Lydon 'exactly fits the gun' Mr Harris then produced a facsimile of the bullet. It was not from an ordinary mould but was made by casting it in a thimble. He had made various experiments on hard and soft substances with the result that a bullet similar to that produced once discharged from the gun, which it fitted exactly, would make a clear wound. If a gun with a larger bore were used, the wound would be greater in size.

On cross-examination by Mr O'Malley, Mr Harris admitted that if a bullet before being used in a gun of larger bore, was encased in brown paper, it would go straight. He added that he could not swear that there were not thousands of rifles similar to that produced all over the country.

Dr Gorham, when examined, stated that the wound in which he found the bullet referred to was small, so small he had to enlarge it to get out the lead. (Considering that this wound was in John Lydon, it seems odd that this evidence was discussed as Walsh was now being tried for the murder of Martin Lydon).

Sub-Constable Sullivan then gave the evidence regarding the time it took to walk from Walsh's house to Lydon's house and from Lydon's house to the wake house. This evidence at the inquest had been given by Constable Kavanagh.[a] In it he stated that walking at an ordinary pace and going part of the way by the road and part by fields, he covered the distance between Walsh's house and

11. ibid.
a. Constable Kavanagh had since been murdered and Michael Walsh, a brother of the accused, was at this time awaiting trial for that murder.

Lydon's in nineteen minutes, and between Lydon's and the wake house in twenty-four minutes. This evidence was used to strengthen the prosecution's claim that Walsh had ample time to commit the crime and still attend the wake.

The Court then adjourned. The Jury spent the night in Morrison's Hotel, Dawson Street, under the charge of the Sub-Sheriff of the City.

The next day, Thursday, a Martin Connolly, examined by Mr O'Malley, stated that on his way to the wakehouse he heard fiddle music coming from Walsh's house; he entered and stayed there for about three quarters of an hour and then he went with Pat Laffey and Pat Joyce to the wake. At about nine o'clock he entered the wakehouse and stayed in the lobby with Laffey and Joyce until twelve o'clock, a quarter of an hour later Pat Walsh arrived but could not get in because there was such a crowd; he turned away and came back again in a quarter of an hour when he got in and stayed. The witness admitted he had been held in jail in connection with the murder of John Lydon but 'they failed in the prosecution'.[12]

Michael Kelly aged about seventeen, stated he saw Pat Walsh in the lobby from about 9 o'clock and was with him until about two o'clock the next morning. He said Walsh could not have gone to Lydon's house between nine pm and two am without his knowing it.

Mrs Mary Mongan who lived near the wake-house and had assisted in washing the corpse, said she attended the wake all night and that she saw Walsh there at nine o'clock first at the door and then turning to the Judge she said 'he never left my sight between 9 pm and 2.30 am'. The Solicitor-General then cross-examined the witness and asked her 'Did you tell Mrs Cassidy (her sister-in-law) more than once, you were sorry there was nothing you could do for poor Pat Walsh because you went to bed at nine o'clock and were asleep until daylight?' 'No sir, she is the last woman I would have a conversation with because she could not keep ...'

'Keep what'. the Solicitor General asked.

'A secret'.

'What secret was there'.

'Any sort of secret'.

'Was there a secret about the wake?'

'No, Sir', she replied.

Sarah Cummins also swore to having seen Walsh at the wake and stated that he could not have visited Lydon's house unknown to her. Francis Garner, employed by Mitchell Henry, arrived at the wake at ten o'clock to paint the name of the deceased on the coffin. After completing the task, he spent the remainder of the night seated on the lid of the coffin. At about twelve o'clock he saw Walsh beside him (on his inside). Walsh he said could not previously have passed him without him standing up to let him by; they both remained there until about two o'clock.

A number of others were called and supported Pat Walsh's alibi. Closing the case for the defence, Mr Bodkin addressed the jury. He relied strongly on the alibi set up in defence of the prisoner and urged that owing to the weak condition of the mind and body of Martin Lydon, his dying identification should not be acted upon by the jury to take away the life of the young man in

12. G.V. August 19 1882.

the dock. Mr Murphy replied on the part of the Crown, he said 'nothing could equal the appalling horror of the tragedy or conduct of the inhuman wretches, the gang of assassins' and he went on to describe the crime. 'In a forcible and feeling address, the learned counsel insisted that there was a consistent and thorough reliable chain of evidence, accompanied by motive, establishing the guilt of the prisoner, and his participation in a well planned and foully executed deed. The alibi so carefully devised by Pat Walsh and his friends had been plainly shattered by a clear statement of the dying man as to the prisoner being one of the men who committed the double murder that night'.[13] The court then adjourned.

On Friday the Judge charged the Jury and having deliberated for two and a half hours they could not agree and were discharged.

Re-Trial

The following Mondy, August 21, Pat Walsh was again put on trial. Again before Judge Lawson and with the same Counsel for the Defence and Prosecution. Mrs Lydon now gave evidence in English although it was admitted 'not with the fluency with which she spoke her native language'. The case for the prosecution continued that day, differing little from the previous trial. That night the Jury spent in Morrison's Hotel and Mr O'Malley opened the case for the defence the next day with the following remarks:

'However painful the conditions of the country might be', he said, 'it should not be drawn like a red rag before the jury to excite their passions, to sway their judgement, and excite their feelings. He asked them not to be carried away by external circumstances, but to act solely on the evidence produced. He contended that the identification of the prisoner by the deceased could not have been reliable and said the evidence given by Mrs Lydon was entirely contradictory of her deposition taken before the Coroner. The finding of the gun was of no weight. There was no motive alleged except indeed an occurance which occurred years before. It might be true that the Walsh's had been fined for trespassing on the lands herded by Mr Lydon but were there not many others in the location in the same plight, and might it not be, Counsel asked, some of these who committed the outrage. There was no evidence to prove the prisoner was either ' a society man' or 'combination man', by which classes all these assassinations in the West were notoriously planned and executed. Counsel then minutely analysed the evidence of the prosecution and concluded by demanding a verdict of acquittal'.

The case for the defence continued as in the previous trial. Mr Bodkin, closing the case for the defence told the jury that after considering and weighting up the evidence which he hoped the jury would do, he had come to the conclusion that 'the evidence was not of a character to justify conviction'. The only solid evidence was Martin Lydon's statement and he went on at length to show that this was 'quite unreliable'.

After lunch, Mr Murphy, for the Crown, advised the jury that if they found that the evidence pointed to the guilt of the prisoner 'their duty to their God and country demanded a verdict of conviction from them'.

Justice Lawson then reviewed the evidence at length and pointed out that 'if

13. G.V. August 19 1882. Reported in full.

they believed the statement of Martin Lydon that the prisoner was at the house that night it was their duty to find him guilty'. 'The uniform testimony of all the witnesses who were not proved to be companions of the prisoners was that he and his companions did not arrive at the wake until eleven o'clock. The deed was carried out at ten o'clock and this gave them ample time to carry out the deed'.[14]

The jury retired at 6.25 pm and returned to court at 6.50 pm. The foreman announced a verdict of guilty, at which the prisoner stood up in a state of excitement, folded his arms and showed an anxiety to speak. The clerk of the court then asked in the usual formal manner if he had anything to say why sentence should not be be passed.

The prisoner proceeded to make a long statement, rendered rather incoherent by his excited condition, in reference to his movements during Saturday April 24 and up to 7 o'clock on Sunday, the night the murder took place. He asserted in the strongest manner his complete innocence of the charge upon which he had been convicted. He insisted 'he had walked from his own house with some boy who had been examined (for his defence) to the wake-house and stood at the door of the house until invited in by some young woman. He declared (with outstretched hands) in the presence of the court and of his God, knowing that he must appear before the Judgement Seat that his hands were clear of this crime. He had been falsely accused (of) the foulest crime of murder. He declared before the world as he was going into eternity, that he was not guilty. He could not leave the dock without saying how falsely the learned Counsel Mr Murphy had been misled about the farm that Lydon was herding. It was not his farm at all'.

Mr Justice Lawson interrupted the prisoner and was commencing to pass sentence when, the prisoner again asserted he had been 'falsely accused, that the charges had been planned by the sister of the deceased and he hoped she would not enter eternity until she had declared the part she took in getting up this false charge'.

Once again, Mr Justice Lawson interrupted and silenced the prisoner. "You have been found guilty by a jury of your fellow countrymen of a most barbarous and brutal murder. I think I never saw a case more clearly proved in a court of justice and your protestations of innocence I entirely disregard, for they only add to your guilt, if that were possible. You spared no one on that Sunday night. You went, leading a party of six or seven men who still remain undetected, and who are now, I suppose, ranging the neighbourhood of Letterfrack. You showed these people whom you attacked no mercy. The case has been proved against you as clearly as if twenty witnesses had sworn that they were present. Under these circumstances I am bound to tell you that your days on this earth are numbered and I can hold out no hope for you. I believe you are a person upon whom any observation I could make would produce no effect and I must now pass upon you the awful sentence of law", — assuming the black cap, the learned judge then pronounced sentence of death, to be carried out in the prison of the County Galway on the 22nd September next'.

The prisoner asked to make a further statement but was immediately removed. The Court was adjourned.[15]

14. G.V. August 23 1882.
15. G.V. August 22 1882.

The Execution

It was hoped up to the last moment that the condemned man would be reprieved, 'as it was looked on by the public and press as most pitiful that so young a stalwart and intelligent man should meet with such an end'. Walsh won the sympathy of anyone who met him during the trial and was known to be a truthful and gentle person. 'A victim of the crime of history', the press declared. But no reprieve came and the execution took place as planned on September 22, 1882.

The prison bell rang out in the early hours of the morning and as the time of execution came closer a crowd began to gather around the prison wall. The gates were heavily guarded by soldiers and police.

Walsh attended Mass at seven o'clock and 'exactly as the clock struck eight he was turned in the direction of the scaffold and walked towards it with a firm tread with his head slightly bent as he responded to the Litany which was recited by the chaplain who walked beside him'. In front walked the Governor of the jail, Captain Mason and Sub-Sheriff Mr Reddington. The procession was watched by Dr Lynam and members of the press.

They halted promptly and Marwood, the hangman, 'stepped forward and strapped down the prisoner's arms. The melancholy procession then moved again as the condemned man prayed God to have mercy on his soul'. As he was half-way up the incline leading to the scaffold, he spoke his last words, 'I am going to my doom and I am innocent. I certainly did not commit the murder. I was not of the party. The witness swore falsely against me', and without the slightest assistance he ascended to the scaffold. 'Marwood then placed the rope around his neck and adjusted the white cap. The words 'Jesus have mercy on me' were repeated by the poor fellow just as the bolt was drawn and he was hanged by the neck till life was extinct'.[16]

Among the crowd gathered outside the wall stood Pat's mother, Honor Walsh, and it was said to have been a heart-rending sight to have seen her face as she watched the hoisting of the black flag that told all was over.

The newspapers the following day reported the execution and described the Lydons as very poor, quiet, inoffensive people, adding the following comment — which seemed to represent the feelings of the population:

'when this is added, that the young man who suffered death on the scaffold yesterday died protesting his innocence, the Letterfrack tragedy became altogether a lamentable affair'. 'Walsh up to the arrest for the murder bore a good character and was popular amongst the people of his own class. What misery therefore has been brought on the two families'. 'The dying depositions of Martin Lydon and the dying deposition of Patrick Walsh are irreconcilable. Let us hope that Lydon was mistaken in his identification of Walsh and that the convict's dying declaration was reliable'.[17]

Kavanagh Murder

On April 25, 1881, Constable Kavanagh was moved from Spiddal to Letterfrack, where he was to try to discover the perpetrators of the crime committed there the previous night. On the following day he assisted in the

16. G.V. September 23 1882.
17. ibid.

Walsh's Cottage, Letterfrack.

arrest of Pat Walsh and gave evidence against him when the case came before the Magistrates on July 1, 1881, after which it was said that Mrs Walsh attacked Kavanagh's house and verbally abused him. Towards the end of the same year another member of the Walsh family, John Walsh, was prosecuted by Kavanagh for 'loitering with intent to commit a felony'.[18]

On the night of February 15, 1882, there were only two constables stationed at Letterfrack, Constable Kavanagh and Constable Nash. The other four constables from that station were attending a wedding in a neighbouring village and were not expected to return until eleven o'clock that night. At about eight-thirty, Kavanagh left the barracks and proceeded to Mrs Noon's public house one hundred and twenty yards away. There he joined a local man, Stephen Coyne, in drinking whiskey and lemonade. The premises normally closed for the night at ten o'clock but on this particular night Kavanagh jokingly remarked that the clock was fast. Lucy Boland, daughter of Mrs Noon, bolted the doors and the two customers continued drinking. Shortly afterwards, footsteps were heard outside and an attempt was made to open the door. Empty barrels were then knocked about in attempt to get Kavanagh outside but it was twenty past ten before Kavanagh left the premises. The night was very dark when Kavanagh and Coyne stepped out the back door into the street. Kavanagh, 'who was smoking a pipe had gone no more than five or six yards from the house, when three shots were fired at him in rapid succession at short range; he screamed, two more shots rang out and Constable Kavanagh died instantly'.[19]

On hearing the shots, Coyne ran back to Noons and asked to be admitted but was refused. Coyne immediately went home and went to bed without repoting

18. G.V. September 30 1882.
19. ibid.

the incident to the police. Constable Nash heard the shots and came out of the barracks and found Kavanagh already dead. Constable Butler and a party of men arrived shortly afterwards; the body had already been removed to the barracks. It was impossible to investigate further in the dark so a guard was placed on the spot and they waited for daylight.

In the morning a footprint was found in a ditch near the body. It had a dent in it and similar prints led across a potato field but were not very clear. They led towards Mrs Walsh's house and here again another clear print with a dent in it was found. One or two more were found close to Walshe's wall.

The left boot belonging to Michael Walsh, a brother of Pat's, was obtained and fitted exactly into the footprints. There was a hole in the top of the boot and Michael's stocking was coloured with the same kind of soil through which the footprints passed.

About four feet from the body a hat was found, said to be the property of Michael Walsh. A neighbour of the Walsh's reported that after hearing the shots she heard someone running past the front door of her house, and stopping outside Walsh's door; a voice called out, 'Open the door, open the door quick'. On this evidence and on a reported conversation between Michael Walsh and John Corbatt, the National School teacher, in which Michael Walsh — on seeing Kavanagh approach them on the street one day — told Corbatt that Kavanagh would soon be removed. When Corbatt questioned his statement, Walsh explained, 'boys who he does not know will gather round him',[20] Walsh was arrested at about seven forty-five on the morning of February 16.

On February 21, 1882, the prisoner, said to be no more than eighteen years of age, was brought before Mr George McCarthy, R.M. at Letterfrack, and charged with the murder of Kavanagh, but there was no evidence given and he was discharged. Asked if he wished to make a statement regarding his movements that night, he stated he went to the house of Stephen Coyne at about seven o'clock and stayed there with John Coyne and John Daly for about one hour. He left the house by himself and went straight home. There was a man named John Mullan staying in the house that night. This man had come from Scotland and had walked from Westport that day. At about eight o'clock Walsh went into the bed beside John Mullan, he slept on the inside of the bed and did not leave it until morning. Walsh was re-arrested on March 14. On Wednesday August 23 the day after his brother Patrick had been sentenced to death by Judge Lawson, he came before the same Judge charged with the Kavanagh murder. The case was adjourned until September 27 five days after his brother was to be hanged at Galway.

The Trial of Michael Walsh

On September 27 the prisoner appeared before Judge Lawson. He was defended by Mr Bodkin and Mr O'Malley, instructed by R.J. Connolly, Clifden, and prosecuted by the Solicitor General A.M. Porter, M.P., with James Murphy Q.C., Peter O'Brien Q.C. and Edward Sullivan, instructed by Mr Bolton, Crown Solicitor. The evidence against him was as previously mentioned; the footprints, the discovery of the prisoner's cap near the body, the conversation with Corbatt and the neighbour's testimony of having heard

20. G.V. September 30 1882.

footsteps leading to Walsh's door after the shooting. Michael Walsh's statement of having spent the night asleep beside John Mullen was confirmed by John Mullen, who said he lay awake smoking a pipe from the time the boy entered the bed until Mrs Walsh came up from the kitchen and told him there was some shouting and roaring at the barracks. He insisted that the boy could not have left the bed without him knowing it. The solicitor for the defence tried every argument to prevent having Mrs Walsh called to the stand; it was only five days since the hanging of her other son and she was overcome with sorrow over the hanging, and this case. But all arguments were overruled and the grief stricken Honor Walsh was put on the stand; her evidence did little more than support John Mullen's.

After hearing the summoning-up of the case by Mr Bodking for the defence, and the Attorney-General for the prosecution, the jury adjourned, returning later with a verdict of guilty with a recommendation for mercy. The prisoner then spoke out, 'I don't allow for being found guilty'. 'There is no plain evidence to pass sentence against me'. He then became very excited and uttered several disjointed sentences, some addressed to the jury, to which he said, 'The day will come when they will account for it — you are standing there and your body and soul will account for my innocent life'. More was addressed to witnesses who had given evidence.

The Judge then said it would have given the jury much pleasure not to have found him guilty but that the case against him was clear, although there was no evidence that he had fired the shot. The Judge then continued, 'I will forward the recommendation of the Jury to the proper quarter and am sure it will be taken into consideration, but at the time I would not be justified in holding out any hope to you. I must now perform a painful duty'.[21] He then assumed the black cap and sentenced Michael Walsh to be executed at Galway on October 28. The prisoner continued to protest his innocence and address abuse to the gallery.

At 12.30 on the night of October 6, Walsh arrived at Galway by train under guard and was conveyed to the County Prison to await his execution. The local paper commented as follows:

'The unfortunate fellow looked fairly well, he was a most innocent cast of countenance and judging from appearance would be the last man in the world that an observer would suspect of having been a party to commit or even abet a foul deed'.[22]

Stay of Execution

On October 9 the scaffold was erected in the grounds of the prison. On October 12 Lady Florence Dixie of Glenlosera Lodge, Ballycastle, Co. Mayo wrote a pleading letter to the Lord Lieutenant for the commuting of the sentence for Walsh. She pleaded on behalf of his mother and begged that his age be taken into account. A memorial was also presented by R.J. Connolly, solicitor on behalf of the people of the district. On October 20 the prisoner was informed that the Lord Lieutenant 'had commuted the sentence of death passed on him to penal servitude for life'.[23] This was a great relief to the public when reported

21. G.V. September 30, 1882.
22. ibid. October 7, 1882.
23. G.V. October 21, 1882.

by the local press and it was expected he would be removed to some convict department with in few days.

Michael was transported and imprisoned for a number of years. His location or exact sentence served is not exactly clear. However, on his release he returned to Letterfrack in poor health and died shortly afterwards.

Assisted Emigration

The idea of transplanting families from the barren rocky lands of Connemara to the wide open prairies of Minnesota came first from Rev Fr Nugent of Liverpool. Aided and encouraged by Bishop Ireland of Minnesota, it seemed the scheme could not fail. The organisers however did not take into account the severe circumstances of the people. Previous chapters have dealt with events which caused the people of Connemara to be in such a complete state of want. Years of bad harvest, loss of land through eviction, loss of credit, lengthy spells of hunger and degrading years of charitable acceptance, left them with little though of the future, except perhaps to wonder whence the next meal would materialise.

Rev Nugent was said to be well known for his 'philanthropic and truly patriotic exertions to alleviate the social conditions of his fellow countrymen in England'.[24] He had in Liverpool 'founded an orphanage and trade school for boys, conducted a total abstinence crusade, and built a shelter for homeless women'.[25] For several years accompanied by some English friends, he visited Connemara during the fishing season. Seeing the worsening conditions of the people in 1879, he wrote to Bishop Ireland of St Paul, Minnesota, and Bishop O'Connor of Nebraska asking them to take fifty families each from Connemara and place them in their recently opened colonies in their respective dioceses. Bishop O'Connor refused to 'accept such destitute families' in their Nebraska colonies,[26] while Bishop Ireland agreed.

Colonisation in Minnesota was well established under Bishop Ireland. In less than twenty years, thousands of Catholics from outside the state took up residence there, taking advantage of the low prices asked for land by the railway companies along their recently laid tracks. Born in Kilkenny, Bishop Ireland had come with his family to America during the famine of 1848. Acting as land agent for the railway company, at first it was his intention that the poor urban dweller of the east coast of America should benefit from these new lands, but soon it was found that only those already possessing some capital managed to succeed. It was therefore with some trepidation that he invited the 'Connemaras' as they became known, into his diocese.

It was agreed that Rev Nugent would cover all their expenses to Boston and the railway companies agreed to transport them from Boston to St Paul free of charge. Once arriving in St Paul they became the responsibility of the Bishop. After an appeal to the people of Minnesota for funds to help finance the venture the Bishop managed to raise five thousand dollars.

'The Bishop (then) instructed Major Ben Thompson, his agent in Big Stone County, to reserve fifty farms of 160 acres each for these settlers, to construct a small frame house on each farm and to break five acres of prairie sod for

24. G.V. January 15, 1881.
25. James P. Shannon: Catholic Colonization on the Western Frontier. 1957, p. 64.
26. ibid, p. 156.

immediate tillage on each farm'.[27]

The people were to be selected by the local clergy. Rev Nugent intended that these families make a promise in writing that they pay the passage money back by September 30 1881 and with this money he would assist others to emigrate.[28]

Arrangements were made for the *'Austrian',* a steamer of the Allen Line of Liverpool, to call at Galway to collect the families. Galway was under consideration by the Allen Line as a port of call on their route from Liverpool to Boston. If the number of passengers was considered good, the possibility of making it a permanent stop would be considered.

Gathered together by the local clergy, the emigrants, said to be three hundred and nine in total, began to converge on Galway on June 10 1880 each group escorted by its own priest. The Rev. Greally, P.P., Carna, had ten families with him, averaging nine persons to each family. Rev. Millett, Killeen, had thirteen families, averaging eight. Five families averaging eight came from Clifden under the care of Mr Thomas Campbell, secretary of the Temperance Association of the Cross, Westminster, London. Mr Campbell was engaged by Rev Nugent to accompany the emigrants to their new homes. Rev. Stephens, Aughagower, Co. Mayo, had five families averaging ten. Besides the families there was a large number, between fifty and sixty, unmarried young men and women. Most of the people, especially the children, were poorly clad. Rev Nugent gave several large packages of clothes to Mr Campbell to be distributed during the voyage.

On the morning of the 11th the emigrants attended Mass at the Pro-Cathedral of St Nicholas. Rev Fr Dooley, who was to have preached, deferred his address until they were all on board the *'Austrian'.* The clergy and several priests of Galway accompanied the people aboard the steam tug to the steamer. On board the *'Austrian'* Mr Ennis, the Manager of the Line

'who came from Liverpool to superintend the shipment of the passengers, showed the clergy and several other visitors over the ship; all expressed themselves highly pleased with the provisions that had been made for the comfort of the emigrants'.

'Just before sailing, men, women and children assembled on the deck and Rev. Dooley addressed them in a touching and eloquent speech in the Irish language. He said they were parting from their own old country for land and new homes that had been prepared for them, such a parting was akin to death because sterile as were the rocks and hills of Connemara, every spot was dear to them. He begged of them never to forget the old country, and to continue to speak the Irish language. They might never again be addressed by a priest in their own language and he hoped his words might not be forgotten'.[29]

Rev Dooley spoke for half an hour and the people were all moved to tears. He asked them to be good practising Catholics and temperate so that their new homes would reflect credit on the old country from which they came.

Rev Nugent then spoke, referring briefly to the many attacks made on him by those against his work. There were many both in Ireland and America who felt the tenants should stay and fight for the land and not be encouraged to

27. Shannon: p.156.
28. G.V. May 26, 1880.
29. C.T. June 19, 1880.

abandon it. The newspaper reported that the people seemed happy, but wept bitterly when parting from their clergy.

The Voyage

Mr Campbell wrote a descriptive letter to Rev Nugent, which was later published in the newspapers, describing the journey to Minnesota and their encounters along the way.

'We sailed on (Saturday) June 11th at 11.15 am under the command of Captain Barrett'. It was a beautiful day and the Clare mountains and Aran Islands were clearly visible. Soon they left these sights behind them and faced the broad Atlantic. Shortly afterwards a stiff breeze set in and caused the sea to rise heavily and this continued during the night and following day. The ship began to rock heavily causing all on board, including some of the sailors, to be sick. By Monday noon the sea had begun to calm and a fog set in with misty rain. The following day the sea was calm and the passengers came on deck and to the music of a flute had a 'lively dance'. All were said to be in good health, and their appetite was said to be increasing; the food was good and there was plenty of it. The children in particular were said to be 'in full glee'.

Soon there were heavy seas again; the ship rolled and plunged heavily into the waves and the passengers became very uneasy. The Captain came to offer them comfort and assurance. By Friday the sea was still 'mountains high', the weather was very cold as they passed large icebergs. On Saturday, fog set in as they passed more icebergs, the sea was getting calmer as they passed Newfoundland. Sunday found the people in good health, Mr Campbell read the rosary and Litanies to them while the Captain carried on the Service of the Church of England. On Monday the weather was very fine and Mr Campbell distributed the clothes Rev Nugent had given him. They landed at four o'clock on Tuesday at Boston.[30]

Mr Dillon O'Brien, Editor of the Northwestern Chronicle, the Catholic paper of the Northwest, a close friend and co-worker of Bishop Ireland came on board to meet them. They were ordered to stay on board that night. During the night crowds came to see them and a 'Cead Mile Failte was given to them'.[31]

Escorted by Mr O'Brien, they left Boston at three pm the next day by train. They passed Albany at midnight and were received well at Buffalo and Cleveland. At Chicago they were met by members of the St Patrick Society, one of whom described them as follows: 'The Famine was visible in their pinched and emaciated faces, and in the shrivelled limbs — they could scarcely be called legs and arms — of the children. Their features were quaint and the entire company was squalid and wretched. It was a painful revelation to all who witnessed it'.[32] They were given bread, milk, cheese and ham. Rev. Fr Cashman gave them a large box of clothes, and a 'sumptuous dinner' was provided for them in Mrs Loftus's hotel'.[33] From Chicago they travelled to St Paul where a great crowd waited with Bishop Ireland, Rev Fr McMullen and Rev Fr Shanley to greet them. Employment was obtained in the city for forty-five young men

30. G.V. June 14, 1880.
31. G.V. July 14, 1880.
32. Shannon, p. 157.
33. G.V. July 14, 1880.

and thirty-five young women[34] while the rest moved on under the care of Rev McMullen to the Connemara Colony at Graceville.

Mr Campbell remained in St Paul, later travelling to Baltimore and then returning to Liverpool. He was full of praise for Captain Barrett and the Allen Line, the crew were kind and attentive to the welfare of the people and to passengers wishing to cross the Atlantic. Mr Campbell advised, 'Choose the Allen Line for comfort, civility and order'.[35]

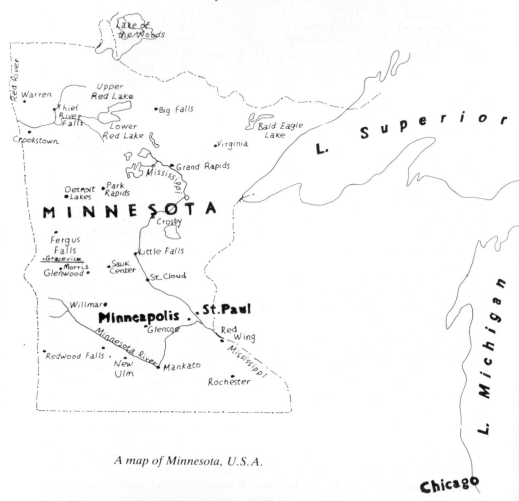

A map of Minnesota, U.S.A.

The Connemara Colony in Minnesota

On arrival at the colony, each family was given a house, a cow, flour, meat, potatoes and wood. Families already established in the colony were instructed to take into their homes an emmigrant family until all the houses were completed.

34. Shannon. p. 158.
35. G.V. July 14, 1880.

Here the friction started. Several of the earlier colonists objected to the 'dirty clothes, rough speech, and offensive manners of the newcomers'.[36]

Soon the houses were completed and the families took up residence. Clothing, furniture and farming implements were supplied by the Bishop along with a year's supply of seed and a year's credit at the Graceville store. Every effort was made to help the 'Connemaras' settle in.

Although their lives as fishermen and 'garden' farmers in Connemara differed greatly from that lived on the wheat farms of Minnesota, the Bishop hoped they would be successful. However, the new settlers became difficult almost as soon as they arrived. Although there was work available as day labourers on neighbouring farms, at wages of 1.50 to 2.00 dollars per day, some refused to avail of it, declaring 'Bishop Ireland was responsible for them until they could grow their own crops'. The Bishop tried to get them to carry out some work about the settlement but 'they preferred idleness'[37]

During a visit to Graceville, in September, the Bishop discovered that the 'Connemaras' would prefer to work as day labourers rather than farm their own land. It was essential that the farmer develop the land and produce bountiful harvests to pay off his debt and own his farm outright. But from past experiences, the 'Connemaras' placed little faith in future harvest, but a wage at the end of the week was something they could rely on. They made little or no preparation for the coming winter. Some sold their seed while others did not even bother to plant it. Some even sold their clothes and farming tools. 'So obsessed were they that having been brought from Ireland by the Bishop they would be cared for by him. They could not be persuaded to do anything for themselves'.[38]

The winter of 1880 was said to be 'unusually early and severe'[39] and although advised to sod up the foundations of their homes in protection against the severe weather, a great number had not done so. The 'Connemaras' suffered greatly during that first winter and it was said that but for the aid given by neighbouring towns the entire population would have died. Hearing of their circumstances newspapermen visited the Colony and later sensationalised their plight in the local press. Bishop Ireland made a collection in St Paul and sent the colony six hundred dollars each month for the winter. Dillon O'Brien went to Graceville to administer the funds and advise the settlers. He later wrote in the *New York Sun:*

> Last winter when the snow was too deep for horses and sleighs, the other farmers in the colony bought flour at the Society's station and drew it by hand on sleds over the snow to their homes. The Connemara men would not take the flour away, although to them it was a free gift. Some of the farmers, when a sum was offered to them to carry the flour to the homes of the Connemara men said they were willing enough to make a dollar, but that they would not turn their hands to benefit such a lazy people'.[40]

Although there were some who took advice and worked hard to succeed, the above were said to be the actions of the majority.

36. Shannon, p. 158.
37. G.V. Jan. 15, 1881.
38. ibid.
39. Shannon p. 162.
40. ibid p. 163.

Commenting on their plight in the *Chicago Tribune,* Mr W.J. Onahan said: 'If their shanties were cold, it was because they neglected to sod them as they were advised to do. If their potatoes were frozen, they had plainly omitted to dig cellars for their protection. If, perhaps, they suffered from the lack of fuel, it must be remembered that they suffered in common with the prairie population of the extreme northwest generally'.[41]

Although many of the newspaper reports were shown to be exaggerated charges of neglect were made against Bishop Ireland and Dillon O'Brien. A committee led by Mr O'Brien went to Graceville to investigate these charges. During the course of the investigation it was found that some of the settlers had hidden extra food and clothing in an effort to support their complaints. Vindicated by the investigation, Bishop Ireland replied to the criticism in an article published in the Pioneer Press. In it he describes the emigrants, 'these people are at best an improvident and worthless class of citizens, and it is perhaps asked how was I induced to bring such people to the State. The families that came to us were not the class we bargained for'. Rev Nugent and he 'hoped that we would have as objects of our beneficiena (sic) industrious, sober, hard-working people, who though impoverished by the famine in Ireland, were still of a mould to make their way successfully in the world, if only the opportunity were offered to them'. He blamed the local curates who selected the people and sent him, for the most part, 'paupers of long standing, totally demoralised and unmanned by years of suffering and unaccustomed to provide for their own wants'.

After weeks of effort the Bishop finally realised he had a mountain of trouble on his hands. 'I had for the past number of years been instrumental in bringing Irish colonists to the State and had noticed their pride of character, their anxiety to work and to be independent, their rapid success amid great difficulties. I had presumed that no family could come to me from Ireland devoid of all those noble qualities'. He went on to say he would not be discouraged, and that it was his belief that the mental condition of the people was the 'unfortunate fruits of oppression and suffering'.[42]

An agreement was reached between the 'Connemaras' and the Bishop. They gave up their farms and in return the Bishop paid their transport into St Paul and secured jobs for them with the railroad companies. The majority settled in what later became known as 'Connemara Patch' in the city. The Bishop then distributed the emigrants' cattle among their former neighbours at Graceville.

The failure of the Connemara colony and the publicity it received was said to be the cause of great 'pain and humiliation' for the Bishop, and the 'strain and disappointment'[43] was believed to contribute to the sudden death in the following year of Dillon O'Brien.

While the dreams of the organisers were never fully realised, the dreams of the emigrants, which were simply to escape starvation and the hardship of Ireland, were fully realised. It is true they did not immediately become property owners but they did survive, one can assume, better nourished, better dressed and happier in their new lives. And by their earnings perhaps improved the lives of many others still left behind in Connemara.

41. ibid.
42. G.V. Jan. 15, 1881.
43. Shannon: p. 166.

The Connemara Girls

Nine months later the newspapers carried an extract from the Northwestern Chronicle, dated September 24 1881. It told of a gathering of Connemara girls, who came to welcome Rev Nugent to St Paul and 'to testify their gratification to him for all he had done for them'. The improved condition of these young girls was striking, 'their dress, manner and self-reliant conduct gave that they had already become most useful members of society'.

About thirty-five girls were employed in private homes and hotels in St Paul, they earned an average of about twelve dollars a month and judging by the report's comments, like all young women everywhere, spent a great deal of it on dress. Their wages 'would make domestic staff in England envious of their conditions'. Their brothers and fathers also worked in St Paul at various forms of labour and they earned between 1.50 to 2 dollars a day.

'It is now evident they are doing well and that their social condition is now such as they would never have attained in Ireland. Each day they became more and more identified with the industrious and energetic people of our progressive state'.

'We feel sure that the noble-hearted citizens of St Paul's will never regret that generosity which they exercised when they offered a home and the opportunities of honest labour in the hour of need, to a suffering and downtrodden race'.[44]

Graceville continued to develop and expand; its history tells that a great many Irishmen succeeded both on the land and in its town, but the story of the dismal failure of the 'Connemaras' still lingers.

The Allen Line

After this successful venture by the Allen Line, it was decided that whenever the numbers were sufficient, a stop-over would be made at Galway. The 'Austrian' called on June 11 and again on July 23, 1880. It called again on October 15 and it was said at the time that there was no doubt 'there is a strong desire on the part of a section of the Irish peasantry to emigrate'.

A Mr Vere Foster went about Galway city offering two pound tickets free to any girl recommended by a clergyman; up to October 16 1880 'he had expended £10,000'.[45] The company hoped that the following year there would be a fortnightly sailing from Galway.

James Hack Tuke

James Hack Tuke (1819-1896) second son of Samuel Tuke, tea and coffee merchant of York, was a Quaker, and like his father before him took an active interest in the welfare of the people of the West of Ireland.

Samuel Tuke had cared and provided for those Irish who arrived in his town during the famine of 1848 while his son travelled the West distributing funds from the Society of Friends. When famine struck again in 1879 James raised funds and backed by English noblemen and gentlemen organised the assisted emigration of nearly 10,000 persons to Canada and the United States up to his death in 1896.[46] He was considered an authority on all aspects of the poorest

44. G.V. October 22, 1881.
45. G.V. October 16, 1880.
46. Frances Finnegan: Poverty and Prejudice. A study of Irish Immigrants in York, 1840-1875.

districts of the West because of his many visits, charity works and writings on the subject over the years.

In 1882 under a special agreement with the Beaver Line, when Mr Tuke had selected sufficient passengers from the numerous applications, one of their steamers would call at Galway. One such steamer, the 'Winnipeg' left Liverpool on Wednesday May 17 1882 and called at Queenstown (Cob, Co. Cork) on Thursday to take on more passengers. There were five hundred on board when she arrived in Galway.

Thursday evening Mr Tuke arrived in Galway with a procession of eighty-six Connemara families, four hundred and thirty three persons in all, many of them recently evicted from their holdings. At six o'clock the next morning they were taken by the 'City of the Tribes' steam tug to the 'Winnipeg'. When the 'Winnipeg' sailed from Galway, of the entire nine hundred and thirty three passengers on board, there were only two who were not Irish born.

Mr P.J. King, Passenger Agent for Clifden, accompanied the emigrants to Galway and rendered valuable assistance in seeing them poperly berthed on the ship.

The newspaper of the day asked respectfully, if he and his colleagues 'could not expand their funds with more advantage to the people by helping them to remain at home than by shipping them off to America'. They suggested that a scheme to 'root the people in the soil' should be taken up by Mr Tuke and his friends and the many other English organisations who pour money into assisting emigration.

'Every man who has land is determined to stay at home' in the hope 'he will have it again on terms that he can live on, not drag out an animal existence as heretofore',[47] they declared. The desire by Connemara people to emigrate is not as great as seems to be believed by outsiders, they insisted. They pointed out that if more money were spent on reclaiming the vast wasteland of Connemara and improving the quality of their land, there would be no need for them to emigrate.

When emigration was inevitable they felt large families should not be encouraged and only the young vigorous ones should emigrate. Sadly this pattern was adopted in the years that followed, when the young, vigorous and ambitious left, leaving the countryside devoid of young men and women.

Reclamation — A solution to Emigration

Great attention was given to the land reclamation carried out by Mr Henry on his Kylemore Estate and it was pointed out as an example to all what could, with a little capital and determination, be done with the vast bogland of the West of Ireland. This project was put forward time and again as a solution to the problems of the West. Alexander Nimmo, engineer of the first roads through Connemara, believed that bringing the roads through the centre of Connemara would lay open to the people 'great wastes to the purposes of agriculture'.[48]

From the very conception of the town it was John D'Arcy's ambition to reclaim and improve the lands of his estate, but althugh pockets of fertile land

47. G.V. May 20, 1882.
48. Villiers-Tuthill. p. 19.

86

appeared, the vast portion of the land still remained either poor quality so rocky or bogland.

Mitchell Henry was first to reclaim on a large scale. He managed to reclaim and make profitable eight hundred acres. Detailed records of the cost and work involved were taken and the idea which at first was purely scientific, developed into a large enterprise when four thousand more acres were drained and improved. A full report was carried out by Mr Roberts, Commissioner to the Royal Agricultural Society of England in 1877 and later Henry was awarded the gold medal for drainage by the Royal Agricultural Society of Ireland.

Before reclamation, the land was said to be valued at two shillings per acre. The cost of reclaiming the land and preparing it for its first crop — this includes roads, small bridges, drains, lime and ploughing — was on average £10 per acre. Four per cent of £10 per acre is eight shillings which added to the original value of the land made ten shillings per acre. After the work was carried out the land was valued at eighteen shillings per acre; this gave a profit of eight shillings per acre.[49]

Mr Henry was first struck by the fact that the bog lies directly on the limestone, just as coal, ironstone and limestone lie in parts of Staffordshire. He believed draining and liming was all that bogland required to yield immediate crops. The main difficulty was to get rid of the water, which kept down the temperature of the land until it produced nothing but the humblest kind of vegetable.

The first step was to cut a big deep drain right through the bog to the gravel between it and the limestone. Then the secondary drains were cut, also down to the gravel; these are supplemented by 'sheep' or surface drains about twenty inches deep and twenty inches wide on top, narrowing to six inches at the bottom. This process was called 'topping the bog', which began to shrink visibly. The surface gradually sinks as the water runs off. When the process was sufficiently advanced, the drains were cleaned and deepened and a wedge-shaped sod, too wide to reach the bottom, was rammed in so as to leave below it a permanent tubular-covered drain, cutting the cost of materials. The surface was then dressed with lime, which the people said 'boiled the bog'.[50]

Henry believed that it was folly to think that once there was grass grown on bogland it should be converted into permanent pasture. 'The land needs a five-course rotation such as ordinary land in England requires', he maintained. He criticised the notion held by the majority in Ireland that the soil ought to produce permanent grass without any layout at all. Grass, oats, potatoes, turnips and mangolds were grown on the reclaimed land, and the celery grown on it was said to be superb.

In 1881 he sent seventy-eight stall-fed beasts to the market in Dublin and England. They were sold at the average price of beef, but six years before, a fat-fed ox was hardly to be found in this part of the world. He told the Government it was a matter of Imperial policy for them to 'dry' Ireland 'for this cannot be accomplished by the unaided efforts of the inhabitants and as long as the land remains like this, permanent prosperity is impossible. 'If you look at the whole question calmly, wisely, but at the same time boldly, there is nothing unreasonable in the suggestion that the Irish Church surplus of about £4 million

49. G.V. April 27, 1881.
50. G.V. November 1880.

be granted along with £15 million 'in the nature of a loan' to fund the reclamation of bogland. He points out that fifty-thousand armed men were at that time required 'to hold Ireland in subject, and hundreds of thousands of Irishmen in all parts of the world are longing for the opportuniy to stake the British Empire in its centre. Every emigrant who leaves these shores — and during the past twelve months nearly a hundred thousand have done so — goes away with hatred in his heart'.

'We may theorise and reform as we like but the commonsense of mankind teaches us that loyalty and starvation are not compatible and in my humble judgement the only hope that remains of producing permanent tranquility in Ireland is to make a strong and well-directed effort permanently to increase the prosperity of the people'.[51]

Money was advanced through the Board of Works to public companies for reclaiming, but this, according to Henry, was doomed to failure from the beginning and should be carried out on a much larger scale.

It was suggested that the Government buy up part of the Berridge Estate, and other wastelands in the West, and reclaim and convert them into small farms; to be leased by families now living in overcrowded areas in Connemara. However, it took some years before the Government achieved just that through the workings of the Congested Districts Board.

51. G.V. April 27 1881.

CHAPTER V

Galway to Clifden Railway

Recovery from the years of famine, agitation and instability came slow to the West. Once again, emigration had helped by reducing the numbers of the population. However the situation was further aggravated by the fall in agricultural prices in 1885, leaving the fixed rents now appearing high by comparison.

The workhouse struggled to cope with the large numbers requiring assistance. Under the Relief of the Distress Act 1886, the Board of Guardians expended a sum of £3,074 on outdoor relief over and above the Grant of £4,442 made to them for that purpose[1]. The Guardians reported that there had been an almost total failure of the crop the previous harvest and gave the severe condition of the people as an explanation for their reduced resources. But upon investigation it was discovered that the drastic financial condition of the Union was due to gross mismanagement on the part of the Guardians. Two months after the final day for collecting rates, May 14, an amount of £1891.1.4d. was still outstanding. The books showed that in one week relief was issued to an amazing number of 18,828 persons in a Union inhabited by only 24,259 persons.[2]

However little attention was paid to these figures as later some members of the Board were charged with interfering with the distribution of contracts for supplying goods for outdoor relief. It was found that contracts were given to relations of Guardians and that these Guardians were themselves involved in the distribution of the food.

In an attempt to reduce the debt incurred by this mismanagement, a new rate of 4 shillings in the pound was levied, but as it was always difficult to collect rates in the district, no attempts were made to redeem the money.

In 1887 a bill was introduced in the House by the Government dealing with certain distressed Unions in the West of Ireland and providing for the payment of their debts. Clifden was among the Unions referred to by the Bill. In July of that year the Bill was blocked in the House of Commons and it became apparent that there was no likelihood of its becoming law during that session. At this time Clifden, along with the other Unions mentioned in the Bill was near bankrupt and it was feared that the Guardians would be unable to obtain enough money to feed the destitute. A loan was therefore arranged from the Bank of Ireland upon a Government guarantee of repayment with interest. £130.13.4d. was borrowed from this fund by Clifden Union.[3]

In 1888 a sum of £515 was borrowed under the Seed Act of that year which was never repaid. In 1890 a sum of £607 was again borrowed for seed.[4] Over the years some small attempts were made to clear these debts, but as the

1. SPO.
2. ibid.
3. SPO.
4. ibid.

Government was well aware of the poor conditions in the Clifden Union, it was believed by the Guardians that if the debt was left long enough the Government would eventually pay it off. However, this was not what the Government had in mind and the Board of Guardians were advised to strike a new rate for the year ending 1893, thereby reducing their debt considerably and this was to continue until all outstanding debts were cleared.

When Arthur Balfour, nephew of the Conservative leader Lord Salisbury, became Chief Secretary of Ireland in March 1887, he was determined to govern by repression and reform. The full effect of the law was enforced in an attempt to stamp out agrarian agitation, with the result he is perhaps remembered more for repression than reform. But in answer to the depression in the West, the many petitioners to the Castle found in him a willing ear. The full extent of his willingness to assist became visible with the passing of the Light Railway Act 1889, under which the financing of the Galway to Clifden railway was obtained.

Railway Proposed

As the construction of railways and tramways spread throughout Ireland, the possibility of a railway link or stream tramway between Clifden and Galway gripped the imagination of every forward-looking man in the area.

First attempts to establish this railway link were made as early as 1872. Mr R. Price Williams, a railway engineer from London, personally surveyed the line and estimated that a railway could be laid for £180,000 excluding the usual stations. Estimates were also made of the probable annual receipts and these were eventually accepted at £26,000 a year, and at least 100,000 passengers a year were expected to use the line.

Attempts were made to establish a private company which would build and maintain the railway. The proposal was sanctioned by the Government and an Act of Parliament passed to that effect in 1872. A large number of subscribers came forward. Mitchel Henry subscribed £5,000 with a promise of a further contribution when work would begin. Mr Eyre contributed £5,000 and Mr John Kendall £1,000. Various sums of £1,000 and £500 were subscribed. A Mr Bagnal, railway contractor, tendered for the work at £180,000 but the amount fell short of the estimate and it was felt that the district was too poor to raise the amount required so this first attempt was abandoned.[5]

When conditions deteriorated in the district in 1879 and charity and Government relief were again sought for the majority of the population, every effort was made to impress upon the Government the necessity of building this railway line. Mr William Acheson of Schanboolard Hall and Dublin was the chief promoter but behind him were the ratepayers and a number of leading men of the district. Mr Acheson attempted to outline the project to the Magistrates and ratepayers at the Baronial Sessions held in the Clifden courthouse in February 1880. It was now felt that a steam tramway would be more suitable for the needs of Connemara and would cost less than a proper railway, and Mr Acheson informed them that this tramway, fully equipped and paved from end to end could be completed for £3,000 per mile or £150,000 in total. But if paved as far as Oughterard only, would cost £120,000. After a lengthy speech by Mr Acheson, the Chairman put the Tramway presentment to the Bench but it was defeated by three votes.[6]

5. G.V. July 1880.
6. SPO.

In July of that year a memorial was sent to the Lord Lieutenant requesting a loan of £200,000 to build the tramway. It was suggested that should the Government wish to dispose of the line upon completion, private companies willing to purchase would be sought. This request was turned down.

Through the summer and winter of 1880 as public works were carried out, the people of the county complained that the work being done by them was temporary and that work of a more permanent character was required. If the railway project were taken up, employment would be given to the labouring classes over a district of fifty miles, saving them from their present want and enabling them to provide against anticipated distress of the next year. The works would amply repay the outlay as commerce of every kind would then come into the area giving employment and the railway would be extensively used by them and the fisheries which would develop along the coast. At present, they complained, Clifden and its surrounding small villages were supplied with all the necessities of life by sea, leaving them for months during bad weather without those necessities, except for small parcels which were conveyed by cart along the road from Galway at a cost of £1.10.0d. per ton.[7] This cost resulted in high prices which could be avoided if the railway were in operation. It was felt that the construction of the railway and the establishing of the industries that would follow would give the people the security and independence for the future that was so sadly missing at present.

Although a Steam Tramway was being proposed, there were those who still favoured a proper railway. As a compromise, Mr Lewis, the engineer, arranged the plans so as to be convertible into a narrow gauge railway should the traffic increase and justify the outlay at a future period. The project was brought before the Grand Jury of the County of Galway at the Summer Assizes but was turned down on a mere legal detail which was later found to be incorrect. When the project was again turned down by the Grand Jury at the Winter Assizes, Mr Acheson withdrew and a Mr Drinkwater took over. Mr Drinkwater was said to be well known for his energy and perserverence; he had reclaimed 9,000 acres of land on the River Fergus in Clare and was at present engaged in the construction of two steam tramways, one from Dublin to Blessington and the second from Dublin to Lucan. He was considered to be one of the most experienced and energetic contractors in the Kingdom.[8] But alas, even the most experienced and energetic were beaten by the Galway to Clifden Railway.

Plans were now prepared by Mr. Griffin, Mr. Drinkwater's engineer, and application was made to the Assizes in July of 1881. This steam tramway would to all intents and purposes be a Narrow Gauge Railway, travelling at a speed of ten miles per hour, picking up passengers along the route at all places, with wagons capable of carrying goods, cattle, pigs etc., and the cost was estimated to be £2,500 a mile.[9]

Mr Townsend, Civil Engineer was appointed by the Board of Works to report upon the engineering merits or demerits of the project. However, all Mr Drinkwater's efforts were in vain; the Grand Jury imposed conditions which Mr Drinkwater said he could not possibly comply with and the project was once again abandoned.

7. G.V. July 1880.
8. G.V. May 7 1881.
9. ibid.

In 1885 John Talbot D'Arcy took up the cause and continued to do battle until the war was won. Once again the great need for employment in the area was stressed and the Government was requested to interest itself on behalf of the people to have the railway built, thereby opening up the west to trade and industry and the area in return could offer cheap but good quality fish to the rest of the country.

The Grand Jury of the County now fully approved and strongly recommended the construction of the line. On its submission, however, for the approval of Her Majesty's Privy Council in Ireland, the Council were of the opinion that the Western district was too impoverished to bear the required tax.[10]

In delivering the judgement of the Council, the Lord Chancellor, Sir Edward Sullivan, expressed the deep regret of the Council at having to reject the scheme, being fully aware of the great necessity of railway accommodation there and fully realising the benefits it would offer. He went on to say that he considered the construction of the line a matter not merely of local but manifestly of Imperial importance.[11]

Although once again beaten, the struggle continued and when in 1889 and 1890 conditions in the West were again brought to the attention of the public and Government, the railway was again viewed as a means of bringing employment and future industry to the district. The Light Railway (Ireland) Act was passed in 1889 and under this Act a free grant of £264,000 was given by the Government towards the construction of the Galway to Clifden Railway. This grant was given to the Midland Great Western Railway Company towards the construction of the line, the work to commence as relief work, on condition that the line be maintained and worked by the Company. If the grant was insufficient to complete the work, the remainder was to come out of the funds of the Company.[12]

The mode of carrying out the work was left entirely to the Company and the Board of Works were only concerned to see that the conditions under which instalments of the grant were to be paid were observed.

The MGWR Company added about £146,000 towards construction and spent between £30,000 and £40,000 on rolling stock. The final result was that the total cost of the line worked out at £9,000 per mile, while £3,000 to £5,000 per mile was generally considered the right figures for the cost of light railways at the time.[13]

Mr A.J. Balfour was then Chief Secretary for Ireland and it was principally through his efforts that this grant was obtained. He was very anxious to improve the conditions of the people of the West and in him John Talbot D'Arcy found a willing ear for his many proposals in these respects.

Disagreement arose as to which district the proposed line would serve. There appeared to be complete agreement regarding the route from Galway to Oughterard but after that opinions were divided. The vast majority of the inhabitants — said to be a population of 60,000 — lived along the coast and as the railway was expected to advance the development of fisheries many

10. SPO.
11. SPO.
12. J.H. Ryan. Paper to members of the Institute of Engineers of Ireland. Read May 1, 1901.
13. ibid.

believed the line should follow the coast through Spiddal, Carraroe, Roundstone and on to Clifden. Great efforts were made to have this coastal route adopted. The Midland Great Western Railway Company stated publicly that they believed this to be the best route. However, the Royal Commission for Irish Public Works disagreed and had the route laid out from Oughterard to Clifden.

Mr James Dillon, C.E., from Dublin, was one of those in favour of the coastal route and offered his services free to the Government should they decide to accept it. He described the hinterland of Connemara through which the Commission planned to lay the line as 'uninhabited bog composed in winter of over sixty-per cent water and cut off from the great sixty miles of coast population by mountains here and there.'[14] However, the interior route was accepted by the Government; their reasons favouring this route were never known. Perhaps the obvious extra cost of the coastal route was unacceptable to them.

Mr Arthur Balfour's visit to the West

In late October 1890 Mr Balfour decided to visit the distressed districts along the West coast of Mayo and Galway to judge for himself the state of the country and the potato crop and the condition of the people. He also wishes to estimate the necessity for public works and to inspect the new railway routes. He planned to speak to as many of the people as possible in order to become acquainted with all the interests of the West and the actual state of affairs in each district. Mr Balfour travelled without a police escort and was accompanied by Sir J. West Ridgeway and Miss Balfour, his sister, and the Member of Parliament representing whichever district through which he passed.

Tuesday October 28, 1890 Mr Balfour and his party arrived at Westport at four o'clock in the afternoon. They started out for Kylemore Castle almost in darkness, stopping at Leenane for tea at Mr McKeon's hotel. They stopped several times to admire the beautiful landscape and Miss Balfour took many photographs. After spending the night at Kylemore Castle they started out the next morning to visit Omey Island and Clifden.

Along the way they stopped off at Letterfrack Industrial School. The school, which had been opened three years before and built at a cost of between £5,000 and £6,000[15] had received a grant from the Government. Brother Flood, Superior, received the group and brought them on a tour of the grounds. The school accommodated one hundred and fifty boys. In the playground the boys were formed in drill order and marched about for inspection. They then visited the workshops where trainee bakers, tailors and carpenters were hard at work. Boots, wearing apparel and other necessities of life were made for the gentry of the area. Carpentry also received outside orders. They next visited the schoolrooms, kitchen and dormitories and after expressing his approval Mr Balfour and his group moved on to Ballinakill.

At Ballinakill they were met by all the important people of the area, led by the Rector, Rev. Canon Fleming. The people thanked them, and pointed out that the railway was practically a present by the Government to the people. On

14. SPO.
15. G.V. Nov. 1, 1890.

93

arriving at Omey Mr Balfour visited a number of cottages and inspected the potatoes and conversed freely with the people he met in the fields, inquiring into their circumstances and general prospects.

At Clifden they were met by a number of townspeople; Rev. P. Lynskey, P.P., Major John Talbot D'Arcy, Rev. W. Nee, Dr Gorham, Mr Patrick O'Hara, Mr John King, Mr Robert Blake, Mr John Burke Clerk of the Union, Mr Brennan C.E. and a large number representing trades of the town. After lunch at the Hotel, Mr Balfour came to the door and was addressed by Major D'Arcy. Mr Balfour replied saying no man was more qualified than Major D'Arcy, descendant of the founder, to convey to him the sentiments of the town. 'He realised that in the past their dream of a railway was a hope against hope but now it was about to come to pass and without any burden on the ratepayers. The railway should be looked at from two points of view, he said, first as a source of employment, and well-paid employment, to the people of the district', the necessity for which was evident. 'This would go far to meet the distress of the crop failure. But this should be looked on as temporary relief work and he believed it would place them in such a position as not to require relief works in the future.' Secondly, he said he was told that the price of meal increased in winter, 'putting it out of reach by those who needed it.' With the railway they would have access to every market, regardless of weather, and this should put an end to unstable prices. Also, the lobster fishing would now have a market in Dublin and should therefore increase. However, he said, 'he did not think he could look with the same confidence, as Mr D'Arcy did, towards making Clifden a great manufacturing centre.'[16]

The group then returned to Kylemore for the night and headed south the next morning to visit the southern coast. On Thursday night they were guests of Costello Fishing Club at Costello Lodge, Derrynee. At Spiddal they called to see Lord Morris and were accompanied on their tour of the district by Mr Byrne, Royal Magistrate, who had an intimate knowledge of the area.

A great number of distinguished Galway men awaited Mr Balfour's arrival at the Railway Hotel, Galway. When he came before them they addressed a number of questions to him regarding the purchase of seed potatoes in the future, an extension of the railway to reach Carraroe, thereby serving the Aran Islands, and the development of fishing along the coast.

In reply to the question on the purchase of seed potatoes by the Guardians of the Unions, to be sold to the tenants of small holdings for cash, he pointed out that this was tried in 1881 and failed. The building of a light railway to Carraroe was out of the question, he said, as the Midland Great Western Railway Company were unwilling to be responsible for the works of light railway. The Railway Commission had already decided on the Oughterard route, he said, and there would be no alterations to this. In regard to the fishing off the coast, he said that Irishmen would have to learn to fish in boats capable of facing and coping with the Atlantic; they would have to train in the methods adopted by English and Scottish fishermen. He pointed out that there were loans already available, which if there were a real interest in fishing, would have been taken up.

After lunch at the hotel they returned to Dublin on the 2.30 p.m. train.

16. G.V. Nov. 1, 1890.

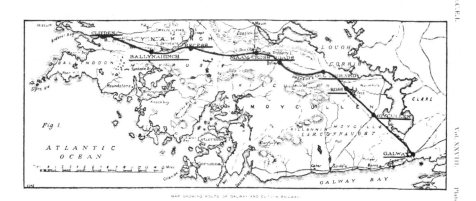

A map of railway route. 1901.

Midland Great Western Railway of Ireland Company. (Reg. No. 42.)

Consignment Receipt for goods to be Received and to be read on the Conditions specified on the back hereof.

Galway Station Dec 12 190

Received the undermentioned Goods from

M Thos Conley of Galway

To be forwarded to Clifden Station, on Ry, via

CONSIGNEE		No of Articles.	Description of Goods and Marks	AMOUNT, If Paid		
NAME	ADDRESS			£	s.	d.
Honery's	Clifden	1 Wgr Turnips		13	2	
			Paid 01 cancelled			
			46	30/12/05		

* If to be paid at destination, write "To Pay" in this column.

Signed,

For the Midland Great Western Railway Co.

N.B.—Complaints of Overcharges, or other Irregularities, should be addressed to JOSEPH TATLOW, Manager, Broad-stone Terminus, Dublin. The Company will not be accountable for correct delivery of Goods or Empties, unless the name of Sender and Consignee is distinctly marked on each Package; nor will the Company be answerable for the loss or detention of or damage to Wrappers or Packages of any description, declared by Sender and charged for by the Company as "Empties."

All Empties must be Prepaid, except Brewers' Empties.

Consignment receipt.

Contractors and Contracts

J.H. Ryan and Mr Townsend of Galway were employed as joint engineers by the M.G.W.R.Co. to lay out the line, prepare the contract plans and estimates etc.

Efforts were made to purchase the land through which the line would pass. In December 1890 the tenants in the Clifden district through whose land the Railway would pass agreed to appoint Bernard J. Lee, Merchant, of Clifden as arbitrator in their claims for compensation and as a tenant himself, Mr Lee appointed Thomas McDonagh of Derrylea to arbitrate on his behalf.[17]

Pending the completion of the plans by the Engineers a provisional contract was entered into in the winter of 1890 with Mr Robert Worthington, of 40 Dame Street Dublin and Westminster Chambers, London.

According to the conditions of Mr Worthington's contract, he was to be paid, if he got the final contract, at the rate specified in the final contract, but if not then at the average of the rates in the several tenders for the final contract.[18]

Efforts were made to start the works as soon as possible in an effort to bring employment to the area throughout the winter. Pressure was brought to bear by the Government on Mr Worthington to commence work. On January 2 1891 Mr Worthington had received plans for executing works at Maam Cross Road, Recess and Ballinahinch and the following day he received plans for similar works for three miles more commencing at about two miles east of Clifden. By January 7, one hundred men were employed on these works at Clifden. Mr LeFanu was in charge of this district.

In early January the Labourers Society of Galway complained that four hundred and fifty men were waiting to be employed on the Railway but work had not commenced. The reason for the delay was that land had yet to be purchased but works were due to start at the end of the month.[19]

By now five hundred men were said to be employed along the line. This work was chiefly confined to boglands, drains were cut and surface formation commenced.

Towards the end of January 1891 the Clifden Board of Guardians complained that the railway had not yet given employment to one-fourth of the applicants for work. As there was a great deal of distress in the area at the time, they were especially worried about the large population along the coast who had not obtained any employment whatsoever.[20]

Mr Worthington declared that he could increase the manpower by double, making it three thousand along the line if the plans were given to him in time, but at present he stated he was held up for days waiting for plans. He complained that the engineers had all the section plotted and as it was only a question of tracing off the particulars, they could give him the necessary information for the entire line in say two days or so. He offered to send his own engineers in to their offices to trace the sections. He went on to say he was now six weeks at work on the line and had only received plans for five miles out of forty eight. Drainage of about eight and three quarter miles of bog was almost

17. SPO.
18. ibid.
19. SPO.
20. ibid.

96

complete and he threatened to reduce men and ultimately stop work if plans were not forwarded to him more swiftly.[21]

However disturbing reports were now reaching the Railway Company regarding the quality of Mr Worthington's work and Ryan and Townsend stated they had forwarded enough plans for Mr Worthington to go ahead with but felt he was choosing his jobs.

They had by now handed over to Mr Worthington the plans for the following:
Clifden: A large rock cutting at Waterloo Bridge Embankments also two very important river diversions necessitating considerable amount of excavation and embankment together with retaining walls all quite close to the town.
Ballinahinch: A large cutting and the formation of embankments together with side cutting drains of five miles of the line.
Recess: The cutting of a large hill and the formation of one mile of railway embankment, the formation and diversion of a public road together with three miles of side drains.
Maam Cross Road: The drains for about four miles of railway.
Galway: A large cutting and embankment at Galway, also plans for the construction of four miles of line starting from the Corrib.[22]

In an effort to offer employment to those living some distance from the works, huts were set up at various points along the track.

By March 1891 there were fourteen huts erected: two at Roscahill, four at Leam, two at (Bunakyle) Lyone, (sic) four at Maam Cross and two at (Bunscauiff) Synche (sic).*

These huts each contained approximately ten beds with bedding and a stove. In some cases although only seven beds were shown to be erected, fourteen men were said to be in occupation. On March 2 one hundred men went on strike at Clifden; they were demanding an increase of six pence per day and a change in working hours from 6am to 6pm instead of the present hours of 7 am to 5 pm. The average wages on the line at this time was twelve shillings per week. The contractor was holding back until the days grew longer but the demands were met and the strike was settled almost immediately.

However, by now it became evident to Mr Worthington that he was not going to obtain the final contract so in order to obtain higher payment for his work, he raised the average by increasing his own tender.

Charles Braddock

The contract was then offered to Mr Charles Braddock. In the week ending April 18, 1891, one hundred and seventy two men were employed on the Galway section of the works but on April 20, these were discharged. All works were closed down during the hand-over to Mr Braddock.

Mr Worthington offered to hand over his plans of the line to Mr Braddock at the cost price of same so as to enable him to get to work with the least possible delay and thereby relieving the distress that would follow from a lengthened stoppage of the works.

Mr Braddock promised full employment to all, which was greatly welcomed

21. ibid.
22. SPO.
    * Place names given in official reports are often mis-spelt making them difficult to recognise.

by the Chief Secretary's office who had continually stressed the importance of giving employment to the area.

Notices bearing the following were posted throughout Connemara: 'Galway and Clifden Railway; — Any man who has not been employed on the above works will find employment on and after Monday 4th May by applying at the works. — Signed C. Braddock Contractor'.[23]

Works were re-opened on the Galway section on May 4. Thirty men were re-engaged with a large number promised work when the contractor had obtained materials etc. It was expected that every able-bodied man who presented himself for work would be employed.

On May 11 works were opened and men employed in the Roundstone area. Work was also resumed at Clifden. By May 19 the following numbers were employed along the line: Galway — two hundred and twenty. Oughterard — two hundred and twenty. Leam — seventy. Maam Cross — eighty two. Recess — ninety six. Clifden — one hundred and sixty six. Along with thirty-five horses.

Although Mr Braddock was anxious and willing to employ every able-bodied man in Connemara it seems he was not so willing to pay them. By May 1892 payment of wages to the labourers was irregular and in some places did not take place at all. The labourers were to be paid fortnightly on Fridays and Saturdays and while the men around Galway were paid, eighty labourers from the Moycullen portion of the works came into Galway demanding their wages; these were told there was no money for them but that they would receive it as soon as some arrived. Fears grew that the works would be abandoned all along the line. The workers from the Oughterard section had summonses taken out against Mr Braddock for non-payment of wages.

The men of Clifden stopped work and by the end of May one hundred and eighteen men along the line went on strike. After some discussion by the middle of June they were all back at work but payment was still irregular.

By now Mr Braddock had run up debts among a large number of traders in Galway. These traders wrote to the Railway Company complaining about his conduct. They listed their names and the total owed to them which amounted to a sum in excess of £1500. The Railway Company denied any responsibility and were accused by the traders of 'bringing a mere adventurer and pauper contractor'[24] into the area who they believed due to his connection with the Railway to be solvent and of good reputation.

However, the Railway Company was adamant in their stand and refused to help the traders.

On July 8 1892 the Midland Great Western Railway took possession of the Railway, the Corrib River Bridge, together with all plant and machinery in the possession of Mr Braddock for breach of contract. All work ceased on the line but the Company stated their intention to resume works as soon as possible.

Mr Braddock then employed the services of a company of solicitors from Liverpool whom he instructed to take certain proceedings against the MGWR Company in an effort to 'if not greatly benefit his estate, at least pay all his creditors'.[25]

23. SPO.
24. SPO.
25. SPO.

T.H. Faulkiner

The contract was then handed over to Mr T.H. Faulkiner who proved more successful than his predecessors.

By December 1892 work was said to be progressing favourably but although the line was to be opened for traffic on December 1, 1892 there was little hope of that objective being realised. Extra time for completion had to be sought under Privy Council orders on two occasions.

In the immediate vicinity of Clifden the Contractor was unable for want of additional land to employ as many men as he would wish but throughout the line there were at that time one thousand men at work on the Railway and as soon as the land at Clifden would have been obtained the number was expected to be increased.

By the week ending November 29 1893 the following numbers were employed:

'Between the 38th mile and Ballinahinch (41st mile) 208 men. Between Ballinahinch and the 46th mile (ie 2 miles from Clifden,) 260 men; between Galway and the 28th mile 1043 men were employed, making a total of 1511'.[26]

By December of that year various sections were completed and drawing to a close. In the immediate area of Clifden works had stopped because nothing remained to be done there except the station works. Plans for these had not then been received. Works in the Roundstone area were also drawing to a close, with about fifty skilled labourers, strangers to the district, still employed there.

When these 'strangers' first came to the district, they found it difficult to obtain supplies owing to the absence of shops in the locality so the contractor started a provision shop, putting up a number of huts in Ballinafad. This store was said to be of great benefit to the labourers and to the locals who came long distances to purchase their provisions.

Due to the presence of so many 'strangers' there was a booming trade in poteen and shebeen houses were set up to accommodate them. Here illicit drink was sold and the local priest complained of the ill-effects this was having on his parishioners. The strenuous efforts by the Contractor and the priest to close the shebeen houses failed and it was not until works were completed and the men had left the district that the houses along with the stores were closed, much to the disappointment of the locals.

Official Opening

The Railway was opened to traffic between Galway and Oughterard on New Year's Day 1895. The Manager of the MGWR Company Mr Joseph Tatlow along with a number of railway dignitaries left Galway on a special train that Tuesday morning at 8 am and inspected the entire route. They arrived at Oughterard at 9.15am. The train then took on passengers at Oughterard and left there at 9.25 am arriving at Galway at 10.18 am. There were only twelve passengers as New Year's Day was a strict Church holiday. Seven were from Oughterard and five from Moycullen.[27]

However at Galway a considerable number of passengers were taken on

26. ibid.
27. G.V. January 1895.

Clifden Station — Courtesy National Library.

when the train left again for Oughterard at 10.45. Two trains each way each day was planned for the route. After returning from Oughterard, Mr Tatlow liberally entertained several gentlemen in the Railway Hotel after which he returned to Dublin.

The remainder of the route was opened with, it would appear, very little ceremony, on July 1 of the same year.

The total length of the line was forty eight miles five hundred and fifty feet. It commenced by a junction with the MGWR of Ireland system at their Galway station, of which system it is an extension and forms an integral part of the same gauge, five feet three inches. It was a single line with the terminus at Clifden. There were seven stations on the line, about seven to eight miles apart. At all stations there were passing places or loops, with up and down platforms, except at Ross, Ballinahinch and the terminus Clifden. The greatest distance of the single line without a passing place was the twelve and a half miles between Recess and Clifden.[28]

Moycullen Station just seven and three quarter miles from Galway had a goods store with internal line, a tank-house, passenger platforms of one hundred yards long and a goods platform.

Maam Cross Station, twenty six and a half miles out, had a cattle and goods platform, a goods store and tank-house.

From Recess station, thirty five and a half miles out, roads branch north, south, east and west.

Ballinahinch station at forty and three quarter miles was the last stop before Clifden.

Clifden Station had one platform, a station building with residence for a station-master, goods shed with internal line, a cattle and goods bank, large engine shed, a turntable, coal stage and a tank.

The station buildings were generally in the centre of the platforms and were said to be very permanent structures with concrete foundations, walls of hammer-square rubble masonry, with vertical and horizontal joints in cement. The stone generally used was limestone, obtained from the many quarries between Galway and Oughterard. Where the local stone was unworkable, they were built of red brick. The roofing was Major's patent red tiles and the overall appearance was said to be very picturesque. The dressing of windows and doors in some station buildings was of brick and in others of cut limestone. The passenger platforms had concrete foundations; their walls were of concrete backing and brick facing and eighteen inches thick.[29]

There were eighteen gatekeeper's houses erected at public road level crossings. They were one-storey buildings and contained a living-room, sixteen feet six inches by twelve feet, and two bedrooms, each of eight feet by ten feet three inches, with fireplaces. There was an outside porch covered by a continuation of the main roof and outhouses consisting of fuel house, privy, and ash-pit. Each house had an English rood of ground attached and was fenced off from the railway.[30]

28. J.H. Ryan paper.
29. J.H. Ryan paper.
30. ibid.

Extracts from J.H. Ryan's Paper read to members of the Institute of Engineers of Ireland, on May 1, 1901.

The Galway to Clifden line was described by one of its engineers Mr Ryan as being the longest and most important railway projects under the Light Railways (Ireland) Act of 1889. In his paper read to the Institute of Civil Engineers of Ireland on May 1, 1901 Mr Ryan gives a very clear description of the track meandering through the rough landscape of Connemara.

'From the station of the Midland Great Western Railway in Galway, the line passes through the eastern outskirts of the town and under Prospect Hill by a tunnel, the only one on the railway, the line thence proceeds over the Corrib River by a bridge, an imposing and elegant structure of steel. A fine view of the town can be obtained from this bridge, as well as of the river. Crossing the bridge, the line traverses for miles, the west side of the River Corrib, passing deserted mansions, breweries and factories,' and on to Moycullen village and station, from there to Ross station and on to Oughterard, where it takes a westerly course. Next comes Maam Cross station and then through the Joyce country to Recess station. After Recess the line passes the southern shores of Derryclare Lake, Athry Lough and the east end of Ballinahinch Lake. 'From Ballinahinch westwards there is a long stretch of wild and rugged country interspersed with many lakes, before reaching the terminus at Clifden.' It was at one time hoped to extend the line to the quay here but this proved too difficult. When the line was opened in 1895 its principal design was to promote and cultivate the fishing industries in the West of Ireland and in his paper Mr Ryan claimed they had succeeded in doing so. 'The Cleggan fisheries', he said, 'which are a few miles from Clifden station, have been considerably increased. It is principally mackerel fishing that they do. In the year 1896 they yielded 398 tons, in 1897 343 tons; in 1898 845 tons; in 1899 861 tons and in 1900, 1437 tons. The figures show what benefit the railway is to the country'.

'The railway involved a very large working expenditure, and it would be years before the line would pay; one of the chief sources of profit would be the tourist traffic'. They established a hotel at Recess and other places and the number of tourists was undoubtedly satisfactorily increasing.

The following extracts from the paper give a more detailed description of the lines engineering features:

Curves and Gradients

'The general alignment of the railway is excellent, with very gentle curves and easy gradients, the sharpest curves being 10 and 12 chains, which occur near the town of Galway, and 2 furlongs in open country. Where reverse curves occur, a straight intervening portion of 5 chains was required by the working company; these requirements entailed in some cases heavier work than would otherwise have been necessary. The worst gradient on the line is 1 in 70, of which there is only one; it occurs at Oughterard, at 17 miles, for a length of about 2,300 feet. There is one of 1 in 72, at Recess, at 34¼ miles, 700 feet long; and one of 1 in 73, at Ballinahinch, 1,100 feet long. In general the gradients are easy, the railway following the watersheds draining into Lough Corrib on the east up to its summit at Lough Boffin, 23 miles from Galway, the Screebe fishery watershed between this and Bunscaniff at 28¾, which latter is the summit level of the railway, and the watershed draining into Kilkieran Bay and Ballinahinch lakes, in the mid-distance, and into Clifden on the west, as will be seen by reference to the map'.

Line Construction

'Throughout the line the slopes of embankments are 1½ to 1, the toes of which are pitched with stone pitching where they abut on the shores of the lakes or banks of rivers; the slopes of cuttings in rock are ¼ to 1. The width of formation in banks is 16 feet, in cuttings 15 feet. In bog lands the land was of a very diverse character, entailing different treatments, the most important step in which, however, was drainage. In some cases, where the surface of the bog was irregular and bogholes occurred, turf sods were cut outside the line of the railway, and the inequalities filled up with them, so as to strengthen as much as possible the natural surface of the bog. Then the material from the side drains, which had become dry, was wheeled on so as to form a cushion, and made thereby a light embankment. In other cases brushwood was laid down on the surface to varying depths, according to the nature of the bog, and the quality of material in the embankments, except in the case of high banks of rock from adjoining cuttings, under which brushwood would be of little use. Owing to the scarcity of timber and brushwood west of Oughterard to the coast line, its use was very expensive. In the case of the banks made of turf, above mentioned, through bog, the top of the bank was made up, for a depth of from 18 inches to 2 feet, to the formation level, with a layer of the stiff clay or marl which generally underlies the bogs. This was found very efficacious, as when this material dries out it becomes quite hard, and renders the bank firm and solid. Where the above treatments did not suffice and the bog was shallow, clay and rock were tipped in until the bottom was found. In some cases rock only was tipped, being more economical, as clay spread very much below the bog surface. The slopes of the peat banks were cased over with clay to prevent them taking fire. If the depth of peat exceeded 4 feet 18 inches of this was excavated and filled in with clay until a bearing was obtained, which was generally attained when about 3 feet of clay was tipped in, the weight of the sides of the cuttings keeping the clay from spreading. This treatment has answered the purpose very well indeed. In some cases a thin layer of brushwood was put on top of formation'.

Rock and Soils encountered

'The nature of the rock excavation from Galway to Oughterard is limestone well bedded, and the best for building purposes was found at Rineen, 10 miles from Galway on the line of railway. This limestone formation is metamorphosed into black marble in the neighbourhood of Oughterard. From Oughterard westward the geological formation varies extensively, and the rock sections exposed by the cuttings have assisted geologists in determining the geological character of rocks, which belong, for the most part, to the schistose series, the origin and age of which have long been involved in doubt; most of the schists are proved to be igneous rocks, which have been altered during successive periods of metamorphism. The principal rock cuttings are, at Oughterard, 16¾ miles, about 700 yds. long, average depth 25 ft, in which is met carboniferous limestone, crushed green quartzite, granite (red and white), hornblende schist, &c. The cutting is traversed by some well-marked fault-planes. Through a considerable part of the cutting the rock is covered with a layer of peat containing numerous tree roots. The cutting north of Lough Shindilla, 27¼ miles, shows chiefly greenish and purplish quarzitic mica schists, and the cutting between Loughs Shindilla and Oorid, 28¾ miles, which is about 12 feet deep, shows crushed quartzitic mica schist with a large vein of normal granite. The cuttings along Lough Oorid show interesting granite intrusions in the schist, and thence, up to Derryneen Bridge, 32¼ miles, most of the cuttings are in hornblende schist with quartzitic bands, while west of this the cuttings are all in quartzitic mica schists. From the neighbourhood of Derryneen an example of folded strata on a large scale may be seen on the side of Letterbreckaun, the most northerly of the Maam Turk Mountains, about 5½ miles distant.

The rock excavation from Oughterard to Clifden was very hard to get through; blasting powder, where the rock was not wet, giving by far the best results, but tonite and dynamite were largely used, the former being the favourite.

The clay excavation varied from very stiff boulder clay in the neighbourhood of Galway to clay and sand of ordinary nature at Ross, 12 miles, showing gravel at Killaguile, 13 miles.

Beyond Oughterard to Leam the clay is intimately mixed with sand showing fairly good pockets of ballast at places, principally at Leam, 20¾ miles. From this, westward, clay does not occur in bulk by itself, except near Clifden and in a few isolated instances, but is generally always found as a covering to the rock in thicknesses of from 1 foot to 8 feet, interposed between the rock and the peat'.

Drains, Fences and Walls

'Side ditches were cut longitudinally on each side of the centre line, and where a double line of ditches occurred, cross-drains connecting them were cut at convenient intervals, generally at every 100 feet, also cross-drains about 25 feet apart from the toes of embankments to the inner longitudinal drain. The cross-section of these ditches had to be continually maintained until consolidation took place, and the experience was that frequent outfalls were necessary to keep the outside drains from closing in and getting choked owing to the bottom bursting up. In some cases, where the line was in cutting in bog overlying hard ground or rock within 3 feet or 4 feet of formation, it was excavated to the hard and refilled with clay.

The fencing in bog lands consists of three wires secured to posts driven sloping every 9 feet in the railway side of the outside drain; that in clay lands consists of ditch and mound, surmounted by posts and three wires 2 feet 3 inches high. Where rock occurs close to the surface, dry stone walling 4 feet 9 inches high by 1 foot 9 inches thick was adopted, pointed with lime mortar and coped; also a seven-wire fence 4 feet high was used on a portion of the line near Galway, where the other classes of fencing were not suitable. This consisted of six lines of 7-ply galvanised strand No. 5 W.G. and one of No. 4 W.G., stapled to posts 6 feet apart, and sunk 2 feet 6 inches in ground, with strainers 200 yards apart'.

Formation, ballast, rails and sleepers

'The formation in general is pitched with broken stone pitching 6 inches deep, set on edge for 12 feet in width, none, however, was laid on some of the bog banks and cuttings, as it was found that the stone cut into and became bedded and choked in the clay surfacing. Coarse gravel, with a slight admixture of clay to make it bond, was substituted, and a border of stone was pitched on each side.

The ballast and boxing on the first division is all gravel ballast; and up to the 27th mile it consists of gravel and a small admixture of broken stone; from the 27th to 35th mile broken stone was first laid down and packed under the sleepers, and then the second lift was made with a top dressing of gravel. From the 35th to 48th mile the ballast consists almost entirely of broken stone and debris from the rock cuttings, as no gravel was available.

The line is single and the stations form passing places, except at Ross and Ballinahinch. The permanent way consists of steel flange rails 65 lb. to the yard, in 30 feet lengths, with a percentage of shorter lengths, with deep angle fishplates, secured to half-round creosoted cross-sleepers by dog-spikes and four-fang bolts; also check rails are used on all curves under 15 chain radius, and tie-bars. A wrought-iron sole-plate is interposed between each sleeper and the flange of the rail; sleepers average 9 feet by 10 inches by 5 inches, laid 3 feet 1½ inches, centres, except at joints, where they are 1 foot 11 inches apart.

A portion of the permanent way over Munga bog, near Clifden, was laid in similar manner to the main line way of the Midland Great Western Railway, viz., with 79 lb. flange steel rails, as it was found that over boggy land this type is much stiffer and better suited than the lighter section'.

Bridges: Foster Street

'Commencing at Galway, the first important bridge is that over Forster-street (on the skew, angle 85 deg.), which consists of four spans — three spans being 30 feet each and one of 36 feet over the street. The clear height from the street is 15 feet 3 inches to the bottom of the girder. The masonry in abutments and piers is heavy squared limestone with drafted quoins and copings all showing the rock face. The main girders are of wrought-iron 3 feet 3 inches deep, stiffened at intervals as shown, and weighing 4½ tons each. Steel trough flooring is laid transversely between the girders and asphalted. The troughs contain the sleepers, which are embedded in clean gravel ballast. The total weight of iron and steel in the bridge is 77 tons'.

Prospect Hill (Tunnel)

'The next work is Prospect Hill Bridge, which is built in the form of a tunnel, but is really a cut and cover. It carries Prospect Hill roadway over the railway, and also acts as a retaining wall to the town service reservoirs. It was thus designed to save the expense of retaining walls of large section, which the great height of open cutting would otherwise necessitate. It also afforded desirable building sites close to the town.

The work is in a cutting, with a maximum depth of 36 feet, through boulder clay, which was so stiff that it required very little timbering, although some was used as a precaution; the sides and bottom were therefore excavated to the exact form of the bridge (or tunnel walls), and the brickwork was proceeded with in 15 feet lengths, and covered in as the arch and haunching were completed for each length. It had to be worked from one face, as the material could be disposed of only in this way. As the excavation proceeded, several springs were encountered, and these were led by 6 inch cast-iron pipes to catch-pits built under the invert, and all connected together by a 9-inch cast-iron pipe running the full length of the tunnel. The invert consists of concrete faced with two layers of brick on edge, and is segmental and laid in cement mortar; the sides and crown consist of five rings of brickwork built in lime mortar, and the haunching is of rubble masonry. The faces are of hammer-squared limestone of an ornamental character. The length from face to face is 240 feet, the extreme width is 17 feet 8 inches, and the height from rail level to crown of arch is 15 feet 1 inch. The whole is situated on a 12-chain curve'.

Headford Road Bridge

'The next bridge of importance is that which carries the railway over the Headford-road, on the skew, by one span of 28 feet 10½ inches. The girders weigh 3 tons each, and the trough flooring is similar to that described for Forster-street Bridge. The total weight of ironwork and steel is 18½ tons. The masonry is coursed rubble in lime mortar; the foundations consist of Portland cement concrete 6 to 1'.

River Corrib Viaduct

'The Corrib Viaduct, which carries the railway over the River Corrib at Galway, consists of three spans, each of 150 ft. clear between bearings, and a lifting span of 21 ft. on the bascule principle to allow for navigation in the river. The main trusses for the large spans are lattice type, the top and bottom girders (or booms) being separated by pairs of vertical struts at 7 ft. 6 ins. centres, and ties at 45 degrees angle. The ties (pillars) at both ends are at 63 degrees angle, and are of similar section as top and bottom booms. At centre span for a limited length, the 45 degrees angle ties overlap for counterbalancing purposes.

The camber in the large spans is 2½ inches. Each pair of vertical struts is wind-braced by a single system of flat bars, and the top flanges or booms are strongly braced over head, and stiffening T-bars are inserted between the top bracing and the vertical struta at an angle of 45 degrees. The flooring consists of Hobson's patent arched steel flooring plates, of a special section ⅜ inches thick, strongly riveted to the side of the trough flanges or booms and resting on the bottom L-iron of the same. The troughs are semi-elliptical in cross-section, rising 9 inches in the centre, and each covering 2 feet 6 inches in length of the span. The actual weight of the 150-feet span is 112 tons 5 cwt., and of the lifting span, with machinery, 36 tons 16 cwt. The total dead load on each span is 213 tons 12 cwt., and the live load was calculated at 1⅓ tons per foot run.

The whole flooring is levelled up to ¾ inch above the crown of trough with tar asphalt; by this method of construction the ordinary cross-sleeper road could be carried across the bridge on ballast 3 inches under the sleepers, and up to top of level of same, except on the lifting span, where longitudinal timbers had to be laid without ballast. The lifting span consists of plate girders with small cross-girders and rail-bearers, the balance weights of the machinery for actuating the span weigh 18½ tons, and drop into slots in the masonry of the pier'.

'In erecting the superstructure the bottom boom was first laid down on a temporary staging, fixed accurately in line, and wedged up to the required camber; the flooring was then put on, the end pillars and struts erected, and the top boom lowered on to these. The riveting was all done by hand.

The bridge is protected by home and distant signals, and is electrically locked from the Galway signal cabin, but it has also a cabin of its own with five levers situated at the western end. By an ingenious arrangement, the bar which locks the opening span, once it has been withdrawn, and the bascule has been lifted the smallest distance, it cannot be shot back until the bridge is again fully closed. The arrangement which cuts off the wire connecting the signals at the east end is also very neat. Each of the large spans has a fixed end and a roller end moving on steel rollers fixed in a frame. Two wheel guards are carried across the bridge, each consisting of a longitudinal bulk 8 inches by 8 inches, protected at the upper inside edge by 3 inches by 3 inches by ⅜ inch L-iron screwed on to balk by coach screws on top and by counter-sunk screws on sides. The angle-iron stands 2¾ inches from outside of rail and rises 3 inches over it.

As to the foundations; those of the east abutment, which were situated clear of the river, are formed of Portland cement concrete; that of the west abutment being full of springs, the concrete was put in in bags. No. 1 pier, at east side of river, was built inside a timber cofferdam, and the foundations are of concrete 4 to 1, with masonry footings on hard boulder clay. The foundations of the two piers carrying the lifting span are each of two wrought-iron cylinders, riveted on a staging over the position they were to occupy when lowered; those in No. 2 pier were the first sunk, and great difficulty was experienced in bringing them to a level bearing all round; owing to the presence of large boulders, they both canted when the internal lining of brickwork was put in, and in straightening one of them the brickwork was so cracked as to require to be taken out and rebuilt; when they canted they were so securely held by the surrounding boulder clay that they could not be lifted up by the Goliath in use, and they were too small inside to enable divers to work with ease at the cutting edge, while the boulder clay was so porous that a 9-inch centrifugal pump and a No. 7 pulsometer, working together, could not control the water; consequently the divers worked down to the cutting edge outside the cylinders, and by blasting and excavating the boulders which were holding up the cylinders, succeeded in straightening them and bringing them up to a uniform bearing.

The excavation thus made around the cylinders was then filled up with concrete in bags, and concrete in bags was also put in the centre chamber, which was filled with concrete by skips. They could then be pumped out, and concrete was put in dry in one of them; however, owing to the disturbance and strain put upon the riveting and joints of the cylinders in the process of straightening them, they could not be rendered water-tight, and in the next cylinder the concrete was all put in in skips, and no attempt made to pump it. The experience gained in sinking these latter cylinders enabled those of pier No. 3 to be got down and filled very quickly; they were hung up by the Goliath and no brick filling was put in until they were finally fixed, except some filling in the annular portion between the inside and outside ring to make them sink.

In this position they weighed about 40 tons. They were then lowered between guide piles until they touched the bottom, and sank through the mud into a foundation that held them; the Goliath was then braked, and they were held at this level until the divers had excavated away the points of support; they were then lowered down, and the next point of support observed and removed, and so on until a uniform bearing was obtained. Then a layer of bags of concrete was put in, and over them fine concrete, and when these had sufficiently set it was found that the pulsometer could control all leakage sufficiently to allow the masons to complete the brick rings up to water level. Caisson No. 4 took 4 days in sinking. Even in these cases it was not considered advisable to put in the centre core of concrete dry, as the cement got more or less washed out by the pump, and consequently the whole was put in with skips. The masonry commenced at low-water level, and was hearted throughout with 4 to 1 concrete. Each cylinder is raised in masonry 2 feet 4 inches to the springing of an arch which connects the two cylinders of each pier. The character of the masonry is coursed ashlar in uniform courses, each stone having an inch draft along courses and on vertical joints, and showing the rock face on the surface between. The ends of each pier are semi-circular, of 5 feet 8 inches radius, and the pier is surmounted by a corbelled stringcourse 3 feet high. The bedstones on which the superstructure rests are of Cornish white granite, and all the remainder of the masonry is of Galway carboniferous limestone, of a dark grey colour. The superstructure was laid down on a timber platform or staging 31 feet wide, carried on rows of piling, three piles of 12 inches by 12 inches to each, spaced 20 feet apart, each row being diagonally braced. Iron rails were laid on this platform, and on it the Goliath crane (span 30 feet 6 inches), and stream derrick could be run backwards and forwards the whole length of the bridge. There was also a low-level timber bridge which accommodated the passage of the contractors' engines with material for the foundations, &c.

The manufacturers of the steel and iron work in the superstructure were Messrs. Cochrane and Son, and for the cylinders Mr. T. Butler, of Stanningley. The signalling was done by the Railway Signal Company of Fazakerly. The contractor for the entire works was the late Mr. Travers II. Falkiner, with whom was associated Mr. E.J. Jackson'.

Woodstock River Bridge

'Bridge No. 5 is that over the Woodstock River, at 4¾ miles; it is 30 feet square span, with wrought-iron plate girder superstructure and steel trough flooring, which carries the road, and is similar to the details shown; it presented no difficulty. The total weight of ironwork in this bridge is about 18½ tons; the main girders are 34 feet long and 3 feet deep'.

Other Bridges

'Bridge No. 6 is 40 feet span on the skew, and carries the railway over the drainage canal at Moycullen, leading to Ballyquirk Lake, at 6¾ miles, with an angle of skew of 40 degrees. The main girders are 48 feet long by 3 feet deep; the total weight of ironwork is about 26½ tons, and the masonry in abutments is squared masonry in cement mortar.

Bridge No. 7 carries the railway over a drainage canal at 8⅛ miles; it is 49 feet span on skew, with cross-girders 4 feet centre to centre carrying 5-inch longitudinal floor troughs. The total weight of ironwork and steel is 35 tons. The masonry is similar to that in other bridges.

Bridge No. 8, at 8½ miles, is the Drimcong River Bridge; it is 30 feet span on the skew of 45 degrees. Here the foundations were rendered difficult on account of water and the depth to which they were sunk. The ground at this place consists of a light layer of peat overlying a considerable depth of marl, evidently an ancient lake bottom. The water came into the foundations so quickly that the lower 6 feet or 7 feet could not be kept dry, and was filled in with dry rubble, which acted as a sumph hole for the 10-inch centrifugal pump. Then several feet of concrete were put in before the masonry was commenced. No traces of yielding in the dry rubble have been detected.

Bridge No. 9 carries the railway over the Knockbane River at 10 miles; the span is 23 feet 1 inch on the skew of 60 degrees, iron plate girders, with trough flooring, carrying the railway. The total weight is 13 tons.

Bridges Nos. 10 and 11 are 30 feet spans of the type above described, and presented no difficulties.

Bridge No. 12 carrying the railway over the Owenriff River near Oughterard, at 17⅛ miles, is 40 feet span, with wrought-iron plate girders, and steel trough flooring carrying the railway. The total weight of iron and steel is 26½ tons. Some difficulty was experienced with the foundations, which were below the bed of the river, owing to the presence of gravel which was waterlogged. The pump working in this could barely keep the water under. About 12 inches of flat heavy stones were put in, then a kind of coarse bag or chamber was formed for the concrete by lining the sides and bottom of the excavation with roofing felt and disused tarpaulin; this effectually prevented the water from flowing through the concrete, and, consequently, the cement was not washed out. The pumps, however, had to be kept working night and day until the masonry reached ground level.

Bridge No. 13 is 20 feet span, No. 14 is 40 feet span, No. 15 is 30 feet span, No. 16 is 20 feet span, No. 17 is 23 feet span, all between the 18th and 28th miles, with wrought-iron superstructure and steel trough flooring, and presented no difficulties.

Bridge No. 18, at 28¾ miles, carries the public road leading to Clifden over the railway at an angle of skew of 60 degrees, and is constructed of masonry, with brick arch of five rings of brick in cement mortar, with dog's tooth on the face. The face work is of blue brindled brick, and the interior of Bridgewater brick.

Bridge No. 19, at 31 miles, is an ordinary river bridge of 20 feet span, similar to those above described. The foundations of this bridge are on gravelly clay, underlying peat about 7 feet 6 inches deep. Immediately over the clay were found several pieces of charred fir timber, suggestive of an ancient forest fire.

Bridge No. 20, at 32¼ miles, carries the railway over a river on the skew with 30 feet span; the superstructure is similar to one of the spans of Forster-street Bridge.

Bridge No. 21, at 33¼ miles, has also 30 feet span; it is similar as to superstructure, and carries the railway over Lissoughter River on the skew; the abutments are very high, with long splayed wing walls and retaining walls to river; the foundations are on rock appearing on general ground surface.

Bridge No. 22 is called Weir Bridge, at 35¾ miles. It carries the railway over a river joining Glendalough and Derryclare Lakes. The span is 30 feet, and similar to those above described. The abutments were built of masonry in mid-river, within cofferdams, on a concrete footing.

Bridge No. 23, at 37¾ miles, is 20 feet span, and carries the railway over a small river.

Bridge No. 24, at 40¾ miles, carries the railway by two spans of 50 feet, over the Cloonbeg River at Ballinahinch, and is built on a curve of 24¾ chains. The superstructure weighs 66 tons; the permanent way is carried on cross-girders and steel through flooring, as described below. The river is shallow, but rapid; the centre pier is built on rock close to the bed of the river, and is buttressed up stream.

Bridge No. 26, at 46¼ miles, carries the public road leading to Clifden over the railway, and is built similar to No. 18.

Bridge No. 27, at 46¾ miles, also carries the public road over the railway. The public road was diverted for this purpose to avoid level crossings. The span is 15 feet 4 inches on the square, and 17 feet 8½ inches on the skew, the superstructure being trough flooring, which supports the roadway and plate girder parapets. The total weight is 13 tons. The abutments were built of blue brindled brick throughout, backed with concrete, with displacers.

Bridge 28, at 48⅜ miles, carries the railway over the river at Clifden by a skew span of 49 feet. The superstructure is of a type similar to the 50-feet spaus above described.

There are 13 small accommodation bridges over and under the railway, mostly under, with spans of 12 feet clear, with iron tops of the trough flooring pattern running parallel with the railway'.

General Bridge Steelwork Description

'Generally in the ironwork superstructure of the bridges, the girders were designed to have a height of one-tenth of the span, and are plate girders with strong stiffening, and up to and including 45 feet span the flooring is steel trough flooring, full height 1 foot 1½ inches, consisting of ½ inch plate with double cover-plates 7 inches by ½ inch at the top and bottom of each trough; the distance from centre of one trough to corresponding centre of next is 2 feet 4 inches, and they are attached to the web of girder by 3½ inches by 3 inches by ½ inch L-iron; they rest on, and are riveted to, the bottom I-iron of flange of girder. A 1-inch screw tap is let into each end of the bottom of each trough for drainage purposes, and in some cases of bridges over public roads, these are connected by cast-iron gutters and down-pipes. The under sides are painted uniform with girders, and the tops are asphalted and filled with clean ballast, into which the sleepers are bedded, thus obtaining a through cross-sleeper road. The 49 feet and 50 feet spans have got cross-girders 15 inches high, consisting of flanges 9 inches wide connected to webs by L-irons and resting on bottom flange of main girders; these are covered by 5 inches corrugated or trough flooring laid longitudinally, and differing slightly from the other flooring described, in this particular, in having no covering plates to the troughs, except where they are introduced for the purpose of joining the flooring together, that is, at every third corrugation. The cover-plates are 4 inches by ⅜ inches. There are holes in the bottom of each corrugation at intervals for drainage. As none of the main girders rise more than 2 feet 6 inches over rail level, they were designed to be placed 14 feet apart centre to centre; where the spans are skew the troughing is cut to a straight line parallel to the abutment face of bridge, and 12 inches inside that face, and the end of the trough is kept from spreading by a 1½ inch wrought-iron bolt, which passes through from side to side of trough. Bed-plates are of cast-iron, 2 inches thick; the bearings vary from 2 feet to 2 feet 6 inches.

The manufacturers of the ironwork of all the bridges, except the Corrib, were Messrs. Joseph Westwood and Co., Poplar, and J. Butler, of Stanningley'.

Tests Carried out on Bridges

'The following are the results of tests made by General Hutchinson, and subsequently by Major Marindin, of the Board of Trade, when inspecting the line. The tests made of bridges between Galway and Oughterard were with three locomotives, each weighing 43 tons, and were recorded by means of rods, and on the Corrib Bridge by the level.

On the Corrib Bridge the results were, for each of the 150-feet spans, a deflection of 1 inch, with no permanent set, and 3/16 in. under trough flooring'.

'In Forster-street Bridge	Deflection
First span, of 30 ft.	3/16 in.
Second span, of 36 ft.	3/16 in.
Third span, of 30 ft.	3/16 in.
Fourth span, of 30 ft.	⅛ in.
In Headford-road Bridge, 28 ft. 10½ in. span;	Girder, ⅛ in.; troughs, 1/16 in.
In Woodstock Bridge, 30 ft. span	Girder, ⅛ in.
In Ballyquirk Bridge, 40 ft. span	Girder, ⅛ in.
In Moycullen Bridge, 49 ft. span	Girder, ⅛ in.
In Drimcong Bridge, 30 ft. span	Girder, ⅛ in.
In Knockbane Bridge, 23 ft. span	Girder, 1/16 in.
In Ross Bridge, 30 ft. span	Girder, ⅛ in.
In Loughtgannon Bridge, 30 ft. span	Girder, 1/16 in.
In Oughterard River Bridge, 40 ft. span	Girder, 3/16 in.
Leadmines Bridge, 20 ft. span	Girder, ⅛ in.
In Glengowla River Bridge, 40 ft. span	Girder, ⅛ in.
In Garibaldi River Bridge, 30 ft. span	Girder, ⅛ in. troughs, 1/16 in.
In Leam River Bridge, 30 ft. span	Girder, ⅛ in. to 3/16 in.
In Letterfore River Bridge, 20 ft. span	Girder, 1/16 in.
In Bunscaniff Bridge, 23 ft. span	Girder, ⅛ in. troughs, 1/16 in.
In Boheshal River Bridge, 20 ft. span	Girder, 1/16 in.
In Derryneen River Bridge, 30 ft. span	Girder, ⅛ in. troughs, 1/16 in.
In Cahir River Bridge, 30 ft. span	Girder, ⅛ in.
Weir Bridge, 30 ft. span	Girder, ⅛ in.
Athry River Bridge, 20 ft. span	Girder, ⅛ in. troughs, ⅛ in.
Cloonbeg River Bridge, 50 ft. span	Girder, 3/16 in., cross-girders, 0 in.
Clifden River Bridge, 49 ft. span	Girder, ⅛ in., cross-girders, 1/16 in.'

Steam Culverts, including brief descriptions of Munga Ravine and Clifden River retaining wall.

'Besides rivers, a large number of streams had to be crossed by culverts varying in size from 2 feet to 12 feet; these are built in rubble masonry in cement with stone inverts. The longest was that in a deep ravine known as Munga Ravine, at about 44¾ miles, and which was about 40 feet deep; a viaduct was originally intended, but as sufficient material was subsequently acquired in the vicinity an embankment was adopted; as the railway crosses the ravine on the skew, it necessitated a culvert of 112 feet in length and 12 feet in width. It is built of rubble masonry in cement, with brick arching; the walls are 5 feet thick, with counterforts 4 feet by 3 feet. Wing walls 25 feet long were built to catch the slopes of embankment. The 18-inch drains are flagged at the bottom with flags 4 inches thick let 4 inches under each wall, and were covered on top with flags 5 inches thick bearing at least 6 inches on side walls. Where the railway traverses very sidelong ground, as on the mountain side, a larger number of culverts had to be constructed than usual, to provide for any sudden rush of water; in many instances these culverts were stepped to suit the declivity of the mountain stream, and a retaining wall, 370 feet long, had to be built on the railway side of Clifden River at 47 miles to meet this case of sliding ground; it is 12 feet high, 2 feet thick at top, 5 feet thick at bottom, and is built of rubble in cement mortar to flood level, and above that height of stone rubble.

The culverts are built of rubble with roughly squared rubble arches, and are almost all coped with hammer-squared limestone from Oughterard, and many of them have quoins of the same. In deep bog lands (where considerable saving might have been effected in foundations by the use of wooden box culverts they were not approved of, except in a few instances, by the working company), the foundations consist of a dry rubble base surmounted by a layer of Portland cement concrete 6 to 1. Earthenware pipes 12 inches and 18 inches have been used in a few cases, the exposed ends being cased in concrete. One or two flat-top culverts are built, the superstructure being 4 inches creosoted timber carried on light iron girders placed under each permanent rail'.

Closure

In the years that followed the railway brought the rich and famous to Connemara to fish, shoot and enjoy the many pleasures the district had to offer. To the poor it was seen as the first stage of that long emigrant trail that took them halfway across the world. It took the boys to the war front and brought back the wounded men and heroes. It carried the Black and Tans on their night of debauchery, when they set the town alight. It had its tracks blown and ripped up by the Republicans, in their attempt to delay the approach of the Free State Army. It did bring with it a confidence and independence to the town that its promoters had hoped for and the town no longer seemed remote and forgotten as it had been in the past.

However, in 1935, just forty years since construction, the owners of the Great Southern Railway Company, announced their intention to close the line. The years of request and demand, of pleading and convincing all seemed wasted somehow, all pointless. The days of excitement and promise, the feelings of achievement by those who worked so hard to have the railway established, seemed removed now from the changing face of Connemara.

The Touring Car was introduced by the Railway Company to facilitate the tourist traffic. They made their way through the beautiful Connemara mountains and along by Killery Harbour linking up with the trains at Westport and Clifden.

The Company declared the line an uneconomic unit of their service and a heavy drain on their resources. The average daily tonnage from Galway to Clifden for some time previously had been only thirteen tons, the Company complained, and the line was in bad need of repair. There was no guarantee that the huge cost of carrying out the repairs would ever be refunded by increased traffic on the line.[31]

Efforts were made by the people to get the Company to rescind their decisions. The Department of Industry and Commerce was approached but all efforts failed and the Company pressed ahead with their plans.

The main argument against the closure was the effect on the roads of the buses and lorries which would replace the Railway. It was thought that too severe a burden would be placed on the ratepayers of the county to maintain the roads used by those lorries and buses. However, the Company answered that the taxes on the lorries and buses of close on £700 per year would go a long way towards the cost of keeping the roads in good order.[32]

All men employed with the Company would be offered either retirement or alternative employment elsewhere in the country. But it was argued that the loss of the total wages of the fifty or so men employed by the Railway, said to be close to £7,000 per year, would be a great loss to the county along with the £1250 rates on the railway company's property. Among the men employed

31. Conn. Trib. April 1935.
32. ibid.

were seven station-masters, Mr Kelly of Recess, Mr Gerrard of Maam Cross, Mr Murray of Moycullen, Mr McKeown of Ross, Mr Murray of Oughterard, Mr Mahoney of Ballinahinch and Mr Grogan of Clifden. These men received wages averaging about £220 per year. There were also two porters and a head porter at Clifden, a signal porter at Recess, a porter at Maam Cross and a porter at Oughterard. There were ten gangs of men working on the line, each gang consisting of a ganger and three men. These men were paid an average of £2 per week. There were also two engine drivers and two firemen.[33]

To replace the Railway a fleet of buses and lorries were placed on the road to serve the area. The buses were light twenty-six seaters, and the lorries would carry no more than four tons, to reduce the effect on the roads. The roads were being tarred in preparation for the service. The lorries would deliver goods direct to the homes and to the shops, thereby eliminating freightage from railway station to house. The buses would provide a house to house parcel service in Clifden, and a bus would now run each day from Clifden to Roundstone. A number of vehicles equipped to carry livestock would be provided for the Clifden, Recess, Leenane, Maam Cross, Oughterard and Moycullen fairs. All in all it was felt by the Railway Company that a far better service would be offered to the people.

The fleet of lorries arrived in the town on Friday April 26 and the drivers, the newspapers reported, seemed confident. Although a large crowd turned out to see them, opposition was still strong and it was hoped that the tracks would be untouched and that perhaps at a later date the railway service would be reinstated. But these were later removed and sold to a German scrap company.

On Saturday evening, April 27, 1935, at five o'clock, the last passenger train pulled out of Clifden. The whistle was blown several times as it pulled away, leaving behind it the station-master Mr Michael Grogan and the station foreman, Mr Edward Stankard 'pathetic figures on the platform'. The newspaper correspondent travelling on the train reported that someone suggested that the occasion called for a speech, 'this was history in the making', but someone else said the less said about this occasion the better, 'it was history in the unmaking!.'[34]

At almost every house along the route, little groups of people were gathered to wave a farewell to the train. Repeatedly the whistle gave back a salute, and at all the level crossings detonators were fired. At the stations, old wagons were hitched on, making the last train from Connemara very long and important looking as it entered Galway station.

Water System

By 1891 there was still no sewage system or water supply in the town. The necessity of installing both was deemed essential before the completion of the railway line and the arrival of the expected increase in tourism.

Up until this, water was obtained from way-side wells, the most popular being the well in Church Lane. These way-side wells were almost on a level with the public road and in wet weather the road surface deposits were carried into them. But the majority of the people obtained their water from the Owenglen

33. Conn. Trib. April 1935.
34. Conn. Trib. April 1935.

114

river, into which sewage from the workhouse flowed, 'causing the supply to be impure, unsanitary and a great danger to the health of the town.'[35]

Several attempts had been made in the past to establish a water system, but these were rejected by the Boards of Guardians who declared the financial conditions of the Union prohibited their construction. Under the direction of Major John Talbot D'Arcy, second son of John D'Arcy founder of the town, a campaign was launched to force the Guardians to take on this work.

Loans were sought from the Commissioners of Public Works, but these were refused on the grounds that the Clifden Board of Guardians had a history of not paying back loans and could not therefore be trusted to repay any loan made to them. However when in 1894 the Medical Inspector for the Local Government Board, Mr Clements, reported that the water used by the people was a danger to public health, the office of Public works relinquished. The works were estimated to cost £1,600, £500 of this was obtained under the Relief of Distress and used to employ unskilled labour. Work commenced in the summer of 1895 and by the end of that year the town boasted a public water and sewage system.

35. SPO.

CHAPTER VI

Landed Families of West Connemara

The following is a list of owners, acreage and valuation for West Connemara as given in Land Owners of Ireland, 1871. A brief history of some of these families appear in the following pages, all of whom resided in Connemara at the turn of the century, and were very much involved in its everyday life.

	Acreage	Value
Richard Berridge, London and Ballinahinch	159,898.1.30	6,321. 0.0
Caroline J. Blake, Renvyle, Letterfrack	4,682.2.10	1,011.15.0
Val Blake (O'Connor) Bunowen Castle	7,690.1.10	2,191. 5.0
Gillman Browne, Rosleague, Letterfrack	1,507.0.10	232.10.0
Bernard Duane, Ballinakill	76.0.30	30. 0.0
J.J. Eyre, Clifden Castle	8,204.2.15	1,526. 0.0
Francis J.Graham Letterfrack	8,641.2.20	354. 5.0
Samuel Freyer, Clachacurra	211.3.15	57.10.0
Thomas Hazell, Doon Cottage	495.1.35	64.10.0
Mitchell Henry, Kylemore	9,252.0.5	639. 0.0
John Kendall, London	2,892.3.35	273.15.0
Alexander Lambert, Derrynaslegane	1,121.0.35	306.15.0
Rev. Anthony Magee, Bollard, Clifden	2,543.2.10	381. 0.0
Anthony Morris, Ballinaboy	1,084.1.5	311.10.0
Frederick Twining, Cleggan	869.0.20	247. 0.0
Thomas Young Prior, Ballinakill	1,084.1.5	311.10..0

Armstrong-Lushington-Tulloch
Shanboolard Hall and Ross

The Armstrongs, descended from an English border clan, came to Ireland during the reign of Elizabeth I. They settled first in County Fermanagh, later in the Midlands and County Roscommon. During the middle of the 19th century, c.1840, one member of this family, John Armstrong (-1888) came to live in South Hill, about three miles outside Clifden.

A local magistrate, John was an active member of the community and was among those attempting to construct a light railway from Galway to Clifden, as early as 1880. John had four sons and two daughters by his wife Letitia Pratt, second daughter of Major Harvey Randall Saville Pratt de Montmorency of Castle Morres Co. Kilkenny. Letitia died in 1882.

Two sons, Elliott (1834-1901) and Harvey, moved to England, married and had families there. The third son John never married. The daughters, Mary and Rose, also married and moved to England, where their descendants still live.

116

But the youngest son William Cairne was by far the most interesting and both his life and that of his wife's go on to make the most thrilling reading in any family history.

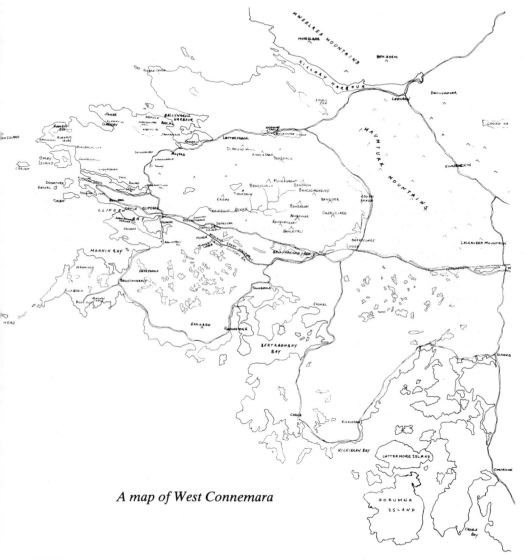

A map of West Connemara

William Armstrong

On October 1, 1881, William married Kathleen (Kate) Mary Lushington, daughter of Charles Lushington of Rodmersham, Kent, and sister to Minna, who two years previously had married William's cousin Francis Graham.[a] William, already acquainted with Moreton Frewer,[b] at about this time became

a. see Graham page 138.
b. see Frewen p. 131.

117

captivated by tales of Moreton's vast holding and of the open ranges in Wyoming. He, along with several other young gentlemen, joined his caravan to the rich pasture lands of Western America.

He purchased land through the Phoenix Cattle Company and taking his young bride, they set forth on an adventure which would either amass them a large fortune or have them scalped by the Indians. By this time, 1881, Wyoming had been opened up principally by the Frewen brothers and was now stocked with thousands of cattle owned by a handful of men known as the Wyoming Cattle Barons. The region was protected by a new post, Fort McKinney, and although said to be clear of Indians, small bands did at times attack the settlers.

The cook, Kathleen Armstrong with daughter Edna, William Armstrong and some Irish Cowboys, outside the Armstrong Ranchhouse in Johnston County Wyoming 1884.

The Armstrongs built their cabin, not in the sprawling style of what became known as Frewen Castle, but nevertheless large and comfortable. It is difficult to ascertain the exact size of their holding, Canyon Ranch, but it was believed to be considerable and of course quite unimaginable by Connemara standards. Their address was Buffalo P.O., Johnston County, Wyoming. When they arrived, Buffalo was a new 'wild town because of the weakness, in will, intellect and knowledge of the law, of the sheriff and his deputy, Nat James and Tom Farrell, who had both been cowboys working for Moreton Frewen when they were given their stars'.[1]

Their first child Edna de Montmorency, was born at the ranch on August 22, 1882 and baptised at St Mark's Church, Cheyenne.

Early years on the ranch were hard and troublesome. Cattle ranching was a long term proposition further complicated by the persistence of the Cattle Barons of the south in pushing their herds ever further north, resulting in overcrowding on the range.

In the years that followed, a number of ranchers thrived and prospered while others failed miserably; falling foul of freezing winters, cattle rustlers and isolation together with associated problems.

1. Allen Andrews: The Splendid Pauper. The story of an Eccentric Victorian Empire Builder, Moreton Frewen. p.65.

While the Armstrongs continued to enjoy the ups and downs of ranch life, Mrs Armstrong's aunt, Mrs Jane Anne Tulloch, was back home in England grappling with stipulations in her late husband's will. Having no children of their own, James Tulloch left it to his wife to select an heir from their six nieces. It is not known what criterion Mrs Tulloch used when making her decision, but perhaps it was her admiration for Mrs Armstrong's strength of character that resulted in her choosing that lady as the lucky beneficiary of a considerable inheritance. One of the stipulations of the Will was that the recipients would take the name Tulloch, so in 1884 the Armstongs assumed by Royal Licence the additional surnames of Lushington and Tulloch. In that year also the family sold up their American ranch and returned to England. They were fortunate to leave before the severe winter of 1884-85 during which a million cattle were estimated to have died on the western range.

William had not amassed a large fortune in America but he had returned with his scalp intact and considerably better off than his contemporary Moreton Frewen. The family settled at Almington Hall, Market Drayton, Shropshire, and there two sons were born, Graham de Montmorency (b.1886) and Kinmont Willie (b.1889).

In 1890 when Shanbolard Hall and estate came on the market the Armstrongs purchased it and returned to Connemara. They now used the names Armstrong-Lushington-Tulloch. They rented Rosleague House while the Hall underwent extensive renovations. Mrs Armstrong-Lushington-Tulloch employed a large household staff; butler, bootman, housemaids etc., including her eccentric cook Mrs Fisher. Mrs Fisher was apparently 'fond of the bottle' and when 'under the influence' dinner was usually served late or perhaps not at all, whereupon Mrs Fisher would immediately be given her notice. Next morning, however, sober and contrite and promising the act would never be repeated, Mrs Fisher would once again be reinstated. Although this little drama was re-enacted many times over the years Mrs Fisher did manage to remain with the family until her death c.1920.

At Shanbolard Hall in 1893 a third son, Eric, was born. In 1894 the estate of the late Thomas Prior was put on the market by his wife Horatia. Kathleen and William purchased this along with Ross House. The estate consisted of about 1140 statute acres, and was situated on the Bay of Ballinakill. It comprised the following townlands: Cartron, Maunfin, Dooneen, part of Cloncree, Knocknahaw, Tirvemore, Ross, Derrylahan, Turvigariff, and Ardkyle, Carrigeen, (Fraighillann Island little) South Freigh Island, Cartron Island in Ballinakill Lough and other islands in the bay, and portion of the bog of Crocknaraw. Along with the land came all the shooting and fishing rights. 'The entire estate abounds with game, pheasants, partridge, hares, rabbits, wild duck and in winter cock snipe, widgeon and teal.

Fishing: herring, cod, haddock and whiting during winter and gunner, mackarel, bream and pollock from May to September' with first rate lobster fishing on the shores and rocks adjoining the land.

The estate was advertised as a 'desirable investment for English purchasers'. 'Rarely so comfortable and picturesquely situated a property with such advantages for fishing, shooting and yachting is in (sic) the market'.[2]

2. Armstrong-Lushington-Tulloch Family Papers.

Shanbolard Hall.

The estate was bounded on the north by the waters of the Atlantic, to the south by Ballinakill Lodge and townland of Garranbaron, to the West by Shanboolard and to the east by Ballinakill Bay. Almost all the lands were completely fenced with stone walls, extensive drainage and other works of reclamation had been carried out at the expense of many thousands of pounds.

Ross, the residence of the Priors, had a number of outbuildings. Three large granaries, new feeding sheds of modern design for seventy head of cattle and stables and coach-houses and piggeries. There were no tenants on the land except for twenty six acres held by Mrs Mathias Burke. The property had in the past belonged to the Grahams. This estate, added to Shanbolard, had increased the Armstrong-Lushington-Tulloch holding considerably. Ross House was leased to a number of people in the years that followed while the family continued to live at Shanbolard.

Kathleen Armstrong-Lushington-Tulloch

Life at Shanboolard for Mrs Armstrong-Lushington-Tulloch was by far more comfortable than in Wyoming. In addition she had the companionship of her sister a short distance away at Ballinakill Lodge. However, the following years were to bring her short-lived happiness and more than her share of sorrow. Her oldest sons Graham and Kinmont were sent to England to be educated at Summerfields and Rugby. Sadly Eric, the youngest, died at the early age of seven in 1900.

Just six months later on January 10 1901, William died from complications arising our of a hunting accident which occurred years before.

Kathleen married again on December 17 1901, James Geoffrey Cave France, a member of the R.I.C. They assumed by Royal Licence on February 25 1902

Letitia Pratt de Montmorency.

Kathleen Armstrong-Lushington-Tulloch with her third son, Eric (1893-1900).

the surname and arms of France-Lushington-Tulloch. However, this marriage was of short duration; Geoffrey died April 17 1905.

A strong spirited lady of high principles and with a deep religious conviction, Kathleen, living the life of a spartan, took over the running of the farm and continued with her breeding stud of Welsh ponies. She was recognised and respected as a horsebreeder and won many prizes at shows around the country. Over the years she made many improvements on the estate. She built many farm buildings, stables and cow-byres and spent long hours attending her garden.

Edna, her only daughter, born in Wyoming in 1882, married on September 2 1908 Walter Marchant of Matfield, Kent. She moved to England and had a family there. Edna lived to see her one hundredth birthday; she died in 1983.

Graham de Montmorency became a Captain in the Connacht Rangers. He served in India and West Africa. However, once again Kathleen was to experience tragedy when Graham was killed in action on November 5 1914 near Neuve Chapelle 'while leading his men in the retaking of a trench captured by the Germans'.[3]

Kinmont Willie married, on March 6, 1913, George Doris, daughter of Henry Arthur Robinson of Letterdyfe House, Roundstone.[c] They went tea-planting in Ceylon (now Sri Lanka) for a time but returned on the death of his

3. Graham Armstrong-Lushington-Tulloch Memorial on Ballinakill Church.
c. and granddaughter of the late George J. Robinson J.P. and Land Agent, Ballinahinch Estate.

Memorial on Ballinakill Church.

brother Graham. Kinmont then enlisted and served as 2nd Lieutenant in the South Irish Horse for the remainder of the war but did not see action.

After the war Kinmont and Doris took over the running of the estate and lived at Shanbolard where they had one son, Graham, the present occupant, and two daughters, Pamela and Ann. A third daugher Romane died young.

Kathleen moved to Cartron House, a short distance from Shanbolard, occupying her time gardening and playing chess, and keeping her grandchildren entranced with stories of the Wild West and their adventures there.

On October 15,1921 the Congested Districts Board purchased the townlands of Ross, Ardkyle, Tievegariff, Derrylahan, Maumfin, Tievemore, Dooneen, for £5,750 plus £287.10.0 commission for agents W.G. Lougheed, Rent Office, Roundstone. Ross House was bought from the Congested Districts Board at a later date by Doctor Alfred Irwin.[d]

Kathleen Armstrong-Lushington-Tulloch died in January 1938. She was taken to Ballinakill Church on a farm cart covered with flowers, with almost the entire population of the district following behind. Mrs Armstrong-Lushington-Tulloch was held in very high regard by the local community as indeed was her son Kinmont and his family. They offered employment where there was little to be had. At one time she had the stones picked from a sloping hill above the Catholic graveyard, between Cartron and Ross crossroads, making the ground suitable for hay while providing much needed employment at that time.

d. Dr Irwin was the son of Rev. Irwin, Rector of Ballinakill for 28 years and brother of Rev. B.C.B. Irwan who returned to Ballinakill as Rector after spending twenty-five years in India and served as Chaplain to the forces during World War I.

Graham Armstrong-Lushington-Tulloch.
(1886-1914)

Kinmont Willie Armstrong-Lushington-Tulloch (1889-1960)

Armstrong by Blood, Tulloch by Name

The family is represented in Connemara today by Graham Tulloch. grandson of William and Kathleen and the present occupant of Shanbolard, and Nicola Goodbody, daughter of Ann Tulloch and great-grandaughter of the Armstrongs. Nicola married Hugh Musgrave[e] and lives at Cleggan House. Another great-grandaughter, Jennifer Cooper, daughter of Pamela Tulloch, married Lord Altamont and lives at Westport House, County Mayo.

Geoghegan and Blake

Bunowen Castle

Bunowen Castle, built at the beginning of the 16th century was one of the seats of the O'Flaherty Clan. The O'Flahertys, from the middle of the 13th century to the 17th century, ruled Connemara. The Castle was a tower-house with a rectangular enclosure attached and was situated on the verge of the ocean at Bunowen Bay.

In 1546, Grace O'Malley, that seafaring lady of legend, married the then owner of Bunowen, Donal O'Flaherty, nick-named 'Donal-an-Chogaidh' Donal of the Battles, because of his warlike nature. Grace and Donal lived at

e. see Twinning Cleggan House p. 140.

Bunowen and also at Donal's castle on the island at Ballinahinch Lake. They had three children, two sons, Owen and Morogh, and a daughter Margaret.

After Donal's death in 1575, Owen succeeded to the lands of Connemara but was killed in 1586 by the soldiers of Sir Richard Bingham, Governor of Connaught. Morogh then succeeded and after his death in 1626, his son Morogh, who was later knighted and known as Sir Morogh na Mart, took over.[4]

Sir Morogh na Mart and his brother Edmond took active part on the side of the Confederate Irish in the Civil War, 1641-1652. After the conquest of Galway by Cromwell's forces in 1652, Sir Morogh na Mart was dispossessed of all his lands and Bunowen was burnt on January 31 1653. Edmond, a Colonel, was captured hiding in a cave near Renvyle and executed in May 1653.[5] Sir Morogh na Mart died in 1666, having lived his latter years in poverty.

On July 25, 1656, Bunowen, along with nine hundred acres, was allotted by the Cromwellian Commissioners to Art Geoghegan of Castletown, Co. Westmeath, in lieu of their forfeited estates in Westmeath. The rest of the O'Flaherty lands were divided among the following:

Richard, Earl of Westmeath, in a grant dated April 26 1678, received Renvyle. This was later lost to the Blakes on May 19 1680. Richard Martin, Dangan, in July 1677 received Ballinahinch. James D'Arcy, Kiltullagh, received the lands at Ardbear Bay where his descendant John D'Arcy afterwards built the town of Clifden.

Geoghegan

In the early part of the 18th century, the then owner of Bunowen, Richard Geoghegan, abandoned the old castle and built 'a handsome residence' at the foot of the hill of Doon. Described by Hardiman as 'a lover of science, and a man of enterprising genius' Richard converted to the Protestant Faith on April 18 1756. After a visit to Holland, where he studied the Dutch method of reclaiming land from the sea, 'he succeeded in recovering a considerable tract of the lands of Ballyconneely, near Bunowen, by erecting a weir or dam to oppose the encroachments of the ocean. This was suitably inscribed in Latin and dated 1758.[6]

In 1780 he erected on the top of the hill of Doon an octagonal building, on the site of an old fortress, as a monument to commemorate the concession of free trade to Ireland. Richard died on January 4 1800, aged eighty-three years.[7] His eldest son John, who succeeded him, assumed the surname of O'Neill by Royal Licence.

A member of the Irish Parliament until 1799 and afterwards Accountant General in the Irish Court of Exchequer, John died August 8, 1830. His eldest son and successor, John Augustus O'Neill, represented the English Borough of Kingston-upon-Hull in Parliament for many years. About 1838 he began to extend the Castle, using the stones from the walls of the original O'Flaherty castle. The expense of this work along with large sums expended by him in various Parliamentary contests resulted in him becoming bankrupt. In 1841 John Augustus left Bunowen and retired in London.

4. Roderick O'Flaherty H-Iar Connaught. p.108. Notes by James Hardiman, M.R.I.A.
5. Galway Archaeological and Historical Society Journal Vol. 2 1902. An account of the Castle and Manor of Bunowen by Martin J. Blake.
6. O'Flaherty, p.109.
7. ibid.

During the famine of 1847 the castle was used as an auxiliary poor house and was in very bad condition when in June 1853 the entire estate was sold in the Encumbered Estates Court in Dublin. John Augustus O'Neill died many years later in London 'in very reduced circumstances'.

Blake

The Castle and lands were bought by Valentine O'Connor Blake of Towerhill Co. Mayo, a cousin of the Blake family of Renvyle. Valentine completed the work begun by O'Neill and converted the castle into a suitable residence for his family to enjoy during the summer season. Valentine's wife Margaret was a daughter of Charles Austin, 3rd Baron Ffrench of Castle Ffrench Co. Galway. They had seven sons and three daughters. After Valentine's death in 1879 he was succeeded at Towerhill by Colonel Maurice Charles Blake his eldest son, and at Bunowen by Charles J. Blake, his second son. Charles, a Barrister-at-Law, also owned Heath House in Queens County. Between 1892 and 1899 extensive repairs were carried out on Bunowen by Charles. By 1902 he resided in Heath House permanently and only occasionally visited Bunowen where his younger brother Thomas J. Blake resided.

The estate and castle were eventually purchased by the Congested Districts Board in April 1909 and the land divided among the former tenants. The castle, stripped of its roof, soon fell into decay and today stands a ruin.

Streamstown House.

Coneys
Streamstown House

James Hardiman, Galway historian of the 19th century, tells us that the first Coneys to settle here was 'Thomas Coney; who, on 21st August, 1677, obtained a "transplanter's certificate for a grant to him and his heirs for ever, of the lands of Towerskehin, Loughana, and Crosslahaine, in Ballinahinch barony"'.

'This Thomas (who appears to have afterwards added an s to his name) was Sheriff of Galway, A.D. 1694'.[8] Little is known of the family's activities for the next hundred years. They continued to live in the district with branches residing at Ballynaleame and Ardbear Bay (Clifden). Mr Hardiman tells us that where the town of Clifden now stands there was in 1809 only one house 'built by Walter Coneys, Esq.[9]

In October 23 1819, a lease was drawn up between John D'Arcy of Clifden Castle and Walter, in which Walter rented 1,000 acres of land at Streamstown and Letternuse, for three lives and thirty one years after, for a rent of £68.14.3d.[10] It appears this land was later purchased from Hyacinth D'Arcy, at the Encumbered Estates Court, in 1850 by Walter's son Edward.

Griffith's Valuation, 1855, shows the townlands of Streamstown, Carmacullaw, Knockannabrane, Doonberg, Corrowbeg, Moumeen, Parks, Prowgarve (or Drumgarve) the greater portion of which belong to the same Edward Coneys. These lands still remain in the hands of the family today. However, this was not due to frugality on Edward's part; he appears to have been a squanderer.

Over the years Edward's cousin Walter Coneys, son of Thomas Coneys and Celia O'Flaherty, a farmer from Fountain Hill, made many attempts to rescue him from his debts but to no avail. On March 11 1848 Walter married Mary Bodkin, a member of the Bodkin family of Omey island.[f] Edward leased out his lands to Walter 'in consideration of said marriage and for a sum of £150 paid to him by the said Walter Bodkin'[11]father of the bride and for £20 per year paid by Walter and Mary. However in 1854 Edward was again in trouble and Walter undertook to pay his debts in exchange for rents from these lands. All Walter's efforts were useless; on November 9 1864 Edward Coneys was declared Insolvent and his lands put on sale 'to satisfy the creditors'.[12]

On March 20 1866 at an auction at Blake's Hotel in Galway Walter Coneys purchased the estate for £340.

Walter and Mary moved to Streamstown House and went on to live a less turbulent life than their predecessor. They had four sons and four daughters. Thomas, the only son to marry did so twice, first to Alice McCollagh from Roundstone, who died just seven years later, they had one son, Walter, who died young, and two daughters, Molly and Maude. Thomas' second wife Mary Wallace came from Maam, they married in 1902 and they had three sons and two daughters Maud and Celia. Their first son Doctor Thomas, emigrated to England; their youngest son Edward drowned in front of the house when just five years old.

The second son John inherited the house and lands at Streamstown and his family continue to occupy these today.

8. Roderick O'Flaherty. Iar-Connaught. p.111.
9. ibid. p.112.
10. Coneys Family Papers.
11. ibid.
12. Coneys Family Papers.
f. Mary's brother, Doctor Geoffrey Bodkin, eloped with Mary Clare Eyre, daughter of J.J. Eyre, Clifden Castle, and they lived for many years at Kilronan Aran, where he was dispensary doctor.

CONEYS FAMILY: Standing, l to r, Mollie Coneys, Mrs. Mary Coneys and her sister, Agnus Wallace. Seated, l to r, The Coneys children, Maud, John, Nanny with Edward in her arms, Celia, Jean Wallace and Thomas.

Thomas Coneys.

John Coneys with his wife Alice.

Eyre
Clifden Castle

The Eyre brothers, Thomas and Charles, first participation in the fate of Clifden town and Castle appears to be in 1837. That year John D'Arcy mortgaged his estates with them for £25,000.

The brothers were English Roman Catholics, with strong Continental connections. Charles resided at Jermyn Street, St. James, Middlesex, and Thomas at Bath, Somerset. It is difficult to ascertain if they were Merchant Bankers or Money Lenders. It is not known if John's debt was cleared before the estates were put on sale in the encumbered Estates Court, or if the Eyres were the principal creditors. But the greater portion of these estates were purchased by Thomas and Charles on November 18 1850 for £21,245. They purchased Clifden Castle, almost the entire town, part of the Sillery Estate and the Kylemore Estates. The townlands were as follows: Sillery Estate: Aughrismore, Grannoughs, Gooreen, Gooreenatinny, Cartoorbed, Claddaghduff, Fountainhill.

Clifden Estate: Eyrephort, Kingstown Glebe, Knockavally, Tooreen East, West Lettershanna, Gortrummagh, Clifden Demesne, Faulkeera, Cloghaneard, Clifden, Ardbear, Rusheenacarra, Malmore, Goulane East and West, Streamstown, Letternush, Derreen, Lettereen, Atticlough, Shanakeever.

Thomas Eyre and J.J. Eyre

Thomas later bought up Charles's share in the estate. It is not known how much time Thomas spent in Clifden; however, extensive renovations were carried out on the castle under its new ownership. He also contributed £800 to the construction of the Convent of Mercy, opened July 16, 1855.

Thomas never married and, on July 16, 1864, left his Connemara estates to his nephew John Joseph (1816-1894). John Joseph (J.J.) appears to have been a man of considerable means and he and his wife, Margaretta, with their seven children spent a good deal of their time moving about the English countryside. Although registered as a magistrate, it has proved impossible to trace any record of him attending a court hearing. However, when they did visit the Castle, his daughters are remembered as being very gay and adventurous.

J.J. had five daughters, three of whom married Irish doctors. Lucy Mary, b.1849 married Doctor Oliver Murphy. Frances Mary (1847-1879) married Doctor Terence Benjamin Brodie on June 30 1875; they had one daughter, Daisy. Mary Clare is said to have climbed out the castle window and down a ladder to elope with her doctor, Geoffrey Bodkin.[g] They were married October 12 1868 and lived for many years in Kilronan, Aran Islands where Geoffrey was dispensary doctor.

Teresa, (b.1844) married James McAndrew. Louisa Mary (b.1839) married first, Edmund Malone D'Arcy (-1867), fifth son of John D'Arcy, founder of

g. Geoffrey Bodkin was a brother of Mary Coneys. See Coneys, Streamstown House. p. 125

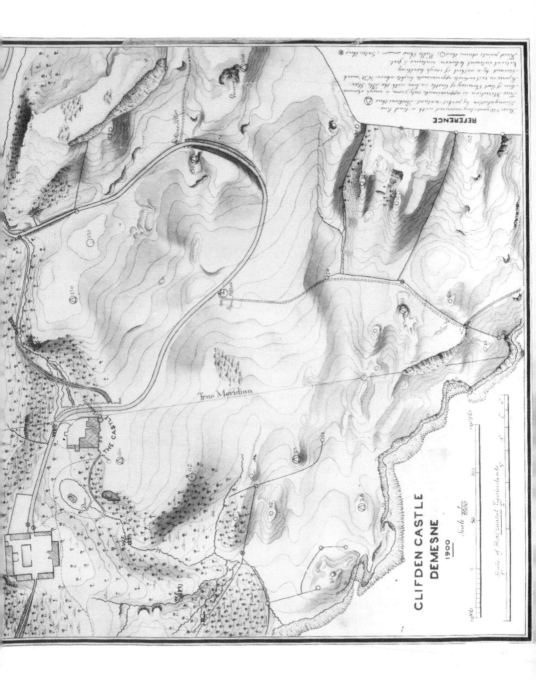

CLIFDEN CASTLE
DEMESNE
1900

Clifden. Although the bride was a Catholic, the marriage took place in the Protestant Church in Clifden on January 15, 1863, and was performed by the groom's brother, Rev. Hyacinth D'Arcy. Louisa and Edmund lived for a time at Knockbawn House near Clifden and later in France, where Edmund died on October 18 1867. The couple had no children. Louisa later married Baron Henri d'Ivoley but again there were no children in this marriage.

J.J. had two sons, Edwin and Stanislaus. Both lived on separate occasions at Clifden Castle and acted as agents for their father. Edwin and his wife Agnes Neill took an active part in local affairs. Agnes was actively involved in fund raising for the destitute during the crop failure in 1879.[h] Edwin worked hard for the construction of the railway from Galway to Clifden and was Deputy Vice-Chairman of the Union in 1880. Edwin and Agnes had thirteen children, almost all of them born in Clifden. Three died there and were buried in the Castle grounds. A small graveyard was created and a tomb erected to the children. Tenant's children who died under the age of two were allowed to be buried there also.

Stanislaus (1851-1896) and his wife Florence (-1893) had ten children. They both died young and the family was split up and divided among their aunts.

Eyre Estate

J.J. died April 15 1894 in accordance with his Will his entire estate, which included considerable business interests in Britain and elsewhere, was put into trust and divided equally among his seven children. The children lived on the income derived from the estate, and in turn passed it on to their children who in turn pass it to theirs, and so it continues.

While the children of J.J. were cared for most handsomely by his will, sadly the town and castle were not so fortunate. Since these were left to no individual Eyre, the running of the Estate was left in the hands of agents; Joyce Mackie and Lougheed of Galway. The castle, then uninhabited, fell into disrepair. The Demesne was leased to local shopkeepers for grazing. Much to the joy of the tenants, rents were not always collected. All land excluding the Demesne was purchased by the Land Commission and divided among the tenants. Finally in 1917 the castle and land were sold to J.B. Joyce, local butcher. But this decision caused great controversy and unrest in the area.[i] Over the years a great number of houses and land were purchased from the estate trustees, but still today rent for houses in the town is paid to the J.J. Eyre estate.

Clifden Castle

This once happy house, built c.1818, in early years bubbled with the activities of the large D'Arcy family and was privy to the dreams and ambitions of John D'Arcy, its builder and founder of the town. It witnessed Hyacinth's despair during the Great Famine, as the tenants gathered on the front lawn; begging for work or food on September 21 1846, and even further as family resources dwindled and he was forced to sell.

It basked in reflected wealth when a new roof was added and its facade altered to the taste of the new owners, in the 1850s. With deep regret it watched

h. see page 45.
i. see Castle Lands p. 166.

Clifden Castle.

the fight for the surrounding land in 1917 without even a thought for the castle. Finally, stripped of its slates, timber and windows, it slowly yielded to nature and now stands bare to the elements, a shelter place for cattle, a roost for birds, but still a place of magic to the mind of an imaginative child.

Frewen
Munga Lodge

Thomas Frewen of Brickwall House, Sussex, wealthy country squire, was the owner of several estates throughout England and Ireland. These he distributed upon his death on October 14, 1870, among the four sons of his second marriage; Edward, Richard, Moreton and Stephen. Their mother Helen Louisa Homan came originally from County Kildare. John, his son by his first marriage, with whom he had fought and disowned, was left no estates but was to receive £50,000 from his half-brother Edward, who received the family seat, Brickwall House.

The division was roughly as follows; Edward received the family seat, Brickwall House; Richard an estate at Innishannon Co. Cork; Moreton an estate in Connemara and Stephen an estate in Yorkshire. The four sons also inherited £16,000 cash each.

It would appear from the outset the young men were well provided for and their futures secure, but the years that followed were not to prove so. The decline of the Frewen family from a position of wealth and prosperity to that of heavy mortgaging and debt was due principally to three things: the dramatic fall in agricultural rents by more than half, the heavy payments by Edward to his brother John and the schemes and ventures of one son, Moreton.

Munga Lodge.

The Connemara Estate

The Frewen estate in Connemara consisted of 3,391 acres situated east of the town, running alongside the main Clifden to Galway road. It comprised the following townlands; Tullyvoheen, Killymongaun, Derrylea and Munga. Thomas Frewen purchased these lands at the Encumbered Estates Court 1850, principally for the fishing and shooting rights. A fine two-storey house Munga Lodge, stood on the land; this was used by the family during the season.

The revenue from the estate would have contributed little to Moreton's style of life, he having inherited them from his father. The construction of the railway through the estate made the Lodge more accessible and it became the centre of true Frewen entertainment when parties of titled members of the British aristocracy arrived to fish and shoot. On these occasions the train made an unscheduled stop close to the Lodge and the party would alight amid the curious stares of the locals.

For forty-seven years the Estate was owned by Moreton; perhaps one of the most diverse and famous personalities of that time to associate with the town.

Moreton Frewen

Born in 1853, Moreton was educated privately and later at Cambridge after which he ran through his £16,000 inheritance in the short space of three years, gambling, fox-hunting, horse-racing and lavish entertainment of the opposite sex.[13] On Friday 13 September 1878 he decided to gamble that which remained on one race, the outcome of which would determine his future life.

The race was the Doncaster Cup. If he won, he planned to spend one or two years as Master of the Kilkenny Hounds; if he lost he would go to Wyoming, 'a territory he had never seen and knew only as an Indian battlefield'.[14] The race was lost. Moreton then persuaded his brother Richard, who still possessed his inheritance, to join him on the Wyoming venture. He sold his stable of hunters,

13. Allen Andrews, The Splendid Pauper: The story of an eccentric Victorian Empire Builder, Moreton Frewen.
14. ibid, p.16.

borrowed what he could and accompanied by four friends who came along for some big game hunting, the Frewen brothers sailed for America.

In late December, after the hunting and killing of many buffalo, the four hunters returned home. Moreton and Richard headed for the Powder River where they went on to establish perhaps the largest cattle ranch in the State. The Powder River country was the home of the Sioux Indians but 'after their extermination of the 7th Cavalry at the Little Big Horn, the Sioux were still in Canada, safe from army vengence.'[15]

At this time, the rich grassland stood devoid of man or beast, with just two trails running through it, the Bozeman Trail which led to the goldfields, and the Wilson Price Trail, which led to the hunting regions. 'There was good cattle range country for a space of five hundred miles north, and certainly two hundred to the east. No one was in occupation. The land was there for the taking'.[16]

The only men to travel the lands were skin-hunters and trappers; there were no homesteaders. Here the Frewens established the 76 Outfit and built the first two-storey cabin in Wyoming. Although not impressive from the outside, the interior was so grand in style and furnishing that it became known as 'Frewen Castle'.

Frewan Castle Wyoming U.S.A.

Cost 40,000 dollars to erect in 1879. The ground floor consisted of; one forty foot square diningroom, with two large fireplaces, a library and office, a small livingroom, a large kitchen and pantry.
"A wide, solid walnut stairway led up to a mezzanine balcony and on to the second floor sleeping rooms".*
The interior was finished with hardwood which, along with almost all the furnishings, was imported from England.

Moreton described his holding as extending from 'the Rawhide near two hundred miles east, to Tongue River, a hundred miles north, the 76 Outfit exercised a benign suzerainty while as yet no dog barked'.[17]

But the cost of stocking and running such a large spread required a far greater capital investment than the Frewen brothers were capable of. Moreton returned to England to obtain financial backing; this he succeeded in doing among his family and friends. He then returned to Wyoming, increased their

15. ibid p. 19.
16. ibid. p.26.
17. ibid. p.76.
*Ernest M. Richardson, Moreton Frewen: Castle King with Monocle. Montana Historical Society/ No. 13.

herd, and established themselves as perhaps the biggest cattle ranch in the State.

Following the opening up of the region by the Frewens, a great many English pioneers followed in their wake.[j] However the Frewen ranch was by far the biggest, estimated to be thirty times greater than any of the others. The Frewens continued to live the life of country gentlemen, they entertained on a lavish scale, both on the ranch and in Cheyenne, where they were members of the famous Cheyenne Club. Each Autumn brought with it a hunting party from England. They came to hunt buffalo and to be entertained in the usual Frewen manner. 'Butlers, maids, valets, continental chefs, served them with vintage wines, whiskeys, English ale, liqueurs, and the choicest food,'[18] all imported and carefully transported for their enjoyment.

On June 2 1881, Moreton married Clara Jerome, daughter of multi-millionaire Leonard Jerome from New York and older sister of Jennie, wife of Lord Randolph Churchill and mother to Winston. Another sister, Leonie, married Sir John Leslie of Castle Leslie Co. Monaghan. Clara lived in Wyoming for a short time but after the miscarriage of their first child she returned to her parent's home in New York and never went west again.

After three years of ranching, Richard Frewen decided he wanted to leave the cattle business and requested Moreton to buy up his share. In order to do this, Moreton formed a company and went to England to promote it and encouraged friends to invest in shares. The company was successfully established with the Duke of Manchester as Chairman and Moreton retained as ranch manager. He held a great number of shares but according to his contract he was unable to sell these for five years: a provision which left him without cash and unable to pay off the debts he incurred when first establishing the ranch. However owing large sums of money to friends and family was fast becoming a way of life for Moreton and was to remain so for the rest of his life.

The ranch now boasted between sixty and seventy thousand head of cattle and employed seventy five cowboys. Over the next two years, Moreton became a leader among the cattle barons of the Cheyenne Club. His political influence in Washington, Canada and London was considerable and his ability as a negotiator brought him much acclaim.

Cattle Rustlers

A regular scourge of the ranchers were rustlers. These lived rough in the mountains, coming down to steal horses or cattle and then driving them to Idaho for sale. Since the opening up the territory, small ranchers and homesteaders had been moving into the region and these were proving more troublesome to the barons than the cattle rustlers. The branding of mavericks by some homesteaders brought about the Maverick Act making it illegal to brand unmarked free calves.[19] So widespread was this practice that the barons employed their own detective force on the range and this act was the beginning of the conflict which was later to develop into a full scale war.

The rich grasslands of Wyoming could carry huge numbers of cattle in the

18. Ernest M. Richardson, Moreton Frewen: Cattle King with Monocle. Montana Historical Society/No.13.
19. Andrews.
j. see Armstrong-Lushington-Tulloch p. 116.

Spring and Summer. It was the practice to leave these cattle on the open range throughout the winter with no extra feed; this was done to thin out the herd and to ensure that only the fit survived, the weaker dying of starvation. The herd was then driven south-east for 500 miles to Omaha; there they boarded a train for Chicago where they were sold, fattened and sold again as meat which for the most part finished up in England.

By 1883, over-stocking was becoming a major problem on the open range, preventing the herds from fattening up sufficiently to carry them through the winter. In the spring of 1884, Moreton was advised that although the winter had been mild, his herd had fared badly. The grasslands in Northern Wyoming had been 'eaten bare' and Moreton recommended to the Cheyenne Club that between two and three million cattle be moved off the ranges fast 'if the cattle men did not move then, the first hard winter would wipe them out at a total loss'.[20]

The winter of 1884-85 was a hard one, 'and all over the West a million cattle were estimated to have died on the range'. Moreton was advised by Murphy the foreman of his Rawhide ranch to move the herds to Alberta. He made contact with the company's directors in London who refused permission for the move. Moreton travelled to London to try and explain the seriousness of the situation but they chose to ignore his advice and by the end of the particularly hard winter that followed, 'half of the Powder River herds were dead of starvation'.[21] Alarm reached the shareholders and they began to sell out; share prices began to fall but Moreton was prevented by his contract from selling. In June 1885 he left the ranch for good and in March 1886 he resigned from the Company.

The management of the Frewen Ranch now passed to a neighbouring rancher and Irishman, Sir Horace Plunket.[k] Sir Horace, along with three other Irishmen, came to Wyoming in 1879 and at this time owned the Union Cattle Company. But the big 'freeze-up' winter of 1886-87 finally finished the Powder River Cattle Company. When the affairs of the Company were eventually wound up and all debts paid, Moreton's shares and those of his friends and relations were worthless.

Moreton was now heavily in debt and a great deal of his time was spent avoiding creditors. Having been forced to lease out his home in London for a number of years both he and his wife spent a great deal of their time apart, Clara living in the houses of friends and relations and Moreton living in clubs and travelling about visiting the country homes of his friends. Their children who saw little of them, lived with Clara's mother in England, and in France.

Chasing success

In the years that followed, Moreton became an influential lobbiest and 'promoter-salesman'. He was constantly living from one new venture to the next. He spent his life on the brink of making huge fortunes for himself, his brothers and those of his friends he had managed to persuade to invest in his latest scheme. He worked extremely hard for the success of each venture, but for one reason or another never seemed to achieve it. The final result usually

20. ibid. p.83.
21. ibid.
k. Sir Horace Plunket returned to Ireland in 1889 and went on to found the Irish Co-operative and became Vice President of Irish Department of Agriculture and Technical Instruction.

meant hugh losses for his friends and his brothers, who could ill afford such losses.

After Wyoming, Moreton became involved in the Indian State of Hyderabad, where he uncovered a million pound fraud. While there he met Rudyard Kipling, took an interest in his writings and introduced him to his friends in the Press. This introduction was to result in the publication of his first book and started Kipling on the road to success.

Once in a letter to his wife, Moreton commented on the financial state of the family: 'It is time some money came into the family coffers, for the present generation of Frewens are in sore need; we have not been as down as now since the time of Cromwell'.[22]

But in his determination to restore the family fortunes, Moreton only succeeded in decreasing them. His venture into the stock market cost brothers and friends heavy losses, as did their sponsorship of a gold-crushing machine. This machine, he believed, was capable of extracting more gold from the refuse ore left after mining, but which, after much expense, did not prove a commercial success.

In 1892, confrontation between the castle barons and homesteaders of Wyoming had escalated into open war. The cattle men now declared all homesteaders cattle rustlers and proceeded with plans to 'clean up Johnston County once and for all'.[23]

```
                    20 East 27th Street
                              May 6th 92




My Dear willy
              Your letter reached me here,I am busy with some mines in the
west & shall be home again the last of July.
                                   Our old cow country is in a state of
siege;the rsutlers have been getting away with the boys,& Fred Hesse Ford & some
more of them started up with fifty men to clean them out,but they got corralsed
instead,& only that the troops came down from Fort MKinney Fred & Co would have
handed in their cheques. But they fired the KC ranche & shot Ray & Nate Champion,
whom you will remember,& are all now in gaol at Cheyenne on a charge of murder
& arson.!
                  Well they were skunks a good many of them,& Fred rustled
from me more than anyone since has from him.
                              My best regards to Mrs Arrmtsrong
& I hope to see you on my return. My wife is in London(18 Alford Street)if you
are intown go & see her.   yours sincerely
                                           Morton Frewen
```

Moreton Frewen Letter. Courtesy Graham Tulloch.

22. Andrews, p.159.
23. ibid. p.168.

In April 1892 the homesteaders surrounded the K.C. Ranch, 120 miles from Casper, trapped inside were thirty cattlemen. During the ensuing battle, it became obvious the homesteaders intended to wipe out the cattlemen. One of the besieged men however, managed to escape and travelled the distance to Casper. From there he sent a telegram to Moreton Frewen who was at the time about to have lunch with Secretary of State, Senator Baline. The telegram informed Moreton that twenty of his friends were held up at the K.C. 'by the rustlers'. 'Can possibly hold them off for three or four days but unless relieved we shall certainly all hang. Can you help us with the President'.[24] Such was their belief in the influence of Moreton Frewen. On reading the telegram Senator Baline sent a mesage through to the troops of Fort McKinney, who went on to the K.C. Ranch and saved the men.

In a letter to William Armstrong-Lushington-Tulloch of Shanboolard Hall, Moyard, an old comrade from his cattle-ranching days, Moreton commented on the event. The letter was typed in violet ink and badly punctuated, as were all Moreton's letters be they to Government Ministers, Presidents or friends alike.

Innishannon, Co. Cork

Richard Frewen died in 1896 leaving Innishannon to his nephew Hugh, Moreton's oldest son. Almost as soon as Hugh came of age, Moreton had him mortgage the property and give him the greater part of the money.

So it continued with Moreton still chasing that fortune; it was now property development in Canada. Not content with almost having ruined his brothers, as soon as each of his three children came of age, he badgered them until 'hey mortgaged their future inheritance, most of which came from their grandmother Mrs Jerome, in his favour.*

While living at Innishannon, Moreton became involved in Irish politics. He succeeded in collecting large sums of money for the Nationalist cause in America and in 1910, sponsored by Tim Healy, he was elected to Parliament for East Cork. However, on discovering that Healy had himself failed to be returned, he resigned his seat and was replaced by Healy.

However Innishannon came to a sad end. During the Civil War it was burnt down and the agent murdered.

Moreton lived out the latter part of his life at his home in Sussex, Brede Place. Thence he continued to write instructive advice to various members of the Government, not least his nephew Winston Churchill. Moreton died on September 2 1924.

Stephen Frewen

Fourth and youngest son of Thomas Frewen, Stephen had in common with his brothers a violent temper. A Colonel with the 16th Lancers he saw action in the South African War in 1899; he 'was twice mentioned in dispatches and led the charge at Klipdrift for the relief of Kimberley'.[25]

24. ibid. p.167.
25. Andrews, p.207.

* Moreton Frewen's only daughter, Clare Sheridan, was a well known foreign correspondent and sculptor. She lived between the years 1947-52 at the Spanish Arch, Galway, and regularly visited her cousin Anita Leslie at Oranmore Castle.

Throughout Moreton's career, Stephen had supported him both morally and financially, bringing himself to almost complete ruin. In Moreton's syndicate, put together to speculate on the stock market, he lost £18,290[26] having already lost on the Wyoming venture. During this time Stephen was serving in the Curragh Camp, Co. Kildare. He wrote to Moreton telling 'I have been sold out and bust'.[27] He discussed the advantages of retiring or staying on in the Army and serving in India. However, the following year found him with his regiment in India and again responding to Moreton's call. Stephen invested many times over the years that followed and as a result of these investments and subsequent losses Moreton was deeply ashamed of the circumstances to which Stephen was reduced. He felt responsible for Stephen's heavy losses; perhaps this is why we find his estate in Connemara being transferred to Stephen's son Layton.

Layton Frewen

Stephen's son Layton, b.1886, received in 1917 the Connemara estate from his uncle Moreton. A retired Army Colonel and local magistrate, Layton possessed extensive fishing and shooting rights with his property and was therefore little liked by the local sportsmen or poachers. He inherited the family temper and is remembered for his term on the bench, where he gave full vent to his inheritance.

In 1922 Layton was given twenty-four hours by local Republicans in which to gather his possessions and leave the country. One important fact which did not appear to be known by the local IRA was that, Layton's sister was the wife of Edward Carson, the Ulster Champion.

The Frewen Estate was purchased by the Land Commission, excluding Munga Lodge and all fishing and shooting rights, for £2,176. Layton and his family returned each summer until the early 1930's. Munga Lodge was later sold to the local Anglers Association who retained the fishing rights and resold the lodge and surrounding land to local farmers. The lodge is now a ruin but the memory of its once eccentric owner lives on.

Graham
Ballinakill Lodge

The Grahams descended from the English border clans, settled along with the Armstrongs in County Fermanagh during the reign of Elizabeth I.

Robert Graham married Elizabeth, daughter of Robert Armstrong of Drumrallagh, County Fermanagh; their son Francis took an active part in the Rebellion of 1798. A grandson, also named Robert, purchased lands at Ballinakill and built Ballinakill Lodge. He also retained his estate at Drumgoon County Fermanagh and divided his time between both. Robert married twice, Elizabeth Davis of Summerhill, who died after the birth of her first child, Francis John, in February 1815. His second wife, Jane, was the daughter and heiress of John Speer, Desert Creight, County Tyrone. Griffiths Valuation of 1855 shows Robert Graham as owning over 10,000 acres including the townlands of Moyard, Ross, Tievegorriff and Ungwee. Robert died in 1859.

26. ibid.
27. ibid p. 142.

Francis John Graham

Francis John, known as Frank, Robert's son and heir, was recently described by one of his former tenants as 'one of the best landlords that ever came into the West of Ireland'. His kindness and concern for his tenants was well known and remembered. He married late in life, on April 3, 1879, Minna, second daughter of Charles Hugh Lushington of Rodmersham, Kent. Minna's sister Kathleen two years later married Mr Graham's cousin William Armstrong and they were to become neighbours in later life.[l] Frank and Minna had one son, Hector, born May 1888. Hector was educated privately and grew to be a quiet retiring man.

Following the death of Frank c.1890, Mrs. Graham left the running of the estate more and more in the hands of her agent Joseph McDonnell, a man not greatly loved by the tenants.[m] McDonnell lived with his sister in Dooneen opposite Letterfrack Quay.

Miss McDonnell and Mrs. Graham were close friends until one evening in 1907. That evening a violent quarrel broke out between Mrs. Graham and the McDonnells concerning estate matters. Mrs. Graham stormed out the house, taking her son and what possessions she could carry and went to Shanboolard and her sister, Mrs. Armstrong-Lushington-Tulloch. The next day tempers cooled and she returned to the Lodge. That night the house went up in flames. Mrs. Graham and her son escaped in their night clothes and, managing to rescue the horses, they drove to Shanboolard. The cause of the fire was believed to be a turf sod lodged on a beam up the chimney which smouldered undiscovered.

Minna Graham (nee Lushington) (1857-1934)

The Lodge was completely destroyed and was never re-built. Mrs Graham then moved to Upper Mount Street Dublin where she lived until her death in 1934.

Hector Graham

Hector married Eleanor Violet Silcock and they had four daughters, Mina, Daffney, Sheila and Iris. The greater portion of the Estate had now been sold off, either privately or to the Land Commission. Hector inherited Summerhill in County Kilkenny from a cousin, John Davis. The family's time was divided between Dooneen and Summerhill, but later Dooneen too was sold. Hector died in Dublin in the 1960's.

l. see Armstrong-Lushington-Tulloch p. 116.
m. see Letterfrack Murders p. 66.

Cleggan House. Photograph by B. Holberton.

Twining and Holberton
Cleggan House

Frederick Twining, a young engineer from London, was a member of the famous Twining tea family. In September 1855 he married Elizabeth Kathleen Nelson, born and brought up in Bermuda, where her father served in the Foreign Office, but whose family were originally from County Tipperary.

The young couple came to Ireland where Frederick had recently purchased almost nine hundred acres of land at Cleggan Bay.

Frederick had inherited capital, making it possible for him to build a fine house, extensive farm buildings, a steward's house and workmen's cottages. The workmen employed on the construction of these were brought from England as indeed were the coachmen and principal house staff.

Twining Family

Frederick and Elizabeth were quick to adopt native ways; they produced ten children, six girls and four boys. Frederick worked his farm and lived handsomely on its income, subsidised by private means. His two oldset sons, Frederick (b.1862) and Horace (b.1866) emigrated to New Zealand, married and had families there but never returned to Cleggan. The third son, Alexander, died young (1887) in a boating accident. Athelstan (1869-1870) and his sister Elsie (1860-1867) also died young. This left the five sisters: Charlotte (b.1856), Kathleen (b.1857), Ellen (b.1859), Julia (b.1861) and Blanche (b.1871) to inherit Cleggan House and farm on the death of their father on February 25 1902.

Under Frederick's Will, Cleggan estate was divided; Julia inherited the house and the greater part of the Estate; Blanche received the steward's house and the three remaining daughters received farm buildings, which were later converted into attractive cottages. They each received a portion of Cleggan mountain.

The daughters lived varied and interesting lives; they all returned frequently to visit and three of them eventually retired to Cleggan. The first three girls were educated at Cheltenham Ladies College, the remainder educated privately at home.

Charlotte Browne

Charlotte, the oldest, married her near neighbour, Gilman Browne of Rossleague House and they had three sons and one daughter. One son died young, one emigrated to Brazil and the other practised medicine in the east end of London.

Following the death of her husband Charlotte divided her time between her cottage at Cleggan and Rosleague. For many years she leased Rosleague House to Miss Robinson, former headmistress of the French school in Bray and suffragette, while continuing to live in a cottage closeby. Charlotte died in 1950 and was succeeded at Rosleague by her daughter Mary.

Mary was born on June 14, 1882 and educated at Cheltenham Ladies College and Oxford; where she obtained a M.A. Degree in Mathematics and Geography.

Cleggan Tower.
One of a system of signal towers built along the coast in Napoleonic times.
Photograph by B. Holberton.

She went to live in South Africa and taught in a school there for some years. Later she returned to England and taught at St Zetazs in Eastbourne: before coming headmistress of a school in Cumberland. In the 1930's she returned to Rosleague to care for her mother. During the Second World War Miss Browne took over the education of her cousin, Evelyn Holberton of Cleggan House, and Ann Tulloch, daughter of neighbour and friend Kinmont Tulloch of Shanboolard Hall. Evelyn was in Cleggan visiting her grandmother when war broke out and it was decided by the family that she should not return to France but instead remain in Ireland; and prepare for entry into Trinity College Dublin. Ann was offered the opportunity of joining her and readily accepted. For Ann, the choice between the enclosed classrooms of her previous school in Dublin and the rugged landscape of her beloved Connemara was a simple one.

The girls lived with Miss Robinson at Rosleague House and each morning crossed the courtyard, to attend daily classes in Miss Browne's cottage. Here they were educated along the lines of a private school, they were to attain university standard, with a broad education on a wide range of subjects. While Miss Robinson ran Rosleague along the lines of a finishing school. After classes each afternoon 'suitable' daily newspapers were read and discussed, and suitable topics of conversation debated. Dinner, like many other persuits, was a formal and sombre affair, after which they retired, silently, to unheated bedrooms; conversation after dark was strictly forbidden. Each Friday afternoon the girls cycled home to spend a week-end of freedom with their families.

At this time Miss Browne organised a Red Cross Division with First Aid lectures at Cleggan and Drilling Parades in Clifden. She also organised sports on Cleggan Beach. On May 14, 1947 she founded the Cleggan Guild of the Irish Countrywomen's Association and each month meetings were held in the old coastguard station there. Among the early I.C.A. members were Mrs Mary Courcy of Cleggan and Mrs Stankard of Clifden. In 1954 Miss Browne started craft sessions on Saturday afternoons for the children of the district, these were continued after her death by Mrs Courcy, and in 1968 she founded the Cleggan Country Market.

Miss Browne died June 19 1974, leaving behind her a wealth of knowledge among those fortunate enough to have worked with or studied under her. She is buried in the family plot in Ballinakill Church.

Kathleen and Ellen Twining

Kathleen became a nurse in the east end of London, much against her parent's wishes. Thence she moved to the south of England and established a home for destitute children at Hayling Island. Recognised as an authority on this subject Kathleen became quite famous in her time. She lived an interesting life of hard work and dedication until her death in 1943.

Ellen became an Anglican nun and lived out her life in Oxford. She enjoyed returning to Cleggan on holidays where she joined her sisters and indulged her passion for card-playing.

Blanche Bailey

Blanche, the youngest daughter, married William W. Bailey, one of the pioneer rubber planters in Malaya, who was originally from the Midlands. Already a wealthy man, William and Blanche retired to Plassey, a stud farm outside Limerick and are best remembered for owning the horse 'Bachelor's Double'.

After William's death in 1910, Blanche continued to run the stud farm for some years, eventually retiring to Cleggan and lived out her life in what was formerly the steward's house, now converted into a comfortable residence.

Julia Holberton

Julia, who inherited the house and the greater part of the farm married on August 11 1884 Doctor Henry Nelson Holberton, an Englishman and her second cousin. After their marriage they went to live in Molesey, Surrey, where

Julia Holberton nee Twining.

Henry practised until retirement in 1921. Julia had never visited England before her marriage and although she reared five children there, four boys and a girl, she longed for her trips home each summer. While Julia resided with her family in England, Cleggan Farm was leased by local men and used as grazing land. About 1904 almost a quarter of the estate was purchased by the Land Commission and divided among local small farmers.

On retirement in 1921, Julia and Henry returned to Ireland, only to be informed shortly afterwards by local Republicans that they had twenty-four hours to collect their belongings and leave. The Holbertons moved to Rhyl in Wales and waited for stability to return to Ireland. Meanwhile Cleggan House was commandeered by the Republicans and the cottage next door utilised as a jail. Here local schoolmaster Mr McLoughlin was interned for some time. He was released on Christmas Day to assist with the carving of the goose; and then returned to jail. Some household furniture and books bear relics of this period; signatures were carved into the wood and scribbled on rare Irish history books.

After the war, Julia and Henry again returned to Cleggan, Julia farmed in a small way but to no great extent. In the years that followed, her happiest times were spent socialising with her sisters Charlotte Browne and Blanche Bailey.

The Holberton Family

Nelson, the oldest of the Holberton family, b.1884, emigrated to Burma and worked in forestry there. He married late in life, an Englishwoman, and had two children.

The second son, Brian, joined the Royal Navy as a cadet at the early age of thirteen and saw service in World War I. After the war he married and had one daughter who died young. He later returned to Cleggan and became a photographer for the Irish Tourist Board. He died in his early forties.

Holberton Family.
Standing L to R: Brian, Frederick, Nelson, Athelstan Leslie.
Seated: Doctor Henry Nelson and Julia Holberton.

Frederick became a rubber planter in Malaya; he never married and retired to Cleggan where he lived until his death in 1968. Athelstan Leslie, and fourth and youngest son, b.1894, joined the East Surrey Regiment at the outbreak of World War I. While serving in France he met and married Yvonne Clementien. After the war Leslie and his wife continued to live in France; they had one son and a daughter, Yves Eric (known as Nickey) and Eveleyn. The children returned each summer to their grandmother for their holidays.

The outbreak of the Second World War found Evelyn and her brother at

144

Cleggan. Leslie re-enlisted and was posted to headquarters in Boulogne. On the occupation of France he was taken prisoner by the Germans and transported to Germany for the duration of the war. Following his release in 1945 Leslie retired to Cleggan. However, his son Yves was not so fortunate; he was killed in action in 1944 at Cassino. Evelyn studied at Trinity College Dublin where she qualified as a medical doctor and emigrated with her husband Doctor John B. Musgrave to London and continued to practice there until retiring in 1984.

On returning to Cleggan, after the death of his mother and his aunt Blanche Bailey, Leslie set about buying up the land, held by members of the family and the steward's house, owned by Mrs Bailey. He and his brother Frederic ran the farm relying heavily on employees. However, it was not until Leslie's grandson Hugh Musgrave, the present occupant, took over the farm in 1973 that the land was once again utilised to its full potential, as in the day of Frederick Twining, one hundred and thirty years before.

Cleggan Megalithic Tomb. B. Holberton.
*This monument is situated on the Northern Shore of Cleggan Bay. "It consists of a gallery, divided into three chambers, the innermost chamber being distinctly narrower and of lighter construction than the other two. The Tomb is aligned ESE—WNW with the front towards the east". 'A large roofstone, set with its heavier end to the east, covers the second chamber'. *

* *Ruaidhri De Valera and Seán Ó Nualláin. Survey of the Megalithic Tombs of Ireland.*

145

Errislannan Peninsula

Mathew French, owner of Errislannan (c.1722) had four daughters. The daughters in turn married men named, Burke, Skerett, Lynch and Lambert. After Matthew's death the lands were left in common to his daughters, each receiving a quarter share.

The lands were held in common until 1843 when a Writ of Partition was taken out and Errislannan was divided.

The Burkes held Boat Harbour and surrounding townlands; this was later sold to the Byrne family from Dublin and held by them until recent years.

The Skerretts held Drimmeen and Emlough.

The Lamberts held Drinnagh; this was later sold to Rev. Richard Wall, D.D.

The Lynch family held Ballinaboy and Maam; this was pased to their daughter Mary who married James Morris of Galway.

James Anthony Morris, Ballinaboy. (1790-1840).

Morris
Ballinaboy House

James Morris (1710-1791) a direct descendant of the Morris's of Galway, one of the fourteen powerful merchant families known as the Tribes of Galway, married Mary Lynch and they had two children. Their son Captain Anthony, (b.1763) commanded a Revenue Cutter on the west coast in 1821, having his headquarters in Westport Co. Mayo. The daughter, Mary, married John Staunton. Both the Captain and his sister inherited half of their grandmother's holding at Errislannan; this holding became reunited with the marriage of their children, James Anthony Morris and Elinor Staunton.

Following the partitioning of Errislannan in 1843, Anthony James (1822-1898) son of James and Eleanor, built Ballinaboy House and took up residence there. Anthony married Elizabeth Hanly in 1843 and had four sons, James, John, Anthony and William, and one daughter, Catherine. During the famine of 1847, Anthony fed all the tenants' livestock and his wife made every effort she could to feed the people out of the produce. After the famine was over the tenants were thus able to make a fresh start. Anthony was 'Barony Constable' at the time and on one occasion a shipload of corn arrived in Clifden for the Government food depot where it was to be stored until further instructions were received from Dublin. Anthony went down to the stores and on his own responsibility broke open the doors and distributed the corn to the starving population.

Anthony James Morris.
(1822-1898).

James Timothy Morris.
(1844-1914).

After the famine, he, like so many of his counterparts, was in financial ruin and forced to abandon his home and lands. John Kendall of London leased these in perpetuity along with other townlands in the district. Anthony then retired to a life of shooting and fishing, living in somewhat diminished circumstances at Ballinaboy Lodge, a short distance from Errislannan.

Anthony's oldest son, James Timothy (1844-1914) emigrated to America.

On arriving in that country with only ten shillings in his pocket, he proceeded on a trail of degrading dead-end jobs for a number of years until he returned home accompanied by his fatally ill brother. James next turned to England and settled in London where he became a shop assistant in Fowns, later John Lewis stores, and went on to become a senior official in that establishment.

In 1881 James married Anna Maria Stacy and had six children, two of whom, twins, died young. The remaining four sons were educated at the Oratory School in Bermingham. A less persistent man would have shaken off his Irish identity and settled for a comfortable retirement in London, but no so James. On the death of John Kendall on August 16, 1890, he managed to buy back the lease, from the Kendall family, of the house and lands at Ballinaboy. In 1896 he returned home and once again there was a Morris at Ballinaboy House. He became one of the last Irish-speaking J.P.s in the west.

In British Naval Uniform.   *In Irish Naval Uniform.*

James Morris changed his name to the Irish, Seamus O'Muiris, and became Commander and Director in 1941 of the Irish Naval Service.

His youngest son also named James completed his early education locally and later followed his older brother Charles into the Royal Navy. Charles was later killed at the Battle of Jutland 1916. James, however, retired in an act of protest, on hearing of the burning of Clifden by the Black and Tans in 1921. He later went on to become a Commander and Director in 1941 of the new Irish Naval Service and changed his name to the Irish, Seamus O'Muiris. Seamus died in Dublin in 1951.

Another brother, Anthony, worked as a Radio Engineer at the Marconi Radio Station Derrygimla. Anthony married Mary Gorham (p. 26) and together they ran a shop in Market Street.

George, the oldest son, joined the Indian Cavalry and after his father's death in 1914 inherited the house and lands, part of which were later purchased by the Land Commission. The house was leased by a number of people until George's son Colonel Anthony Morris retired there in 1968.

Errislannan Manor.

Wall and Heather

Errislannan Manor

Rev. Richard Henry Wall, D.D. of Bormount Manor, Wexford, rented a shooting lodge at Errislannan from Colonel Lambert, c.1832. In the early 1840s the Reverend purchased the Lodge along with 1100 acres of land. Following renovations and extensions the Wall family took residence and re-named the house Errislannan Manor. However, in 1850 the estate was put on the market and the publicity drawn up for the sale gives an interesting description of the house and buildings:

'a commodiously staunchly-built house comprising hall and porch, three sitting rooms, eight bedrooms, housekeeper's room, dairy, kitchen, scullery, pantry, laundry, turf house, water closet etc. all constructed in the most permanent manner'.

The outbuildings were said to be extensive —

'comprising stables, coach-house, piggery for five brood sows, barn, fowl-house, Steward's rooms and extensive storage'.

149

The land was 'half under cultivation and the remainder consisted of pasture, bog and mountain'.[28]

For family reasons the sale was withdrawn and the Manor remained in the family for a further one hundred years.

Heather Family

Reverend Wall and his family worked closely with Hyacinth D'Arcy and the founder members of the Irish Church Mission and later with the Clifden Orphanage. In 1853 the Reverend built the small church at Errislannan, partly with the help of the Irish Church Mission but mostly with funds collected after a begging letter was circulated in Dublin by the Reverend. Following the death of the Reverend's three sons in active service; Henry and George, an Army surgeon, were both killed while serving with the Army in India, James died of yellow fever while serving with the Navy in Jamaica, and the death of the fourth son Walter, the estate was inherited by their sister, Henrietta. Henrietta married Reverend George Heather in 1866; the service was the first wedding service in the little church at Errislannan and was to be the last for one hundred years. The Heathers had four sons and three daughters. Two of the sons, Major Dean and Major George, served in the South African war and later in the Sligo Militia, and lived at the family estate at Knockadoo, County Sligo. Their brother Walter lived for a time in Warwickshire England and later at Knockadoo. The fourth brother John lived with his sisters Jane and Edith who had inherited the estate, at Errislannan. The third sister Eva was a missionary in India and China but later retired to Errislannan.

The sisters Jane and Edith are remembered with great fondness in the neighbourhood; they were kind and cheerful, and after Church services in summer, would invite the entire congregation to the Manor for refreshments. John ran the farm for them but after his death they found it difficult to continue. On the death of the sisters, the Manor, now heavily mortgaged, was inherited by Walter's two daughters Medara and Kathleen. A great portion of the land was purchased by the Land Commission and, much to the regret of the sisters, the Manor was sold in 1958 to the present owner, Doctor D. Brooks.

28. Medara Bent. Manuscript. 'A Connemara Family .

The above regatta pony races and other athletic amusements came off on Thursday, the 17th inst, in the beautiful demesne of Cleggan Tower, kindly given by the owner, Mr Frederick Twinning, whose munificent support and patronage secured the success of the sports. Appearances in the morning did not at all favour the idea of a particularly good day. There was fog and gloom and threatening clouds, and considering the unsuitableness of the tiny crafts and curraghs of the fishermen of this ... most built for other purposes than fast poverty in many instances unable their ... provide, also the untrained unprepared condition of the native ponies riding helter skelter in all directions but where they are required to go, I was asking myself at Leenane whether I would accompany some friends to the races, whether they were worth going to, whether anything even approaching to mediocrity in horse racing or boat sailing might be expected, or whether chance or fortune if so guided, held in suspension the threatening storm, and the perils of the race course. I was informed by the weather wise that those signs or facts need occasion neither alarm or surprise, that the elements were kindly disposed, that a foggy morning oft turns out a sunny day and though rough weather was not an improbability in the near future the day would hold up. This decided me to go and their forecast of the day proved correct. A strong sun and a nice wind dispelled the fog, the gloom, and the threatening clouds, giving to the pleasure seekers a most enjoyable day. The drive from Leenane was beautiful. Skirting Kylemore Castle the princely residence of Mr Mitchell Henry, whose son and daughter patronized by their presence the sports and whose steam yacht was gay with flags and bunting, on through the village of Letterfrack where a philanthropic Englishwoman far from home and friends on an elevated spur of the Diamond mountain built herself an iron house and dwells therein and employs at basket-making and wick r work poor people in the village. Another of those compassionate ladies was pointed out to me at the meeting, this time it was an Irishwoman who has fixed her abode in a place called Ecrisflinin, near a fishing station at Bunowen, who is interesting herself in the promotion and development of the fishing on this coast. If heavens choicest blessing are reserved for particularly good people I should certainly award it to those whose whole lives and fortunes are devoted to bettering the condition of the poor and wretched. I doubt if reference to those good ladies needs an apology, if there be any who think so I beg to apologize.

Well, digressed I was on my way to the races at the village of Letterfrack which is built on the foot of the Diamond Mountain, linked on both sides hip and thigh with other mountains forming an amphitheatre in which the village nestles at the head of Ballinakill bay. The village contains several large shops, a hotel, a courthouse, police barracks, the parish priests

pretty house and the doctors, besides the residence of the Christian Brothers, the large Industrial School under their management, adjacent to which are several other buildings and scores of detached limewashed cottages, they whole forming a pretty rural picture. Passing Letterfrack we continued our drive along the head of Ballinakill bay where are some of the country seats notably those of Mr Gelman Browne, Mr Russell, Mr M'Donnell, Ballinakill, with its pretty lakes, Loughcartron and Shanboolard Hall, the residence of Mr Armstrong Pollock, arriving at the racecourse about 12 o'clock, when the first event of the day commenced the starting of some small sailing boats in which only four competed. Then followed the starting of others of a smaller class, and others still smaller followed, and so on until there was a good sprinkling of boats in the little bay.

The yachts of the local gentry who patronized by their presence the races with their families, and the local Coastguard Station were gaily dressed with flags and bunting people interested and boat-owners were cheering and shouting their own boats and every boat as well ... and peddlers balled singers, rarce-shows, trick aloop, wheel-a-fortunes and pitch and toss players and others, every kind of entercy... craft was represented there, and gesticulating wildly and noisely plying their trades, while the pretty brass band of the Letterfrack Industrial school discoursed sweet music on a neighbouring hill. Altogether it was a gay and animating scene and thousands witnessed it, and mingled in it and enjoyed it too. The whole programme as previously notified was fairly but tardily carried out under the management of local gentlemen, conspicuous amongst them were the District Inspector of police and the Medical Officers of the districts who by their courtesy untireing efforts contributed not a little to the success of the sports. The Band of Letterfrack Industrial School relieved the tedium, (for tedium there was) by a close selection and contributed largely to the days enjoyment. Despite my fears in the morning I enjoyed it much, I was not run down by the wild unmanageable ponies, tho' I hear there were some hair breathescapes and the elements true to the prediction of the sage held the storm in suspension until night, and as a ... enjoyed the sport, dc ... fur my thanks to the Committee of the races in general, and to Mr Twinning in particular, the worthy owner of the Cleggan Tower Estate, a man to all his neighbours dear, my meed of praise for a most enjoyable days outing in his beautiful demesne, with the close of the days enjoyment. Cheers were given and many a fervent wish and aspiration to heaven that he would be long spared for his good health, and for the welfare of those most dear to him.

TRAVELLER

, 23rd August 1893.

J A PEACEFUL MOOD

Newspaper report on Cleggan Regatta, 1883. Courtesy Dr. E. Musgrave.

151

CHAPTER VII

Monsignor McAlpine — Parish Priest and Politician

The turn of the century saw Clifden somewhat more prosperous than it had been since its foundation. The railway works brought spending capital into Connemara, and upon completion offered access to outside markets and an increase in tourism and trade. The Local Government Act of 1898 enabled the middle classes to take a more active part in local politics, while, under the many Land Purchase Acts, the tenant farmers now became owners of their lands and in many cases increased their holding. Living conditions and education had improved greatly over the previous thirty years. Under the Chairmanship of John Redmond, the Irish Party united and a relative political stability followed. With political stability people now devoted their time to improvement and self-advancement.

The town had about it a style, amounting almost to arrogance; it gave off an air of superiority — not always appreciated by the surrounding communities. It became known as a pro-British town, a belief strengthened by Padraig Pearse describing it as 'Clochán na nGall'.

There was a great deal of British influence in the district. Each season brought the annual influx of Irish and English gentry, who came to fish the many lakes and open sea. They gave the town notoriety and were always assured of a hearty welcome. Townsmen were actively organising sporting occasions; regattas, races, etc., which were strongly supported by the local gentry. Local dances and social occasions were frequented by employees of the Marconi Company and the Coastguard service, and many of these married local girls.

Rural District Council

Under the Local Government Act 1898 the grand juries were replaced by publicly elected County, Urban and Rural District Councils. In Connemara, indeed throughout the country, the grand juries were dominated by the local Protestant landlord or his land agent, while the Rural District Council had for its members the local publicans, shopkeepers, and solicitors; all with Nationalist sympathies.

The Rural District Council held their monthly meetings in Clifden. The first meeting was held on April 15, 1899. At this meeting a resolution was adopted, copies of which were sent to the Chief Secretary, their local Member of Parliament and the several District Councils in the province:

    I. We record our conviction that nothing less than National Self-Government will satisfy the needs and aspirations of the Irish people.

    II. That while regretting the disabilities imposed by the Legislator on

Clergymen in making them ineligible for the ordinary rights of Citizens we hereby give it as our opinion that their presence at our meetings we shall always think of not as a pleasure but an honour.'[1]

R.J. Connolly was in the Chair, with the parish priest Canon McAlpine close to hand.

At a further meeting held on May 6, a resolution calling upon the Government for a grant for the cost of erecting a fishing pier at Doughbeg, Clifden, or an extension of the existing pier, was adopted. They recommended their proposal be brought before the Galway County Council and the Congested District Board.

They requested that the Congested District Board give this subject their favourable consideration with a view to establishing at Clifden a fishing and curing station, thereby promoting the fishing industry in this 'congested district.'[2]

A meeting of the townspeople on the same subject was held soon afterwards. A resolution put forward by R.J. Connolly Solicitor and seconded by John J. D'Arcy, Merchant, calling upon the Government to construct the pier, was passed unanimously. At the time a number of boats landed their catch at Clifden, but an even greater number landed their catch at Cleggan and other more suitable piers in the district. The fish were then delivered by cart to the railway station at Clifden. It was the Council's opinion that with the improved pier at Clifden all boats would land their catch there and the fresh condition of the fish, on arrival at the station, would be preserved by the avoidance of the long road journey. Despite their arguments the project was rejected and over the years the number of boats fishing out of Clifden Harbour diminished because of its dependancy on tides.

The names of the first Councillors are unknown, but on August 20 1902 the following list of members was published in the local newspapers. They were:-

Bernard J. Lee, Chairman. R.J. Connolly, J.J. D'Arcy, Peter O'Toole, John Kane, A.J. Lydon, P. Lydon, William Lydon, Joseph Gorham, J.P. T. O'Flaherty, P. O'Hara, J. Burke, M. Lavelle, Thomas Canavan, J.J. Vallely, Michael Mannion, William Gorham, John D'Arcy.

Royal Visit

When it became known that King Edward VII planned to include the Congested Districts of Connemara on his itinerary during his visit to this country in 1903, the Clifden Rural District Council and Board of Guardians passed the following resolution: 'That in view of His Majesty the King visiting the Congested Districts of the West, on his visit and tour through Ireland, we the Rural District Council and Board of Guardians beg cordially to invite His Majesty to Clifden, the capital of Connemara; and it is further resolved that An Address of Welcome be presented to His Majesty by the Rural District Council and Board of Guardians, as the representatives of the people of this congested district: and we hereby direct our clerk to forward a copy of this resolution to the Lord Lieutenant for submission to His Majesty.'[3]

1. S.P.O.
2. ibid.
3. Galway Express June 27, 1903.

King Edward VII at Kylemore Castle

King Edward VII among the people.

Recess Hotel.

Some years before, in 1890, John Talbot D'Arcy wrote to Dublin Castle suggesting Clifden Castle as a possible site for an Irish Royal Residence. At the time Clifden Castle was on the market and he suggested Edward VII, then Prince of Wales, should purchase it for his son the Duke of Clarence; to use as a shooting lodge in the Irish Highlands, similar to those owned by the Royal Family in Scotland.[4] The suggestion however, appears to have gone no further than Dublin Castle. This time it was not a Royal Residence that was being sought, just a Royal visit. However when the route His Majesty was to take became known, Clifden was not included. Instead the King, accompanied by the Queen and Princess Victoria, arrived by Royal yacht at Leenane travelled to Kylemore Castle and from there to Recess; where they boarded a special train for Galway.

The Royal group landed at Leenane quay on Wednesday July 29, 'amidst the cheers of thousands of spectators, while a crowd of schoolchildren, grouped on a hill overlooking the quay, sang God Save The King, the refrain was taken up by the adults and rang over the waters. The scene was picturesque, impressive, cordial and loyal in every respect.' They were greeted with an address of welcome by Rev. Curran C.C. and the local Rector Rev. O'Connell M.A. To which His Majesty replied: 'Gentlemen. The Queen and I are most grateful to your loyal welcome to this most picturesque part of our demesnes. We are confident that we will greatly enjoy our visit to your district, which we have not previously seen, but of whose natural beauty we have often heard. I am very pleased at the spirit of progress and industrial activity which is among you, and the Queen and myself join in hoping that all your anticipations for the future will be abundantly fulfilled.'

After receiving an address by the Earl of Lucan and Lord Kilmaine on behalf of the Magistrates of Mayo, the group entered their cars and drove through the village of Leenane, 'which was handsomely decorated for the occasion.'

On their way to Recess they passed through Tully, where a large crowd assembled. 'An arch spanned the road, bearing the words "A friend of the Pope", at each side of which a Roman Catholic Clergyman stood waving a red flag.' Arches were also erected at Kylemore and Letterfrack. 'At various points along the road cheering crowds of country people assembled.'

The group entered Kylemore Castle, where they were received by the agent and his wife. From there they moved on to Recess. At Recess Railway station they were met by 'forty men riding bareback on Connemara ponies and flaunting favours in red and green ribbons.'[5]

'Cries of Long Live the Queen were heard.' The riders escorted the Royal group to the hotel were they lunched. After lunch the couple 'preceded by the mounted cavalcade' visited the marble quarries at Lissoughter, at one point their carriage had to be pushed up the steep and narrow road by the crowd. The Royal train left Recess for Galway at 4.15 p.m.[6]

At Galway among the many addresses presented to the King was one on behalf of the people of Clifden. This address was presented by Bernard J Lee and John J D'Arcy.

4. SPO.
5. Galway Express August 1, 1903.
6. ibid.

Congested Districts Board

For Connemara, one of the most important steps taken by the Westminster Government at this time was the setting up of the Congested Districts Board (1891) whose aim was to enlarge the small uneconomical holdings in the west. The Board also helped to improve the breeding of livestock and poultry; it also aided and encouraged weaving, spinning, fishing and similar industries.

Over the years, the Board's powers were increased under several Acts of Parliament until 1909 when the Land Act of that year empowered it to acquire estates and land compulsorily. Over the following years almost the entire lands of Connemara were purchased by the Board. These were then divided among the previous tenants and where necessary houses provided, or improvements made to existing dwellings, thereby improving the conditions of the inhabitants. The tenant, having agreed to purchase the land from the Board, the purchase price was spread over a number of years and every effort was made to assist and encourage the new owner to work his land to full advantage and increase his agricultural knowledge.

In a great number of cases, the Connemara landlords, heavily in debt, were only too willing to sell part or all of their estates, but for others parting with land on which a good deal of money had been expended on improvements and drainage, came hard. The Congested Districts Board was replaced by the Free State Government having its duties divided between the Ministeries of Fisheries Industry and Commerce, and the Land Commission.

Education

Following the death of Archbishop McHale (1881) and the support by his successor Dr McEvilly, of the National School System, National schools were opened up in every community and village. The Clifden boys school, situated on the Sky Road, was run for many years by Mr. Vesey[7]. In Ardbear the Franciscan Brothers ran a free school which was pupilled by local children along with some from the town. This school was later recognised and financed by the Government. Following the death of Mr Vesey in 1924, the Clifden school came under the care of the monks. The girls of the town attended the Convent of Mercy school, established in 1855. In all other districts the schools were co-educational.

Right Rev. Monsignor McAlpine. P.P.V.G.

Patrick McAlpine was Parish Priest of Clifden from 1898 until his death on November 13, 1932. Born in 1847 at Keelogues, County Mayo, he was one of a family of thirteen and had a twin brother named James. In the pages that follow he will be referred to as Canon or Monsignor McAlpine.

He studied for the priesthood at Maynooth and Montreal, Canada, and was ordained in 1877. He then returned to Mayo and became curate of Kilvine at Irishtown, County Mayo, birthplace of the Land League. The son of an evicted tenant, the Monsignor in the historic years that followed, became closely

7. S.P.O.

Monsignor McAlpine.

associated with that organisation and remained a lifelong friend of Michael Davitt. Over the years his reputation grew and he became a regular contributor to newspapers and attended at public meetings. The Monsignor moved to Ballindine, Aughamore and Milltown parishes before becoming, in 1898, Parish Priest of Clifden. Recognising the Monsignor's background, it is easy to understand why he took the positions he did, and reacted so strongly to issues which arose during his term in Clifden.

The Monsignor took to all aspects of live with the same zeal he showed in his pastoral duties. Two things were most important to him; the Roman Catholic Church and the land of Ireland. During his youth in Mayo he experienced at first hand the emotional and traumatic fight by the people and their clergy on both these issues. The renewed proselytising campaign by members of the Protestant faith in the 1870's brought bitterness and bigotry to the fore. The fight for the land by the Land League showed all those involved the power of organised protest and meetings. Previous conflicts of these kinds had made the Monsignor intolerant of any attempt by the Protestant churches at proselytising and of any man who acquired land over the heads of their tenants.

In his treatment of both he was determined and effective, often carrying his actions beyond what was considered acceptable by his Bishop or Dublin Castle. Frequently rebuked by both, he continued with singleminded determination to destroy whatever individual or organisation had attracted his wrath.

A gifted orator and enjoying a position of influence in the community, the Monsignor was a force to be respected and feared; he used his oratorical power to gain advantage from the pulpit, for whatever cause he espoused, from a captive audience at Sunday Mass.

Though feared by most, he was still sought by the poor or wronged to plead their case; he was loyal to his parishioners and tireless in his efforts on their behalf. Whether it be pleading for the life of one about to be hanged, raising funds for those hungry and in need, or simply needing support in a political election, all were met with the same energy and drive he exhibited throughout his life.

The Monsignor came to Clifden with a reputation for 'church ornamentation already well established.' He quickly completed the spire on the new church so that 'from the ground below to the summit there was a distance of 200 feet. A beautiful tower clock was then put up and a cross dominating the whole was electrically lighted, and could be seen in the darkness of the night far out to sea.'[8]

Sadly a storm damaged the upper portion of the spire and this had to be taken down and rebuilt. The spire was built in 1898 and the clock installed in 1899. A bell was erected and first rang out on St Patrick's Day, 1899 while the organ was added in 1900.

A new Town Hall was built in 1908. Hitherto the old church, St. Mary's, was used as a hall. The architect was R. Butler and the builder T. McWilliams. The seats were American oak and purchased in America by the Monsignor while there on one of his many fundraising trips. These trips were organised by emigrants from the town. The Monsignor addressed many meetings and functions and the contributions increased greatly thus helping the completion of the church and the building of the hall.

The Politician

Throughout his career, the Canon was a strong supporter of William O'Malley M.P. for Galway, and the Irish Party. Not long after arriving in the

8. Dalton: History of the Archdiocese of Tuam, p.251.

ST. JOSEPHS. CLIFDEN. 6761. W. L.

Interior St. Joseph's Church — courtesy National Library.

town he became involved with the United Irish League, a political organisation set up to promote the dissolution of large grazing farms and division of these among poor farmers.

At one of their meetings held on August 16 1902 he displayed a disregard for the RIC which was to surface on many occasions in the years that followed.

The day was wet and the meeting was to have been held in the open. The League decided to take over the Courthouse and conduct their meeting on that premises. As the Courthouse began to fill, Head Constable Green arrived and insisted that the premises be cleared. Just then Canon McAlpine appeared on the scene and instructed the people in a 'quiet but firm tone' not to move. After a hurried conversation between the Canon and the District Inspector, Mr Glasgow, at which the Canon pointed out that the police had not objected to the use of the Courthouse on the previous day by Mr Hazell, land agent, as a rent office. 'We claim the Courthouse as the property of the people; we are here now and here we will remain until evicted by sheer force,' he said. The District Inspector then retired, leaving behind four constables and a sergeant who took notes throughout the meeting.

Among those present were members of the County Council, the Urban District Council and shopkeepers from the town. During his speech the M.P. William O'Malley denounced the system of fixing 'fair rents upon holdings not worth any rent whatever.' He spoke on the 'grabbers and graziers' and told the people 'to create such a public spirit that graziers would find it to the advantage of their pocket to throw these grass farms onto the shoulders of the landlords.'[9]

1904 saw an increase in land agitation throughout the country. Every effort was now being made to force landlords to sell their estates to the Congested Districts Board under the 1903 Land Act. In Connemara a number of these estates were leased by local shopkeepers for grazing. A campaign of intimidation was organised and encouraged by politicians to force them to give back these lands, making them unprofitable to the owner, thereby forcing them to sell at the Board's price.

Connemara was once again suffering the effects of a poor harvest but it is only fair to mention that the vast majority of the population were now in a much more secure position to see themselves through to better times. However alongside a prosperous town and developing farms, Connemara always carried — perhaps more than any other district — a large number of the very poor. These people usually occupied poor land in districts where rock and bog were more prevalent than arable land. They still dependend on the workhouse for relief and assistance. Those involved in the campaign to inform the Congested Districts Board of the need to purchase the privately held estates, and divide and distribute them among the farmers, often used the circumstances of the poor and increased their numbers to strengthen their case.

At a further meeting of the League held on December 18 1904 the Canon was once again in the Chair. This meeting was attended by Michael Davitt and the Canon's speech was widely publicised in the press and brought to the attention of Dublin Castle.

'Now I say and I accept the fullest responsibility for my words, that in a crisis like this, should the State fail to discharge the first duty which it owes to the

9. Galway Observer, August 23, 1902.

Town Hall, Clifden — courtesy National Library.

community — namely, to preserve and to support life — our people would be the veriest fools if they allowed themselves to starve, so long as fat sheep were grazing on the hillside, or sleek kine were browsing on the plain'. This 'was greeted with loud cheers.'

The meeting went on to condemn land grabbers, and advised their members to be prepared to give the life of the damned to any person who is condemned by the organisation. Councillor P.J. Kelly of Galway County Council advised 'whenever a man was found going into the enemy camp he should be brought down.'[10]

All this was reported to Dublin Castle and the police requested advice on what action should be taken. The Chief Secretary's Office however advised that no action be taken, and acknowledged that a state of outrage prevailed throughout the county no more in Connemara than elsewhere.[11]

During 1906-07, conditions again appear to have deteriorated in Connemara. At a meeting held in the town square on Sunday September 2 1906, the Canon was moved to the Chair and declared the following: 'Our turf is mud, our hay rotten and the potatoes gone'. 'In Connemara distress looms, trouble is near', he told the meeting, 'it is highly incumbent upon the Government to take proper and effective measures at once to cope with the situation.'

'They do not want relief work at one shilling a day', he says, calling them 'starvation wages' with no other result but the demoralisation of the people and promoting jobbery. Nor did they want assisted emigration, 'another pet project of the powers-that-be,' leaving 'our piers unmade, our fisheries undeveloped, our quarries unworked, and our lands unattended.' 'Give us back our Parliament of which we have been robbed'.

The Land Act of 1903 was a great step in the right direction, he told them, 'who can deny that here in the west, owing to the landlords' exorbitant and prohibitive demands, it might as well have never been passed. Here in Connemara it practically remains a dead-letter and at the coming Commission on the Congested Districts, it will be very easy for us to show that it is not with the people the fault lies or the blame rests.'

The meeting resolved that the 'demands of landlords in Connemara prove conclusively that compulsory sale becomes a matter of urgent and absolute necessity.'[12] February 1907 and the priests of the Clifden Deanery drew Dublin Castle's attention to circumstances in the district: 'Failure of potato crop has caused distress acute and widespread now prevailing all over Connemara'.[13]

They, along with the Board of Guardians of the Clifden Union called upon the Government to proceed with the erection of the pier at Dougbeg and to make a grant available to the Union with which they could purchase good potato seed and make these available to the poor at a price they could afford. However the pier at Dougbeg was never erected.

Street Preachers

The Open Air Mission for Ireland, a Methodist organisation, had a base in

10. Freeman's Journal, December 19, 1904.
11. S.P.O.
12. S.P.O.
13. ibid.

Oughterard and time and again their members came to Clifden to preach to the public. By law these preachers were entitled to preach where they wished and could only be checked or restricted by the police when it became obvious their presence would lead to disturbance.

Street preaching in Clifden led to many unsightly rows and physical outburts in the town. However, the report that a member of the Mission was tarred by local men on the Clifden Streets was completely unfounded.

The first record of violence was on May 2, 1903, when two ladies, Mrs Clara Millard and Miss Florrie Mendie, arrived on the eleven o'clock train from Oughterard. It was market day in the town and the ladies went to the Market Square and began to sing hymns, while one of them played the concertina. This continued for about ten minutes. The Head Constable was advised of their presence and, anticipating trouble, went directly to the Square. He was informed that Rev. Thomas Brett, C.C., who along with Canon McAlpine was known to be extremely bitter against street preachers, was aware of the ladies' arrival and was on his way to organise the people against them.

Following a conversation with the ladies, the Head Constable managed to persuade them to leave. The ladies, accompanied by the constable, left in the direction of Lower Market Street but just as they passsed William Gorham's shop some water was thrown over the three. A large crowd had gathered about the group, making it impossible to identify the offender.

The ladies then went along to the Errismore road and sat on a fence, awaiting the next train out of town, but a large number of boys and girls followed them and began throwing clods. Canon McAlpine and Rev. Father Brett arrived at the head of a crowd and ordered the ladies to leave the town at once. The priests continued to threaten and abuse the ladies, while sods werre thrown by the crowd, until eventually the ladies had to be escorted to the railway station under the protection of Sergeants Murphy and Cunningham and Constables Mangan and Wellwood. The caught the one-thirty train back to Oughterard.

Mrs Millard reported the incident to the Chief Secretary; who investigated the police reports. The County Police Inspector informed the Chief Secretary that the police had 'taken whatever steps were seen to be necessary to maintain the peace'. He complained 'the crowd were encouraged and provoked by Canon McAlpine who told the crowd to "get the preachers"'. 'The police were stoned and mud was thrown at them.' 'The Canon was very excited and pushed one of the constables away from him. He went to attack another when the constable tried to prevent some stone-throwing.'[14]

Mrs Millard was advised to inform the police in future when she intended visiting the town, and that preaching on the Square was forbidden as this would be seen as incitement. The following Sunday at Mass the Canon told the congregation that he hoped 'the people would deal properly with these street preachers in future and not be waiting for their priest to arrive on the scene'.[15]

However, contrary to advice and without informing the police, on July 25 1903 Mrs Millard was back in town, this time accompanied by a man and a woman. They arrived at 12.35pm and went straight to the Market Square. The constables arrived at the same time as Canon McAlpine. The Canon ordered

14. S.P.O.
15. ibid.

the preachers to leave. He then went a few yards away and returned, informing them that dead or alive they would leave the Square in five minutes. Again it was market day and there were about five hundred people in the Square. Mud and stones were being thrown in all directions. The police tried in vain to protect the preachers. Philip Boylan, a Clifden man, then struck the male preacher with a box on the side of the head. As one of the policemen got hold of Boylan, Canon McAlpine rushed at him and threatened to strike him. The crowd then closed around the group of preachers and police, and within minutes the group were covered with mud and dirt, and were struck with stones. The Canon continued to urge the crowd on, but somehow the police managed to get the preachers free and took them to the station. The preachers left on the next train.

Philip Boylan was prosecuted for assault on the male preacher; all others, including the Canon, were bound over to the peace.[16]

A complaint was sent to Archbishop John Healy D.D. regarding Canon McAlpine's behaviour, who replied he had advised Canon McAlpine to 'keep within the law and to take legal advice'. He hoped the Canon had done so, 'if not, let him take the consequences.'[17] He himself would interfere no further nor play the part of policeman for the street preachers.

On August 8, 1903, Mrs Millard and two ladies returned, this time having advised the police of her intentions. Policemen were drafted in from other regions in anticipation of further trouble. Ten policemen came from Oughterard on the same train as the preachers and twenty men were present from the area. They were advised should trouble brew to take the preachers to the railway station and protect them until they left on the train. They were to warn the people against acts of violence and take the names of any offenders. Again it was market day but the day was wet and very few people were at the market. Canon McAlpine was ill and Father Brett was away at the time.

The police stood about as the ladies preached and sang hymns; there was no trouble and the day went by peacefully.

The following Sunday, Father Brett in his sermon said that, if they were prepared to send an army to protect the preachers, then the people should leave the preachers to preach to the police.

For the next three years preaching on the marketplace was forbidden and the preachers came regularly to preach at a spot near the police barracks, at the top of the street leading from the railway station, without interference. They continued to request permission to preach in the Market Square but this was refused.

However, on September 1, 1906, four preachers arrived on the 12.45 train; one, a Mr Knapman, went to the usual spot and started to preach. The others, Reverend William Harpur, a man and a lady went to the Market Square. The police were not aware they were going to preach in the Square and stayed protecting Mr Knapman. After a short period Reverend Harpur began singing a hymn and the people at the Square at once attacked him. The police then went to the Square and informed Reverend Harpur they could not protect him on the Square; he then returned to the usual spot and began to preach. The crowd soon dispersed.

16. S.P.O.
17. ibid.

Later, all the preachers except Reverend Harpur left on the train. In the afternoon, Canon McAlpine, having discovered his identity, went up to Reverend Harpur on the street and asked for one of the books he held under his arm. The Reverend refused but the Canon then caught hold of the books and a struggle took place. The preacher went to the ground and the crowd moved in to attack; Reverend Harpur was kicked and stones were thrown. The police asked the Reverend to come to the station and after a little while he agreed. The Canon along with a crowd followed them. The Reverend was struck several times and cut, and in the scuffle lost his hat. It was with great difficulty the police managed to get him onto the train.[18]

The incident was reported in several papers and varied considerably in accordance with the religious leanings of the paper. Reverend Harpur was urged by the police to prosecute, but refused. However, the Chief Secretary felt that due to the publicity already given to the incident, some form of action should be taken.

Those who were seen to assault the preacher were brought before the court and fined sums of five shillings and two shillings and sixpence. In the case of Canon McAlpine the Attorney General advised that in cases such as these it was usual to prosecute only against the most serious offenders. Proceedings were not taken against the women, 'who were probably more violent than the men but less effective with their missiles'.[19] It was not considered 'necessary or desirable' to include the Canon in the prosecutions.

Reverend Harpur was summoned to appear at the court but was not called upon to give evidence. When the Canon took the stand he declared that the 'preachers language is highly insulting to the Catholic community and eminently calculated to lead to a serious breach of the peace. If they want to talk, let them hire a field or rent a hall.'[20] The Open Air Mission complained to Dublin Castle about the 'biased' court but were advised that as Reverend Harpur refused to prosecute, he had little grounds to complain.

According to the Chief Secretary's office, 'Street preaching in Roman Catholic districts is most irritating to the people and these preachers were but little under the control of the Church and their references to Dogmas cherished by Roman Catholics are often calculated to cause bloodshed. These preachers worked throughout the country almost always causing trouble wherever they went. Usually they had no contact whatsoever with the Protestant community but they invariably left behind them division, resentment and lack of trust in the community.'[21]

The Castle Lands

The Demesne of Clifden Castle consisted of two hundred acres. It was some of the first land in the estate to be reclaimed and drained by its first owner and founder of the town John D'Arcy. The land surrounding the castle left vacant by its owners, the Eyres, from the late 1890's. After the death of John J. Eyre,[a] in 1894, the property along with the rest of Mr Eyre's personal estate was left

18. S.P.O.
19. ibid.
20. S.P.O.
21. ibid.
a. see Eyres p. 128.

in trust for his six children. This resulted in the Castle being left vacant and the running of the estate left in the hands of agents. Over the years several attempts were made to sell the property but these met with no success. The agents, Joyce, Mackie & Lougheed, Galway, leased the lands for grazing to local shopkeepers but their purchase by the Congested Districts Board was much sought after by local tenants.

Beside the Castle Demesne, in the townlands of Faulkeera, Gortromagh and Cloghanard, lived a number of small farmers, tenants of the Eyre estate. For generations their families had tenanted these lands; some of their names can be traced back to Griffiths Valuation, 1850, and even before that time. The average holding was about twelve acres. One tenant told a newspaper reporter: 'He, his wife and nine children had twelve acres, rented at £4.10.0 per annum'[22] This holding he held in a 'quilted patch' type system and the land was said to contain more rocks and swamp than arable land. There was no hope of these holdings being increased as there was no land available. So it was that in 1913 when the lands were offered to the Congested Districts Board at £2,100.00 the tenants looked forward anxiously to their purchase and possible division among them.

Although interested in purchasing the lands, the Board took their time over the negotiations. By 1917 the land was still for sale. Mr James B. Joyce, Victualler, made contact with the auctioneers and 'speedily completed the purchase'[23] at the asking price of £2,100.00. As news of Mr Joyce's purchase became known the disappointment of the tenants turned into frustration and even anger. Sympathising with their plight and angry with what he saw as the underhanded way Mr Joyce conducted the purchase, Canon McAlpine orchestrated a severe and sometimes violent campaign against him. While the Canon may have had the best interests of his parishioners at heart the issue did become something of a political football in the months leading up to the 1918 General Election. The Canon was a strong supporter of the Irish Party and for years carried the bulk of the town behind him in support of that party, while Joyce had the local Sinn Fein Clubs on his side as two of his sons were prominent members in the local club. The conflict outlasted the election and went on for almost four years until it was finally settled in the courts in 1920.

Public Meetings and Demonstrations

Almost immediately after Joyce had purchased the Castle lands the Canon, without naming him, denounced off the pulpit the recent purchase of the Castle and lands. He called him a 'land-grabber' — a name that carried with it a stigma since the land war of 1879. Mr Joyce and his two sons Toby and P.K. were in the church and heard the Canon tell his congregation that he had recently returned from Mayo where he 'had passed the graves of grabbers, the same as the Clifden Grabber and within six months he would pass the grave of the Clifden Grabber and that there would be six feet of clay over him.' The entire population of the town turned against Joyce and his family; his shop was boycotted by the people who believed that he was 'under the Priest's curse.'[24]

22. Conn. Trib. March 9, 1918.
23. ibid., January 17, 1920.
24. ibid.

The Sinn Feiners stood by Mr Joyce and their club passed a resolution condemning the Canon for interfering in the matter.[25]

A public meeting was held in St. Mary's Hall to protest against Mr Joyce's action. Mr E.J. King, local publican and shopkeeper and Chairman of the Clifden District Council presided. The tone of the meeting was militant; Mr King opened by saying 'they must show him (Joyce) they were prepared to fight this to the bitter end, and he assured them that if they presented a solid front they would make him give in.'

The local representative, Mr W. O'Malley, M.P., gave a rousing speech, saying that 'in a country like Ireland where agriculture was the only industry the people had to support them, land-grabbing was always an intolerable offence' as they fought to get 'the British Government to enact laws for the restoration of untenanted ranches to the tillers of the soil, and one would imagine if only through a sense of shame, nobody would stoop to land-grabbing in Ireland now.' He condemned Sinn Fein for their support of Mr Joyce; 'It was rather amusing to see young Joyce calling on the young men of Connemara to cry down the Irish Party and to throw their caps in the air for an Irish Republic while his father took the land from under their feet.'[26] Michael Lavelle, District Councillor, told the meeting that if they were determined to win their cause they would have every man of principle at their back: 'Referring to the Irish Party he said they had a record to their name (hear, hear). They had achieved a wonderful success for the Irish farmer and in season and out of season had come to their assistance and it would be simply foolish for the farmers to throw them over.'

A Memorial was then drawn up and signed by Canon McAlpine, Rev. W. O'Connell, the tenants[b] and almost every businessman in the town. It was addressed to the Trustees of the Eyre Estate and protested 'in the strongest possible manner against this outrage on the rights of your tenants'.[27] An offer on behalf of the tenants was made to rent or purchase the lands, pending their purchase by the Congested Districts Board. The price was guaranteed by a number of shopkeepers and businessmen of the town.

As the date of take-over of the land by Joyce drew near a pit was dug outside the gate of the Castle. It measured seven feet by two feet and two feet deep. It was described as a 'bad imitation of a grave,'[28] such graves were recognised as threats. Tenants stock were driven onto the land and the gates 'heavily barricaded.'[29]

A further public meeting was held at 2 p.m. on March 3 1918, at which the Canon was characteristically eloquent and audacious. Supporters came in organised carloads from all over the county. Three Members of Parliament and a large group of Sinn Fein supporters were present. Fearing trouble, District Inspector Barry placed his Chief Constable Fitzpatrick along with fifteen men outside the hall where a group of about forty Sinn Feiners had gathered.

25. ibid., February 14, 1918.
26. ibid.
27. Conn. Trib. February 14, 1918.
28. ibid. January 17, 1920.
29. ibid. March 9, 1918.
b. M. Browne, Faulkeera; Joe Keady, Faulkeera; M. Conway Gortromagh; John Staunton, Cloghanard; John Whelan, Gortromagh, Patrick Quinn, Faulkeera; Ellen Mannion, Gortromagh, James O'Toole, Gortromagh, Penelope Folan, Cloughanard, P. McDonnell, Gortromagh, James McCann, Pat Lydon, Patrick McGrath (all Faulkeera).

The meeting commenced with Canon McAlpine taking the Chair saying: 'Here we are again', and 'once more in our own humble way, fighting the people's battle, pleading the people's cause and as far as we can, resisting to the utmost all the sundry who dare to interfere with the legitimate attainment of the people's rights, (cheers)'. He recalled the foundation and aims of the Land League and talked again of the twenty or so families whose hopes were dashed by the actions of Mr Joyce. 'What excuse may I ask can be offered for Mr Joyce's grasping actions? None whatever. (cheers) Could he plead injustification of his conduct, that in the pursuit of his vocation he was cramped or limited or circumscribed? On the contrary, his farms can be reckoned by the score; they extend from Ballyconneely to Clifden from Clifden to Leenane and from Leenane to Meath. History tells us of Alexander the Roman Emperor who wept and lamented because for him there was not another world to conquer (laughter and cheers): it is so with our local Shylock, not satisfied with his already wide possessions, he has declared that he will not die easy, contented or happy until he ends his days in a castle (laughter). Let us wait and see (cheers)'.[30] He declared that 'the grabbing of these lands are the first fruits of Clifden Sinn Fein'. This caused some disturbance among the audience. He then suggested that Mr Joyce be sent out 'with a bottle of water and like Ismael that every man's hand would be against him and that' Joyce 'was a Clifden Shylock, that he might get his pound of flesh but that a cabbage plot of the demesne he would never get.'[31]

Mr O'Malley during his speech declared that a great many Sinn Feiners, on account of their 'absurd political beliefs, are proper subjects for the lunatic asylum'.[32] He said he looked forward to meeting them at the Election and was confident of his success.

At the end of the meeting an appeal was made to Mr Joyce to reconsider 'the error of his ways' and consider the conditions mentioned by the tenants in their petition to the Trustees of the Eyre Estate, and abandon the sale.

Following the meeting, scuffles broke out between the Sinn Fein supporters and the R.I.C.; stones were thrown at the police, injuring three of them, but the crowd retreated when the police baton-charged.

Agreement

On July 8 1918 four men appeared before a special court in Galway charged with driving Joyce's cattle off the Castle lands. The case came before Mr Hill, R.M. but was adjourned. Mr Hill then asked Mr Joyce and Mr Connolly, solicitor for the four men, to meet him in his room. Once alone, Mr Hill advised Mr Joyce to 'yield to the agitation as the police would not be able to protect him'.[33] Mr Joyce agreed to sign an agreement to sell the lands for their purchase price of £2100 plus £200 and costs, and to have the rent of these lands until they were divided up among the tenants by the Congested Districts Board. Soon afterwards Mr Joyce contested this agreement claiming he was taken by surprise and had no independent legal advice before signing. However, it was January 1920 before the case came before the courts and was settled with the

30. Conn. Trib. March 9, 1918.
31. ibid., January 17, 1920.
32. ibid., January 9, 1918.
33. ibid, January 17, 1920.

P.K. Joyce

Toby Joyce.

James B. Joyce
(1852-1928)

Barbara Joyce (nee Keeley)
(1858-1943)
with her daughter Margaret.

Judge ruling in favour of Mr Joyce with costs and an injunction that he was not further to be interfered with.

In his judgement, Judge Power pointed out the lands were untenanted land on the Eyre estate and the Trustees had the power of sale. He criticised Mr Hill for encouraging Mr Joyce 'to surrender his legal rights in order to put an end to the intimidation', and gave Canon McAlpne a thorough dressing-down.

'Canon McAlpine,' he said, 'seemed to have allowed himself to be carried away by his feelings and to have used language, in his church and elsewhere which it was the Judge's duty to say was wholly indefensible'. He could, the Judge believed, have tried to dissuade Mr Joyce from purchasing before he denounced him from the altar, 'it should have been a fairer thing to have done'.[34] He felt that on several occasions the Canon used language in his church, 'calculated to produce a very bitter feeling towards the defendant' (Joyce).[35]

Despite the court case and the Judge's warnings, the fight went on. Canon McAlpine's name no longer appeared in newspaper reports of further attempts to persuade Joyce to sell; it may well be that having been appointed a member of the Congested Districts Board in 1918 the Canon's campaign from within the organisation was found to be more beneficial. For whatever reason the principal mover was now E.J. King, Chairman of the District Council and strong supporter of the Irish Party.

The intimidation continued and Joyce's cattle were once again driven off the lands. Six men were charged with this offence in September 1920 under the British law system, even though one of Mr Joyce's sons, Toby, was an official in the Sinn Fein courts which were in progress throughout the country at the time.

However, it was the decision of the Sinn Fein Arbitration Court of September 1920 that was eventually accepted by James P. Joyce. Under an agreement reached in that court, Clifden Castle and Demesne were sold by Mr Joyce for £2,300 plus costs and £150 compensation for damages done to him, to Trustees preparing to establish the Clifden Co-Operative. These trustees were James J. Cloherty, County Councillor, Roundstone, Alice Cashel, P.C. and Mrs Bridget Gordon.

One of the terms of the agreement was that the wood and Castle were to be preserved as the property of the Clifden people.[36] The Co-Operative was established on November 19 1921 and the estate was purchased from these by the Land Commission on May 12 1935. In the meantime the land was divided among the local tenants and under the Land Commission the Castle passed to the tenants and held under their combined ownership. With hindsight the wisdom of such a decision has often been questioned.

The contents of the castle had previously been sold by public auction, and the roof, windows, slates, lead and timber were now stripped and taken away. Today it stands a ruin.

Although the conflict was now settled, the original campaigners were not at all pleased that credit for its success should go to the Sinn Fein Courts.

The following chapters tell more of the Monsignor's political and social

34. ibid.
35. Conn. Trib. January 17, 1920.
36. ibid., September 25, 1920.

influence on the town and district. In 1910 he was appointed Vicar-General of the western portion of the Archdiocese of Tuam, and in 1915 he was appointed a Domestic Prelate with the title of Monsignor.

The Monsignor died on November 13 1932 and was buried in the grounds of St Joseph's Church.

Marconi Wireless Station, Derrygimla

While searching for a suitable location along the east coast of the Atlantic for his wireless telegraph station, Guglielmo Marconi, the Italian pioneer of wireless telegraph, viewed many sites along the coasts of England and Ireland. In July 1905 he finally decided on Derrygimla, three miles outside Clifden, just off the Ballyconneely road.

The site was a bleak desolate bogland, devoid of vegetation with some lakes a little to the west. Three hundred acres were leased from James Timothy Morris and work commenced on the construction which was to revolutionise the world of communications and bring a degree of fame to Clifden the extent of which it had never previously experienced.

The station took two years to construct and was still not fully completed by 1907, the year operation was to commence. Up to that year, world communications were operated by cable telegraph. However, on October 17 1907 with the opening of the station at Derrygimla, the first commercial wireless messages were transmitted and received across the Atlantic. Messages from the United Kingdom were received at the station by ordinary telegraph from Galway, and from there transmitted by the Marconi system to Cape Breton, Nova Scotia. Marconigrams received by wireless at Derrygimla were in turn transmitted by line to Galway and from there to the United Kingdom.

There was little ceremony to acknowledge this historic occasion; competition among competitors resulted in strict security being enforced. Newspaper reporters and members of the public had to receive an official pass from the Marconi Head Office in London before being permitted on the site. The British, Canadian, Italian and United States flags were raised on the masts. But only a priviliged few were present when those first messages were being transmitted. Marconi was supervising operations at the Canadian station at Cape Breton.

The first messages were received from Canada about nine o'clock and 'throughout the day the officials were busy engaged in receiving and transmitting dispatches.' The first transmission received was believed to be one of congratulations from Mr Marconi in Canada. 'All messages dealt with were regarded as private property, and none of them were shown to the visitors present.'[37]

At first only press messages, previously arranged by contract, were dealt with at a cost of two and a half-pence per word. The private messages were at a rate of five pence per word. This was considerably cheaper than cable companies who charged five pence per word for press and one shilling for private messages. The service was also faster; Marconi system could transmit thirty to thirty-five words a minute while cable companies transmitted at twenty-two words per minute.

37. Irish Times, October 18, 1907.

Approximate Layout Of Marconi Station At Derrygimla, Co. Galway.

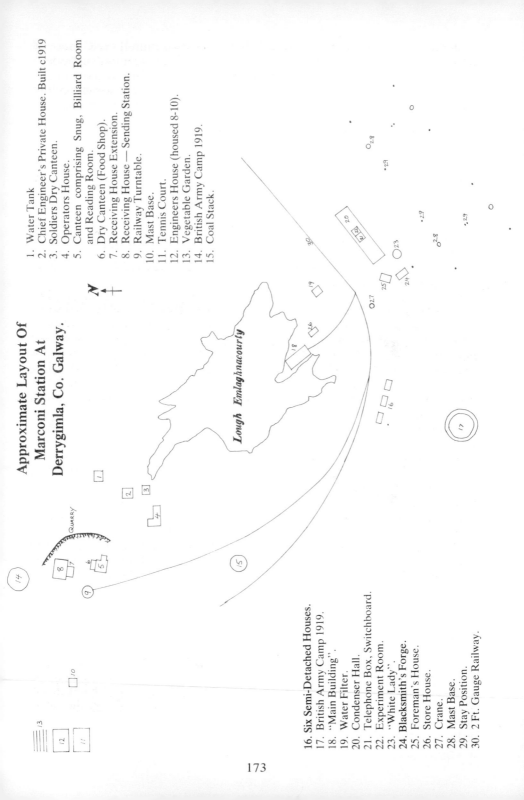

1. Water Tank
2. Chief Engineer's Private House. Built c1919
3. Soldiers Dry Canteen.
4. Operators House.
5. Canteen comprising Snug, Billiard Room and Reading Room.
6. Dry Canteen (Food Shop).
7. Receiving House Extension.
8. Receiving House — Sending Station.
9. Railway Turntable.
10. Mast Base.
11. Tennis Court.
12. Engineers House (housed 8-10).
13. Vegetable Garden.
14. British Army Camp 1919.
15. Coal Stack.

16. Six Semi-Detached Houses.
17. British Army Camp 1919.
18. "Main Building".
19. Water Filter.
20. Condenser Hall.
21. Telephone Box, Switchboard.
22. Experiment Room.
23. "White Lady".
24. Blacksmith's Forge.
25. Foreman's House.
26. Store House.
27. Crane.
28. Mast Base.
29. Stay Position.
30. 2 Ft. Gauge Railway.

Lough Emlaghnacourty

Among the first private messages to be transmitted was one of congratulations from Mr Lloyd George, then President of the Board of Trade:-

'Every improvement in the communications between various parts of the British Empire helps to consolidate and strengthen it. All well-wishers of the Empire will welcome therefore, every project for facilitating intercourse between Britain and the great Dominion across the Atlantic.'[38]

Another was sent by H.M.A. Murphy, Solicitor and County Councillor, Galway, to President Roosevelt, Washington:-

'On the opening of the Marconi Station here, allow me, on behalf of this country, to congratulate you on the success of your Presidency in the United States and hope Ireland, in her struggle for a just measure or self-government will have the encouragement and support of yourself and your liberty-loving people.'[39]

Tuesday October 24, and the Chief Secretary Mr Birrell and his party were given a tour of the Station by the Chief Engineer Mr Entwhistle. Mr Birrell was touring the west and spent the night at the Recess Railway Hotel.

Station Buildings

The compound was surrounded by a well constructed fence of barbed wire. At the entrance was a large wooden shed which acted as a locomotive shed, store and sentry box. The mile and a half climb to the main buildings was over bog and rock alongside which was constructed a narrow-gauge railway line, to facilitate the transport of equipment and materials onto the construction site. The first buildings erected to house the works, accommodation for the operators and engineers, 'with the exception of the Condenser House', were 'all of temporary construction and give a shanty town appearance.'[40] These were later replaced by attractive red-brick constructions. There were eight wooden masts, each two hundred and ten feet high and separated from each other by about twenty yards and had a tremendous extension of aerials. These were later replaced in 1918 by four steel masts. The noise from the spark transmitter could be heard for many miles around and the electric spark was plainly visible and resembled lightning. An engine-room housed two large stationary engines which alternately provided the electricity which charged a considerable number of batteries housed in the battery room.

The Chief Engineer Mr Entwhistle lived in a bungalow built nearby. Later, more permanent residences were built for the operators and engineers. This was a large red-brick bungalow which houses the single men; married men rented houses in the town or close to the station. Six semi-detached houses were occupied by maintenance men and their families.

The station had a total permanent staff of fifty, among these were twenty-five operators and ten engineers. These were much sought after on social occasions and added a certain colour to the local dances, dinners and sporting events. The maintenance men lived in the station precincts. Thomas O'Rourke, in charge of the engine room and fitters workshop was a mechanical engineer who came to Clifden a widower in 1908. He married a local girl, Miss Madden from Ballinaboy Bridge, and they have five children. Festus Sweeney, the head rigger, along with local men maintained the mast system.

38. Irish Independent, October 18, 1907.
39. Connaught Champion, October 26, 1907.
40. Irish Independent, October 18, 1907.

Boiler house. Courtesy Paddy Clarke.

Chief Engineer's bungalow with the six semi-detached workmen houses in background. Courtesy Paddy Clarke.

Mr Johnston, the carpenter, Mr Quinn, the engine driver, a Mr Helpson and Mr Grogan, also lived here with their families, who grew up on the station and attended the local national school at Errislannan. Their houses were quite roomy and comfortable; they all were electrically lit and had hot and cold running water. On the ground floor there was a living room, a back kitchen and bedroom and there were two more bedrooms upstairs. There was an outside privy and turf house. The men kept shift hours and were called to work each morning by a steam whistle on top of the engine house.

Seventy men were employed full-time working the turf. Usually from February to September another two hundred casuals were employed cutting and saving the turf, large quantities of which were used in the boilers. Turf, it was estimated, could be cut, saved and stored for five shillings a ton, whereas coal cost thirty shillings per ton.[41]

The wages at the station were high and with such large numbers of locals employed, the benefits to the district were tremendous and contributed greatly to the prosperity of the town at that time.

In 1910, 'Receivers of a much more sensitive type were installed.'[42] By 1913 with the use of an ordinary gramophone record, transmission was now increased to anything from eighty to one hundred words per minute. This year also saw the erection of a Receiver Station at Letterfrack and one in Canada at a place called Louisburg. Clifden now became a transmitting station only, the receiver there having ceased to operate. The operators at Letterfrack continued to live at Derrygimla and were transported there each day by the Station car.

Throughout World War I a company of British troops were stationed at Derrygimla; these occupied one permanent and two temporary buildings. The separate receiving station at Letterfrack proved uneconomical and was closed down and the receiving station at Derrygimla re-activated. In the years that followed, the Black and Tans regularly used the stations Social Club bar.

Residential Bungalow, Condensor house with aerial system and the boiler house. Courtesy of Marconi Company.

41. Irish Independent, October 18, 1907.
42. Conn. Trib. August 19, 1922.

The 'Marconi Express' narrow-gauge railway line. Courtesy of Marconi Company.

The Station Destroyed

On Tuesday night, July 25 1922, three local men, members of the Republican forces, were watched by an eye-witness as they set fire to the receiving station at Derrygimla and fired shots into the condenser house, causing serious damage. At this time Connemara was in the hands of the Republicans but Free State troops were moving in from the north. That same night Republicans in Oughterard burnt the workhouse and police barracks there. The act was condemned by the clergy and seen by the press as a 'preliminary to the retreat of the Irregulars (Republicans) from Clifden.'[43]

The ostensible reason for the burning was that it was 'regarded by the Irregulars as a British concern, the rights of which they claimed were withheld from Ireland under the Treaty.'[44] Later it was claimed the station was destroyed in retaliation for having transmitted a request by the local RIC for assistance on the night on which two of their members were murdered, March 16 1921; this request was answered by a trainload of Black and Tans who proceeded to burn, murder and plunder the town.[c] However, none of these explanations were acceptable to the estimated one thousand local people who had lost their livelihood as a result of the damage.

On the Sunday following the burning, Monsignor McAlpine condemned the act. Sometime before the Company decided to close this station and it was principally through representations made by the Monsignor and public representatives that the decision was rescinded. The Monsignor paid tribute to the Marconi men who he said 'always comported themselves in a manner highly creditable to any body of men.' 'I never thought,' he told the congregation, 'that I would live to see the day when our own boys would descend to the level of the Black and Tans.'[45]

In the week following the burning it was felt that the station would once again be operable as repairs got under way. As time passed however, more and more

43. Conn. Trib. July 29, 1922.
44. ibid.
45. Conn. Trib. August 5, 1922.
c. see page 211.

Jack Phillips was born in Godalming, Surrey, He was a wireless operator at Derrygimla from 1909-1912. A British long-jump champion, he helped to foster interest in that sport locally. However, he found life in the West rather dull and requested a transfer back to sea.

Following a brief refresher course on the S.S. Oceanic he was assigned as senior wireless officer to the S.S. Titanic on its maiden voyage.

Up to this the international distress call was indicated by the call letters C.Q.D. In the interest of clarity, and by international agreement, the distress signal was changed to S.O.S. in early 1912. Within weeks, on the night of 14/15 April, 1912 following the collision of the Titanic with an iceberg, Jack Phillips made history by being the first man to sent out a genuine S.O.S.

His call resulted in seven hundred and fifty lives being saved. Unfortunately Phillips himself was among the one thousand five hundred lost.

Operator Jack Phillips senior wireless officer on S.S. Titanic.

Local workmen.

Codes MARCONI WESTERN UNION & A.B.C. 4TH & 5TH

Marconi's Wireless Telegraph Company. Ltd

Head Office.
MARCONI HOUSE,
STRAND, LONDON.W.C.

Telegrams: EXPANSE, CABLE, LONDON
Telephone Nº CITY 8710 (10 LINES).

FEB/FJC

Clifden,
Connemara
Ireland Oct. 1st. 1923.

TELEGRAMS:
CLIFDEN, c/o EXPANSE LONDON.

PLEASE ADDRESS THE COMPANY
AND REFER TO

T
MFT   930

R. J. Connolly Esqr.,
Solicitor,
Clifden.

Dear Sir,

I have to thank you for your letter of even date
re Club Licence. With regard to the last paragraph, we
understand that negotiations are proceeding between the
Company and the Government re the reopening of the station,
which we understand will take place as soon as a favourable
decisio n has been arrived at.

With reference to the Honorary Members, there are
about 40 of our Staff, who are now on the Unemployment list,
who could be included as they might be looked upon as being
only temporarily unemployed.

We are sending you in our Copy Of Rules by Mr. Kehoe,
and shall be obliged if you will return us same when dealt
with.

I hope to go in to Clifden on Wednesday next.
                    Yours faithfully,

Marconi Letter. Oct. 1, 1923.

men were transferred from Derrygimla by the Marconi Company and it became evident that the station would be permanently closed. Commercially the station at Derrygimla was very successful but because of the improvements in transmitting equipment, the need for a station so far west was eliminated. The more modern Marconi station in Wales could take over the Derrygimla traffic quite easily, so the burning had merely advanced its closure by only a few years.

Mr Mathias, Chief Engineer, was transferred to London in February 1923. On the night before his departure a farewell party was given in the Social Club by the members of the 'very depleted staff',[46] past employees and their families. Mr Mathias, who had married a local girl, Miss O'Flaherty from Ballyconneely, was presented with an engraved silver-mounted tantalus by the staff.

For the local community the loss in revenue was considerable and for many employees the only answer to the problem created by the burning was emigration.

A skeleton staff remained and the contents of the station were from time to time auctioned off. In the 1930's the company eventually sold out to the Land Commission and the land was divided among local farmers. Today this once historic site is difficult to locate and poorly marked, but its influence and that of its employees is still remembered by older members of the locality.

Alcock and Brown

On Saturday June 14 1919 at 5.13 BST (4.13 GMT) a Vickers-Vimy two seater biplane, left St John's Newfoundland Canada. Its destination was Galway Bay, over one thousand nine hundred miles away, its quest: to cross the Atlantic non stop within the specified time limit of seventy two hours, and thereby collect the prize offered by The Daily Mail newspaper of £10,000. On board were Capt John Alcock D.S.C., the pilot, and a navigator named Lieut Arthur Whitten Brown.

The prize of £10,000 was first offered in 1913; with the object of securing improved aircraft and engines. This was suspended during the war but had now been renewed, and competition among airmen to collect was keen.

Some hours before, as the airmen prepared for the gruelling hours ahead, an accident took place which almost prevented their take off. There was a strong wind blowing across the field and the plane was tied down with ropes and pickets. Suddenly one rope became loose and was driven by the force of the gale around the petrol pipes and, caught in the under carriage, was pulled tight across the copper piping, severely indenting them. The pipes had to be removed and the mechanics set to work replacing them.

While the work was in progress, 'stretched on the ground in the shadow of the Vimy's wings' the airmen took their last meal in Newfoundland. Lunch consisted of 'tongue, bread, potted meats and coffee.' Both men were in high spirits and told reporters: 'With this wind if it continues all the time' said Lieut Brown 'We shall be in Ireland in twelve hours.' 'I am steering a straight line for Galway Bay and although I shall do my best, I do not expect to strike it off exactly.' Capt Alcock told them: 'This wind amuses me, for a few years ago it would have put the wind up me badly. In the very early days, long before the

46. Conn. Trib. February 24, 1923.

Capt. John Alcock and Lieut. Arthur Whitton Brown at Clifden.
— *courtesy Michael Freyer.*

war had taught us what flying really is, we used to scatter pieces of paper and if they blew away we would not dream of taking a bus out.'

By 5.13 p.m. however all repairs were complete and against a forty mile westerly wind, they took off and turned out to sea. 'As soon as we got clear of the land we had the wind in our tail and it remained like that practically all the way over.' Both men were experienced flyers, and airplanes had been their love and their life from an early age.

Capt John Alcock D.S.C. was just twenty six years of age. He was born in Manchester and as an engineering apprentice had worked with the British Westinghouse Company and afterwards with the Empire Company. He soon became a noted flyer and was the first man to fly across the country at night. In

Vickers-Vimy plane at Derrygimla.

1913 he took part in the London to Manchester flight. 'Shortly after the outbreak of war he became attached to the designer depot of the R.M.A.S. he was sent to Mudros, on the island of Lemnos, where he earned a big reputation and set up a record for a long-distance bombing flight.' While on a flight to Constantinople he was forced by engine trouble to bring down his plane in the Gulf of Saros. 'After swimming about for hours they reached land, but were taken prisoners by the Turks'. Capt Alcock was released on the signing of the Armistice and was awarded the D.S.C. for his service. He joined the Vickers company and 'devoted himself especially to the problem of Atlantic flying.'

Lieut Arthur Whitton Brown was thirty two years of age. He was born in Glasgow but his family moved to Manchester when he was seven. After completing his studies at the Manchester College of Technology, he joined the British Westinghouse Company and worked for them in South Africa, Germany and France. When war broke out he tried to join the Flying Service but was 'turned down', so instead he became a second Lieutenant in the Manchester Regiment. However in 1915 he was transferred to the Royal Flying Corps and was twice shot down but he escaped. 'When he was shot down over Bapaume, Brown crashed his machine to prevent it being used by the Germans. It took fire, though he was badly burnt he escaped into the British lines. Later he was brought down in the German lines and was so badly injured in the foot that he will be lame for life.'

He was taken prisoner but later handed over to the Swiss Commission 'as one not likely to recover.' Once back in England he volunteered for service and became an instructor at Petersborough.

The machine used by the airmen was a Vickers-Vimy two seater biplane, 'its principal feature being that it is of all steel manufacture, its length from fueselage to tail is forty two feet eight inches, and its width across the wings is sixty seven feet. It is fitted with two Rolls-Royce engines of seven hundred horse-power, and is capable, fully loaded, of an ordinary speed of ninety miles per hour and with the throttle wide open, of one hundred and fifteen miles per hour.' For the first hour out it was quite clear but soon they hit thick banks of cloud. 'Most of the time we were compelled to fly between clouds, and very thick banks of fog. Indeed the conditions were anything but pleasant for flying.' Capt Alcock told the Connacht Tribune reporter. They started to loose their transmitter, the receiver worked all night but the wireless messages were not for them. They 'did not exchange a signal with anyone on the outside world during the entire period' of the flight. The radiator shutters were frozen up and the petrol gauges soon covered over with ice. They climbed to eleven thousand feet. 'We climbed all that we could at the outset to try and get out of the clouds, but without avail.' The crossing was rough and bumpy, and the wind was blowing 'hard right down to the water.'

Although the average speed of the plane was ninety mph, with the following winds they managed to average one hundred and twenty mph. 'I believe that the great secret of long distance flying' Capt Alcock said 'is to nurse your engine. I never opened the throttle once.' They only caught sight of the sea about six times on the way across and had just two sightings of the sun, just two hours from landing. 'Our only guide was the stars and we got occasional sights of the moon'. At one time they 'spiralled down to within ten feet of the water and flew as if upside down, without any sense of horizon.'

During the flight the men ate sandwiches and chocolate and drank ale and coffee. Communication between the two was difficult; with the roar of the engine, they conversed by means of notes and signals, but the darkness kept even this to a minimum.

When asked how he felt flying over such a vast ocean in the dark, Capt Alcock replied: 'We have done a considerable amount of night flying in the past, the sense of loneliness that might be supposed to accompany it has long since worn off. Indeed I do not think that either of us had ever thought of what we were flying over, being merely intent on getting the machine across.' 'We were jolly pleased, I tell you, to see the coast.' They first spotted Turbot Island and then circled the town before spotting the Marconi aerials. They headed towards Derrygimla and landed behind the condensor house at the station. 'Our landing would have been a perfect one only that we happened to come into the bog. It looked quite all right from the air, but as soon as we touched the ground the machine began to settle down to the axles, and the wheels suddenly stopped, and the machine went down nose first. We were not hurt or shaken, but only a little damage was done to the under plane of the machine.' The time was 9.40 a.m. BSM (8.40am GMT). From take off to landing the flight had taken sixteen hours twenty seven minutes, but from coast to coast the time was fifteen hours fifty seven minutes. Their arrival was witnessed by some of the town's inhabitants but a great number were attending Mass and only heard the roar of the engines.

The operators on duty at the station went out to greet the flyers as they stepped out of the plane. 'I'm Alcock — just come from Newfoundland' Capt Alcock announced, while Lieut Brown remarked; 'That is the way to fly the Atlantic.' On discovering the identity and achievement of the flyers, one operator requested their autograph. 'Now' Capt Alcock said 'If we had a shave and a bath, we should be all right.' Only two thirds of their fuel had been used up, and had it not been for the poor landing conditions, the flyers had intended taking off again and continuing their journey to London.

As the men relaxed at the station social club, a Royal Flying Corps light airplane, piloted by Capt Bowen with Lieut Bradley as observer arrived at Oranmore. They circled the Vickers machine and landed about fifty yards from where it stóod, but they too got bogged down. Large crowds flocked to the station during the day, but the military refused admission. However some people did wade ankle deep through the bog to see the plane, which was carefully guarded by the military. Despite this souvenir pieces of the wings were on sale in the town that evening, and are still in possession of some town families today. Monsignor McAlpine P.P.V.G. and E.J. King, Chairman of the District Council, were among the first outsiders to meet the airmen. They 'bid them Céad Mile Fáilte to Ireland; hoping that their visit was but a prelude to the opening of a regular service across the Atlantic to the nearest point on the European side.'

That evening the men were taken to Galway by the Marconi motor car. They carried with them 'a little white mail bag with lead seals unbroken,' this contained 'eight hundred letters, including correspondence for the King and many nobilities.' 'This is the first Atlantic aerial mail.' Alcock explained.

At Galway they were given a hero's welcome and were entertained late into the night at the Railway Hotel where they stayed. Next morning they went shopping for fresh clothes and souvenirs. One Galway jeweller presented each of them with a Claddagh ring, 'I shall always keep it and always wear it as a lucky charm' Captain Alcock told him. People stood in the rain for hours outside their hotel to witness their coming and going. At one o'clock they were given a civic reception and 'addresses of welcome and congratulations were presented from the Galway Urban and District Councils.' Capt Alcock thanked the people for their kindness and Lieut Brown said 'Thank you very heartily for the extremely kind welcome you have given us, and I think that it is a much greater welcome than has been deserved,' 'after all even though the voyage has been a long one it was straight forward flying all the way.'

Captain Alcock left this message for the Irish people before leaving for Dublin on the mail train on Monday evening. 'I thank you for your great kindness and hospitality, and hope that the new link forged today between Europe and America will become a chain around the world for good-will and amnity.'[47] Later the men fought their way through a dense crowd gathered on the platform of the Railway station, to bid them farewell. From Dublin they travelled to London where the celebrations began in earnest.

On Friday, at a luncheon at the Savoy Hotel, the prize of £10,000 was presented to Capt Alcock and Lieut Brown by Winston Churchill, on behalf of Lord Northcliff proprietor of the Daily Mail. Next day they went to Windsor Castle to have their knighthoods conferred upon them by King George V. Sadly Sir John Alcock was killed in December of the same year, on a flight from England to France, and was buried in Manchester December 27, 1919. Sir Arthur Whitten Brown died in 1948. A memorial to commemorate the flight was erected in Ballinaboy on a height overlooking Derrygimla bog.

47. Conn. Trib. June 21, 1919.

Newspaper Scoop

The story of the Alcock and Brown landing was to have been a Daily Mail exclusive; a special correspondent had been in Galway for weeks awaiting the arrival, to be circulated afterwards, free of charge, to all newspapers who wished to use it. However the editor of the Connacht Tribune, Tom Kenny, managed to get to Derrygimla before the Daily Mail correspondent and interviewed Captain Alcock. He sold his article internationally, and was later congratulated by the Press Association on his 'scoop'.

CHAPTER VIII

Fighting Men All

As the nation waited for the enactment of the Home Rule Bill of 1912, the Ulster Volunteers declared their opposition and drilled openly in defiance of a political concept repugnant to them. In Dublin in 1913 the Irish Volunteers were founded and they too drilled and were trained in the use of arms. They declared their willingness to uphold Home Rule against any threat from the North. Throughout Connemara, young men enlisted in the Volunteers and took part in the exercises and drilling in the months that followed.

At the outbreak of World War I, Home Rule was postponed until the war was over and John Redmond, leader of the Irish Party, encouraged the Volunteers to join the British Army and fight for the freedom of small nations. Thousands of Volunteers enlisted but many objected and so the organisation split.

Those who followed Redmond called themselves National Volunteers and as their members swelled the ranks of the British army, their former comrades, the Irish Volunteers, continued to remain in readiness. The Irish Volunteers were usually also members of the local Sinn Fein Clubs. In Connemara, as elsewhere, they had few arms and any man who possessed a gun guarded it well.

National Volunteers

Here a large number of men answered 'Redmond's call'; they joined mostly the Connaught Rangers and the Irish Guards. Recruiting for the Connaught Rangers was opened at Renmore Barracks Galway on August 6 1914. By September the military declared the 'recruiting has been most satisfactory, and best of all is that the men are eagerly asking when they can get to the front.'[1] Between August 10 and October 11, one thousand six hundred and twenty-three recruits had enlisted at Renmore; included in this number were ex-soliders who had re-enlisted. The breakdown was as follows; five hundred and ninety-six came from the counties of Galway, Mayo and Sligo; six hundred and ninety-three came from other parts of Ireland and three hundred and seventy-four came from England and Scotland. But already the list of wounded printed in the local press increased weekly as did the tributes to those killed in action.

In September the Royal Irish Rifles Detachment who were stationed at Marconi Station, Derrygimla, were posted to the front. A huge crowd under the leadership of 'Dr Pit Gorman and several other gentlemen assembled at the railway station' to bid them farewell. Dr Pit made a 'most invigorating speech' and this was replied to by Captain Manders and Captain Chatterton, 'who spoke from the carriage window' and 'averted to the very kind manner in which he and his detachment had been received during their stay in Clifden. This

---

1. Galway Express, September 5, 1914.

splendid send-off which they were receiving would be an encouragement to them in the grey times they had to meet'.[2] The train pulled out amid cheers and expressions of goodwill. Encouraged by Monsignor McAlpine, recruiting rallies were organised in the town hall; these were well-attended and had the support of almost the entire population of the town.

From all works of life they joined and from all backgrounds; strengthened by the knowledge that both the clergy and politicians applauded them. Some joined for political reasons, some joined for the pay, but most joined for the adventure. Some were never to return; the survivors were met with a hero's welcome. On all, however, this adventure would leave a permanent scar. Over the years their magnificent efforts were diminished by politics and politicians but in 1914 they were the men of the moment.

Capt. Leo King.
Photograph taken in Deccan India 1921.

Lieut. Jack King.

Leo and Jack King

Leo and Jack King were the sons of John King, Clerk of the Petty Sessions, and Lena Casey, sister of Dr Joseph Casey, local dispensary doctor. The brothers were educated by the Franciscan monks at Ardbear and later at St Jarlath's College in Tuam. They both received their commissions in the Connaught

2. ibid September 19, 1914.

Rangers; Leo became a Captain, Jack a Lieutenant. Neither brother was wounded and after demobbing, returned to complete their education and both graduated in law. Leo later married and lived in Dublin where he worked for the Electricity Supply Board. He was killed in a motor cycle accident on July 28 1935 leaving a wife and children. Jack joined the Civil Service but contracted T.B. and was advised to try a warmer climate; he moved to South Africa and died there.

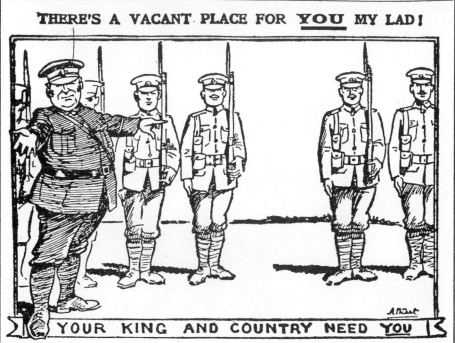

THE GALWAY EXPRESS, Saturday Morning, November 14, 1914

THERE'S A VACANT PLACE FOR YOU MY LAD!

YOUR KING AND COUNTRY NEED YOU

Lord Kitchener has obtained 900,000 recruits, and only 100,000 are needed to make up the first million. So take *your* place in the ranks, young man, at once, and enlist at the nearest recruiting office, for the sake of your King and Country.

Advertisment: The Galway Express Saturday November 14, 1914.

Michael Lavelle

Michael Lavelle, son of a small farmer from Streamstown, became Master of the Clifden Workhouse in 1914. His younger brother William (Willie) had returned wounded from the front when Michael declared his intention to enlist. Willie quickly recovered and returned to the front, but their father, named Michael too, an old Fenian, then Distict Councillor and member of the Board of Guardians tried to persuade Michael not to enlist. Michael however was adamant and he received his commission as Lieutenant in the 4th Battalion of the Connaught Rangers in July 1915. After the usual course of training he went to France. He became attached to the 9th (Service) Battalion Royal Inniskilling Fusiliers and while with them he won the Military Cross. News of his award left

Michael Lavelle (1883-1951)   *Lieut. Michael Lavelle.*

Clifden 'ringing with joy' reported the local press. A 'more popular distinction combined with a more popular officer there could not be'. 'Lieutenant Lavelle is a type of officer to whom honour would come as a matter of course. Brave to a fault, possessed of a daring that might be mistaken for rashness, a born leader of men, ever solicitous for the welfare of men under his charge, and imbued with the ardent spirit of a deep patriotism'.

Extracts from a letter written by Michael to friends in Clifden recount the circumstances under which the award was won.

'Some days before the raid a particular serious annoyance was occasioned by machine-gun fire and other forms of attack. A surprise party of volunteers was called upon to storm the position. The storming party consisted of Lieutenant Kempston (son of the late Rector of Roscommon) with three other officers, myself included, with a party of seventy to eighty men. We did the journey to enemy trenches in record time, with little or no casualties until we arrived there. Then, before the rattle of machine-gun fire, the explosion of bomb shells, hand-grenades etc. it was a veritable hell, we requisitioned and bombed them with their own bombs which we captured. We did give it to them! In coming out of the German trenches the first thing that attracted my attention was the lifeless body of my dear friend, poor Kempston, of whom I will say, a better or truer-hearted man did not exist. He was a soldier and a man. I had his body carried back to our lines. His grave is marked with full particulars of identification. Out of the four officers that went out, only

Harvest Thanksgiving in Clifden.

On Wednesday last the annual Harvest Thanksgiving service was held in the Parish Church, Clifden, which was well filled by a large congregation which had come from far and near—in fact from all parts of Connemara, and including a good muster of the Royal Irish Regiment, under the command of Captain Percival. In the procession we noticed the Rev. Canon McCormick, D.D., Rev. Thomas Nee, Rev. B. Shea, Rev. J. Mortimer, Rev. Canon Fleetwood Berry, and the Rector, Rev. W. O'Connell. The musical portions of the service were sweetly rendered and very hearty, and included Stainer's anthem, "What are these," and also a solo, "Thus saith the Lord," from the "Messiah." Miss Murphy, daughter of the late revered Rector of Clifden, presided at the organ with her usual ability.

Evening prayer was said by the Rector and the Rev. B. Shea, and the Lessons read by Rev. Canon McCormick and Rev. T. Nee, and the sermon preached by Rev. Canon Fleetwood Berry. The offertory, which was in aid of the Connemara Orphanages, and was collected by two members of the Royal Navy, was, we hear, a substantial and fitting thank-offering for the blessings of harvest. After the service the visitors were all entertained to tea at the Schoolhouse by Miss D'Arcy, whose father had been for many years Rector of Clifden.

We congratulate the new Rector, the Rev. W. O'Connell, on the great success of his first Harvest Festival since his recent institution to the parish, and we take this opportunity of wishing him much happiness and prosperity for many years to come in his new sphere of labour.

Galway Express October 12, 1916.

one (myself) returned. The men suffered severely; every man did his duty'.[3]

What Michael did not tell was that, upon completion of his assignment, he returned to no man's land, against the advice of his Commander, and recovered the body of Lieutenant Kempston. He took the body on his back and crawled on his stomach back to his own lines. He was fulfilling a pact made between the two men the previous night; neither man was to be left on no man's land should the other survive.

Within a month of Michael having received the award, his youngest brother Joseph enlisted in the Irish Guards. Their father was heard to say; 'If there was a war in hell, they would be there'.

190

When Michael next returned home on leave he was met with a hero's welcome. The railway station was crowded with friends and well-wishers, at the head of which was Monsignor McAlpine. He was lifted shoulder high and carried triumphantly through the town. A dinner in his honour was held in the Railway Hotel and there among his friends many speeches were made and toasts proposed until the early hours of the morning.

Later, Michael was transferred to the 5th (Service) Battalion of the Connaught Rangers on September 20 1917 in Egypt; the Regiment had arrived in Alexandria just four days before. They moved on to Palestine and there he saw active service against the Turkish enemy. After the Armistice in 1918 he was transferred to the Royal Army Ordnance Corps and promoted to the rank of Acting Captain. On December 11 1919 he was decorated by George V at Buckingham Palace. He retired in 1919 and returned to take up his position as Master of the Clifden Workhouse.

Michael was the only brother to return unscathed; both Joseph and Willie received minor wounds. Joseph died in 1939 unmarried. Willie inherited his father's farm at Streamstown, married and had one daughter. He died in 1959.

Michael married first Mamie Cloherty[a] who died childless on June 16, 1945. Later Michael married Teresa Joyce from Coolacly and they had one son, Michael Joyce, and two daughters, Barbara and Kathleen (the author). Michael died November 19 1951.

Sinn Fein

Although a branch of Sinn Fein was formed in Clifden as early as 1908, as with the rest of Ireland, it was not until after the Easter Rising 1916 that its numbers increased to any extent. Sinn Fein's aims were to create an independent republic. Its members included shopkeepers, businessmen, but the vast majority were the sons and daughters of small farmers from the outlying districts. Meetings were held regularly in the old jail, newspapers and pamphlets were read and rousing speeches by visiting speakers were given. Topics such as the possible introduction of conscription into Ireland and the re-distribution of the remaining private estates were prominent. The main activities were fundraising and political awareness. With the supression of the organisation in July 1918 some members resigned, but the dedicated remained. The club vacated the jail and moved instead to a premises further along Market Street.

When the war ended on November 11 1918, a General Election was called shortly afterwards. The previously restrained energy and drive of the Sinn Fein members was now harnessed and put into use to the success of their candidates. In Galway the contest was between the sitting M.P., William O'Malley, who had represented Galway for twenty-three years, and Padraic O'Maille from Kilmilken in the Maam Valley.

Padraic O'Maille

Padraic O'Maille, son of a sheep farmer, was born in the Maam Valley, Leenane, in 1878. He came from a family with a deep interest in learning. His father was a Latin scholar and had insisted that his children continue their

a. See D'Arcy, p.22-24, 24n.

education beyond the local National School standard. For this purpose a tutor was employed and Padraic, along with his four brothers and two sisters joined his cousins in a private classroom either at his home, Muintireoin, or nearby at the home of his cousins.

His brothers went on to attend University College at Galway where Thomas later became Professor of Irish Studies. His cousins became well-known surgeons in Galway and London. Padraic remained on the family farm and became active in local politics. At an early age he became organiser for the Gaelic League. He joined Sinn Fein in 1906 and was on its Central Council for over four years. He helped Padriag Pearse to establish the Volunteers in Connemara in 1914 and was a member of that very secret organisation, the Irish Republican Brotherhood. On Easter Tuesday 1916 he fought under Liam Mellowes in Galway and was among those arrested and interned in Frongoch, North Wales. It is believe that while there, a young Welsh girl fell in love with him and helped him to escape, disguised as a priest. However, he was later re-arrested and interned in Wandsworth prison in England until his release under the general amnesty of 1917.

With this background and ability, Padraic O'Maille seemed the obvious choice as Sinn Fein candidate for the coming election. Sinn Fein declared their intention to abstain from Westminster if elected and instead to set up a Parliament in Dublin.

The Irish Party

William O'Malley M.P. relied on the old machine and in Clifden that meant Monsignor McAlpine. For years now the Monsignor had held the town for O'Malley and the Irish Party and with this new threat he was more determined than ever to succeed.

The first meeting held by local party members to voice their support for their candidate and prepare for the coming election was on November 10 1918 and was chaired by Monsignor McAlpine. The venue was the Railway Hotel and on this occasion the Monsignor gave a short speech and then retired on his doctor's advice; he was suffering from a flu. He told supporters:—

'We can't forget the sacrifice which the Irish Party have made; the battles they have fought, the victories they have achieved and the lasting benefits and priceless advantages to the tenants which they have secured. It would be strange at this critical period of our country's (fortunes) that we should follow the thoughtless crowd, whose rainbow-chasing policy, no matter how well-intended, will cause defeat and spell disaster, whose aims are impossible of achievement', 'whose whole tout ensemble considered in the light of the present character of many of them, shows their present action to be fraught with untold evil to our country and its cause'.

'To me it is simply sickening and disgusting to find that our people don't open their eyes to see for themselves that many of the apostles of the new (gospel) were bred and reared in the rent office, that they were the plied tools and willing agents of the Landlords and the sheriff when the poor people were evicted and that these who are now the most prominent against the constitutional movement owe their present position what they have been and what they are, to their receipt of government moneys which to this hour they gladly accept and don't dream of refusing. How much some of us might forget and how much some of us could learn'.

He cautioned the supporters not to use language or actions which might 'cause discredit to us as Irishmen'. The Monsignor then took his leave. When William O'Malley, M.P., spoke, he told his supporters that:—

'the country was face to face with a crisis greater than they had known, even during the Parnell split. They were asked to decide between two policies, one of which would bring only ruin and disaster to Ireland and Ireland's cause (applause). He stood as the standard-bearer of the old cause that had won so much for the farmer, labourer and townsman of Ireland'. He 'believed the Irish people if they understood the question did not wish to follow a policy of shadows and phantoms and would resolve to stand by the party that had solid achievements to show' and 'whose methods could win the ultimate freedom of Ireland. The movement for an Irish Republic was impossible of attainment and could only result in the destruction of the national movement, the division of the forces of the nation into warring sections, with the inevitable consequences of loss in productivity and national effort towards progress and many years of that resolute government that Sinn Fein had already brought upon us'.[4]

Among Mr O'Malley's prominent supporters were, H.G. Connolly, solicitor and Election Agent; E.J. King, J.P., County Councillor and Chairman Clifden District Council; Mr Walsh D.C., Bartley Rutledge, D.C. Oughterard; James J. Valleley, and John Walsh Tullycross; Martin Holleran and Patrick O'Connor; Mr Killanin, Walter McDonagh, Cleggan; R.J. Dowd, P. Duane, A. Walsh, J. Lynch, M. O'Connor, M. King D.C., C. McDonagh J.P., County Councillor; James Reddington, Sub-Agent and T.J.W. Kenny representing Galway National Club. An election fund was opened and the Monsignor headed the list of subscriptions with five guineas.

At a public meeting held in the Town Hall on Sunday November 17 the Monsignor advised the voters of his parish to support O'Malley. He said it was 'nothing short of an insult to the intelligence of the Connemara people to ask them to support a man who never did anything for the people'. He believed 'Connemara would teach these men the lesson, for he was confident that Mr O'Malley would be elected by such a majority on the day' that 'Sinn Fein would never dare to contest a seat again (applause)'.[5] But he advised them they must work hard to ensure such a success.

In the evening a meeting for the ladies was held in the hall; they were addressed by the Monsignor and Mr Connolly. An election committee was formed and the ladies undertook to canvass all the electorate of the town and district. The following ladies were appointed: Mrs F. King, President; Mrs M. O'Connor, Secretary; Mrs Fintan Cavanagh; Mrs G.I. King, Mrs James Casey; Miss Ward; Miss M. King; Miss H. King; Miss L. Lee; Mrs A.D. McDonagh; Miss Daley; Miss Deacy; Miss Moynihan; Miss Keady; Mrs W. Gorham; Mrs J. O'Connor; Mrs Whelan; Mrs M. O'Malley and others.

Eyre Square Galway was the venue for a large meeting to launch the campaign of Padraic O'Maille on Sunday November 24. A fife and drum band

4. Conn. Trib. November 16, 1918.
5. ibid, November 23, 1918.

headed by two pipers paraded the streets prior to the meeting. As supporters gathered, a force of armed military arrived from Renmore Barracks. Dr T. Walsh presided over the proceedings; he told the crowd they were asking them to vote, not for Padraic O'Malley or Eamon De Valera but 'for the cause of Ireland and to show the world that they were united in their demand for Ireland's right to decide the form of government which the country should have. John Dillon and his party were worse unionists than Carson and his followers', he said, 'Sinn Fein was the first party since O'Connell's time that had advocated the abolition and complete severance of the Union'. 'What Sinn Fein wanted was to show to the Peace Conference that the Irish people wanted the right to govern themselves and decide on their own form of government'. Professor Thomas O'Maille, brother of the candidate, addressed the people, telling them: 'Sinn Fein asked the electorate to do nothing for England, but to live and die for Ireland. Sinn Fein stood for Ireland's independence and to prevent the race being crushed out. (applause)'.

Rev. Griffin, Curate from Rahoon, referred to the opponents' meeting to be held that afternoon in the square. 'Around the platform would be assembled the forces of England's Johnnies who put out their Union Jack and got drunk when the war was over and shirked the fight themselves'. He was 'sorry that some of the soldiers were not at home; he had been speaking to some of them who were determined to be on the right side in the election'.[6]

The election was held on December 14 1918 and the results declared on December 28. When news of the result broke in Clifden, Sinn Fein supporters were overjoyed with their success. Over the whole country, seventy three seats out of one hundred and five were taken by Sinn Fein. In Galway, Padraic O'Maille was elected with a majority of 8,432 votes. O'Malley declared later that Sinn Fein were more enthusiastic and professionally organised. 'I am afraid there was a deplorable lack of moral courage in the Nationalist ranks, in many cases the shouting of small boys, the wearing of flags and the Soldier's Song had the intended effect on the voters. Nothing will convince me that, if the undue influence and the intimidation that they deliberately persisted in were absent, the electors would not have voted for Sinn Fein to the extent they did'.[7]

But the majority had voted for Sinn Fein, expressing their lack of faith in the Irish Parliamentary Party. Bonfires were lit in Clifden and supporters burnt candles in their windows throughout the night. It was as much a victory over Monsignor McAlpine as over the Irish Party. At a triumphant meeting held in Eyre Square Galway, Sinn Fein declared they would never be satisfied with anything less than an Irish Republic and 'if need be were prepared to fight and to die for it'.[8]

Dail Eireann

In keeping with their pre-election promise, the Sinn Fein elected members, that is, those not in jail, set up an Irish Parliament soon after the election. The first sitting of Dail Eireann took place on January 21 1919. The British legal system was to be ignored and local Sinn Fein courts set up; these dealt with land claims and disputes. The Dail were declared illegal in September 1919 and the

6. Conn. Trib. November 30, 1918.
7. Conn. Trib. December 11, 1919.
8. ibid, January 4, 1919.

Volunteers now became the Irish Republican Army and within a year entered into guerilla warfare with the military and the RIC.

A new force was formed to support the RIC and began arriving in Ireland about the middle of 1920. These were called the Black and Tans because of their dress; they wore a khaki coat and bottle-green RIC trousers. The majority of them were demobilised soldiers earning ten shillings a day. Another force, the Auxiliaries, were made up of ex-officers and were dressed in a dark blue uniform; these began arriving in September of the same year. Although house searching and harassment of Sinn Fein supporters and known Volunteers was carried out, it was not until the arrival of the Black and Tans that a degree of disturbance was reported from Clifden.

Local Power

As the authority of the government was threatened by the new regime throughout the country, in Clifden the year of 1919 saw little violence, except for a continuation of land agitation and conflict between RIC and Sinn Fein supporters. Raids were periodically made on supporters' houses. The young men usually spent most of their time away from home. They travelled the mountains or stopped in 'safe', remote houses, returning late at night to their families.

At a meeting of the Clifden District Council on June 14 1919 the old regime were unanimously re-elected to their positions of local power: E.J. King, re-elected Chairman; M. Lavelle re-elected Vice-Chairman. To the Board of Guardians, M. Joyce J.P., re-elected Chairman, J. Lee elected Vice-Chairman, John King elected Deputy Chairman. When, however, the elections came round the following year, an all-out effort was made by Sinn Fein to replace these with their own men.

The election took place on June 1 1920 and was said to pass off so peacefully that there were no police present. Order was kept by the Volunteers who also guarded the boxes in the boardroom that night. Sinn Fein flags were displayed in and near the booths.

All seats were taken by Sinn Fein except one at Clifden which was taken by James J. Lee who topped the poll. James B. Joyce and Martin Mongan were returned for Owengowla, Thomas O'Flaherty Jr. and T. Joyce were returned for Roundstone. William Diamond was returned for Renvyle. Seventy-five per cent of the voters cast their votes and counting began at eight o'clock on Wednesday morning and continued until eleven-thirty that night. Counting was carried out by Mr F. King. Clifden had four seats with ten candidates and six hundred and four votes cast. The following were elected — all Sinn Feiners except James Lee.

James J. Lee, P.K. Joyce, Thomas Heanue, M. Vaughan.

Volunteer Activities and Sinn Fein Courts

On Sunday night, August 8 1920, bonfires blazed on all the surrounding hills and the town was illuminated as crowds paraded about the streets, 'singing patriotic songs', in a display of solidarity with Archbiship Mannix, who was refused entry to Ireland by the Government, as he travelled along the west coast. Suddenly 'a bright glow in the western sky caused various surmises as to its origin; the truth was learned in the morning'.[9] The unoccupied coastguard station at Belleck had been set on fire and was partially burned. The station had not been used for a number of years but was undergoing repairs. The four houses on the east were completely gutted but the chief officer's house at the western end remained intact. Other buildings representing the British presence came under the torch in the area. On August 20 at two a.m. the vacant RIC Barracks at Cleggan was burnt, as on September 4 Tully Coastguard Station was similarly destroyed.

In early August, three houses in the Ballyconneely area were raided and money stolen. The Volunteers made some enquiries into the robberies and later arrested three men. These were taken to a secret place and held there for two days and then released after 'establishing their innocence'.[10]

The local Volunteers were said to be successful in a number of minor larcenies. Their actions were a deliberate attempt to undermine the authority of the RIC and render them helpless in the performance of their usual duties.

Agrarian agitation was rampant; the owners and lessees of grazing lands were constantly threatened and had their cattle driven off the lands. Every effort was made to force the owners to sell these lands. Neighbouring farmers seeking lands held by shopkeepers of the town or farmers whom the former felt already held more than their share of local land, were subject to threats, cattle drives and intimidation.

At the first arbitration court held under the auspices of Sinn Fein at the club in Clifden on Tuesday August 31, 1920, such a case came before the court. John M. Lyden claimed damages of £40 against John Ward, J. Davis, T. Ward, P. Walsh and J. Mulkearn from Claddaduff 'for injuries to his cattle in the recent drive on his land in Fountain Hill' and for trespass of thirty-two cattle, belonging to those mentioned, on Lydon's land from August 9 to date of court.

Mr Connolly, Solicitor, appeared for Lyden and Mr Nicholas, Solicitor from Galway appeared for the defendants. The Court was presided over by J.J. Cloherty, County Councillor, Roundstone, Mr Cosgrove and J.M Lyden (prosecution) and Miss Cashel, County Councillor. Lyden did not adjudicate during the hearing of this case.

The land in question was situated in Fountain Hill and consisted of forty-three acres, three roods. Lyden had bought it seventeen or eighteen years previously from Anthony Walsh for £160 plus fees. Lyden used the land to rear stock to supplement his dairy herd which supplied milk for his customers in the town. Up until July of that year he had had no difficulty with his neighbours. However on July 31 1920 his herd, a man named Lacy, received a threatening letter warning him to cease herding for John M. Lyden or be prepared to take the consequences. The letter was presented to the court. On August 9 the defendants, in a 'most arbitrary and summary manner' drove Lyden's cattle off the farm and immediately replaced them with thirty-two of their own.

John M. Lyden proclaimed himself to be one of the most prominent members of Sinn Fein and told the court how, fourteen years previously, he had surrendered an eleven-months take he had held on the Twining farm at Cleggan to facilitate the tenant's purchase. When approached by the RIC to

9. Conn. Trib., August 14, 1920.
10. ibid.

prosecute the defendants, he immediately refused and took the case to this court instead.

Mr. Connolly declared that the Sinn Fein organisation 'strongly objected to this high-handed action on the part of individuals with a lust for land'. 'In other places, such actions were severely dealt with and were speedily brought to a full stop'. The Sinn Fein hall was packed for the proceedings and order was kept by the Volunteers. The verdict was not publicised but it was said that all concerned 'left expressing entire satisfaction with the justice and impartialment meted out to them'. The public agreed that 'the court's conduct and judgement contrasted favourably with that of the British court'.[11]

The successful conclusion of the lengthy dispute over the Castle lands was a major achievement by the court that September.[b]

Padraic O'Maille, T.D. (1878-1946).

Gerald Bartley

Gerald Bartley and his brother Paul were the sons of an RIC Sergeant. They were born in Cloghans, Ballina, while their father was stationed there; Gerald in 1898 and Paul in 1900. Following the death of their father, Mrs Bartley returned home to Clifden with her family. Both boys attended the National School under Mr Veasey and later Gerald was sent to Dublin and attended the Christian Brother's school. While in Dublin he joined the Volunteers and Sinn Fein. On returning to Clifden he took up a position as Clerk at the Marconi Station and became very active in both these organisations locally. Paul followed his brother into these organisations.

Gerald, along with Mattie Joyce, also from Clifden, was sentenced to one month in Galway Jail for lighting a fire on the John D'Arcy monument. The fire was lit to celebrate the Sinn Fein victory at the Longford By-election in May 1917. At about this time he was dismissed by the Marconi Company; the order came by wire direct from Head Office in London. Gerald believed the disclosure of his involvement with Sinn Fein and the Volunteers was the cause of his dismissal.

He then became Clerk in the Galway County Council, returning home each weekend. During his absence one weekend, the Black and Tans raided his lodgings and shot his friend Seamus Quirke. Following this incident Gerald joined fellow Volunteers in the hills.

11. Conn. Trib., September 4, 1920.
b. see Monsignor McAlpine p. 157.

Connemara Flying Column
Left to Right: back row; Patrick Wallace, Letterass; Gerald Bartley, Clifden; R. Wallace,
Letterass (brother of Patrick); Patrick O'Malley, (ex-R.I.C.) Cleggan; Dick Joyce,
Leenane.
Front Row: Jack Conneely (ex-British Army); Jack Feehan, Leenane; S. Stanton, Martin
Conneely, Leenane; Jim King Roundstone; Eugene Gillon, Carraroe

Jack Conneely

Jack Conneely a native of Letterfrack was a sergeant in the Royal Engineers
during the First World War. At the end of the war he returned to Connemara
and took a job as driver at Leenane Hotel. He joined the Volunteers and
throughout the Black and Tan regime he accumulated information and
transported arms and men throughout Connemara. Because of his war record
he was seen by the Black and Tans as a friend and they regularly accepted lifts
from him in the hotel van.

On one occasion while on the road with an assignment of arms, he was
stopped by some Black and Tans seeking a lift to Leenane. Jack readily agreed
and the men climbed into the van and spent the remainder of the journey seated
on crates of guns and ammunition bound for the Volunteers. The men alighted
at Leenane and Jack continued with his assignment to a 'safe' house along the
coast. Later that night, Mayo men arrived by sea, collected the arms and
returned back up the coast.

Military Activities

Throughout the year, military detachments came and went, often stopping for
some days, sometimes for just a few hours. For however long their stay, they
managed to intimidate the people, generally disrupting the peaceful pursuits of
the people and angered the most staunch supporter of the Union.

On Sunday October 10, 1920, a detachment of military came into the town.

After conducting what was now becoming a regular search of the homes of Sinn Fein supporters, they took up quarters in the Workhouse.

Some time later, a group of the soldiers strolling about the town were jostled and some youths shouted 'Up Sinn Fein' at them. They immediately returned to the barracks and emerged fully armed. They marched into town, ordered all indoors and fixing bayonets they proceeded to break into the Sinn Fein hall and smash pictures of Pearse and the executed men of 1916. They then searched Mrs Bartley's house looking for her son Gerald, but he was not at home; they later called to the house again but he was still not at home. On both occasions the officer in charge was said to be 'courteous'. Next a search was carried out on Mr McDonnell's hotel on the Main Street; here they carried out a showcase 'containing, the proprietor said, over £200 worth of marble ornaments'.[12] The showcase was not found until the following morning with the contents broken and strewn around the street.

The soldiers continued to patrol the town, shouting and terrorising the inhabitants until about five o'clock in the morning.

The following night, Monday, about ten or twelve of them arrived at Bernard Lee's public house. They ordered the bar cleared and saying they were 'out for blood', forced the assistant to give them drink. Next they broke into O'Hara's pub where they held up the owner with a revolver and helped themselves to drink. 'They then selected the dearest boots in the shop and carried them off'. Mr O'Hara later said they also took money and did damage to the amount of £50. They next stopped at Stanleys drapers on the corner of Market Street. They smashed the shop window, climbed inside and lit the lamps. They then proceeded to loot the shop, passing its contents to their colleagues outside. The noise of the broken glass and the wrecking of the shop terrorised the five female assistants living on the premises, two of whom fainted. The Stanley children screamed in terror. 'This was the first time I had ever heard an English accent', one of them, Percy, later recalled.

The owner of the premises, Gerald Stanley, told the press: 'I hope I never again undergo such an experience. I feared every minute the shop would be set on fire. Next morning I found my shop to be topsy-turvy, everything strewn about — large quantities carried off. I cannot yet form a correct estimate (of what) I have sustained, but it cannot fall short of £600. Thank God the house was not burned.[13]

The soliders next called to Nee's; here shots were fired and one assistant who was standing by the window had a near miss; one bullet passed by his head and lodged in the wall. They kicked the door down; Mr Nee ran down to try and stop them but a revolver was pointed at him and the shop keys demanded. He was then forced to hold a candle and watch as they helped themselves to drink and carried off a number of bottles of whiskey. Mr Nee's mother became hysterical and begged them to carry off whatever they wished but not to burn the house or kill any of her family. One soldier said ' 'tis alright, we won't hurt anyone'.

'I will never forget the sensation I had when I found the revolver put to my face,in the hands of a drunken soldier. I thought my hour had come; imagine my relief when they left', Mr Nee told the press.

12. Conn. Trib., October 16, 1920.
13. ibid.

MARKET DAY. CLIFDEN. 5350 W. U.

Market Day, Clifden — courtesy National Library.

200

They next broke into and looted Thomas Lydon's. An officer now appeared on the scene and ordered them back to camp. They left next day, 'to the great relief of the townspeople'. The local RIC halted their departure at Recess and succeeded in recovering some of the stolen property.

Tuesday night, October 12 and the people were now looking forward to a good night's rest when two lorryloads of RIC auxiliaries arrived in the town at about nine pm and began firing indiscriminately. The firing continued all night but fortunately no one was hurt. 'The people of Clifden had reason to be grateful to the local constabulary for restraining the passions of the soldiers and there is no doubt that the town would have fared much worse only for their exertions'.[14]

The following Monday, October 18, a warship landed a detachment of soldiers at the town. Once again, houses were searched. John M. Lydon, William Clancy and Mr Lydon's assistant, a Mr Walsh, were arrested. Mr William Clancy was later released but the others were detained in the barracks until midday and were then removed under heavy escort to Galway. Mr Kelly, law clerk, had his rooms searched but nothing incriminating was found. He was also arrested but later released. Again, Mrs Bartley's house was searched 'but her sons were not at home'.

The officer in charge warned the people that should any policeman be shot, 'he would return with troops and burn the town before twenty-four hours'.[15]

A military inquiry was then held in the barracks into the damage done on October 10 and 11 by the looters. Here shop-owners gave details of their losses. Later a sum for compensation was agreed by the Military but this was never paid, so the business men were forced to take their claims before Civil Courts. In January 1922 Gerald Stanley was awarded £565 and Pat O'Hara £112.

Early December and plain-clothes policemen again raided the homes of Gerald Bartley, Bertie King and Alex Higgins but these were found to be not at home.

Mid February 1921 saw a 'good deal of military and police activity' taking place in the district. The houses of J.M. Lydon, Alex Higgins and Mrs Bartley were searched for seditious documents but nothing was found. Enquiries were made for 'wanted young men' at Higgins' and Bartley's but they were 'not at home'. The houses of Mathew Vaughan, Fall, J. Ward, Kingstown and Pat Madden, Ballinaboy, were searched but nothing incriminating was found, except two bullets found at Madden's. One son Patrick Madden was arrested and enquiries were made about another, Thomas, but he was not to be found. Patrick had served in the war, and was severely wounded; the bullets, he told them, were souvenirs.[16]

Bloody Sunday

Sunday November 21 1920 became known as 'Bloody Sunday' because of the number of killings which took place that day in Dublin. In the early morning, eleven British Officers believed to be intelligence men, were killed and several wounded and in the afternoon indiscriminate firing by the Military at the football spectators in Croke Park left twelve dead and sixty injured.

14. Conn. Trib., October 16, 1920.
15. ibid, October 23, 1920.
16. ibid, February 26, 1921.

The incidents sent a wave of shock through the country. However, its far-reaching effects on Clifden could scarcely have been imagined at the time.

The pattern was the same for all the morning's shootings; one or two men arrived at the door of the hotel or boarding house, requested the victim by name, and on being admitted, several others followed in their wake. Guard positions were taken up at the door and hallways and the intended victim was sought out and shot, either in his bed or, when more than one was sought, were rounded up and shot altogether in one room. The men, members of Michael Collins's Execution Squad supported by picked Volunteers, then walked slowly from the houses and disappeared into side streets.

The alarm was raised at one house in Mount Street when the 'raiders' were still there and a street battle followed between the 'raiders' and the soldiers. During the morning, eleven officers and civilians connected with the Crown were killed and four wounded, while six attackers were declared to be wounded.

That afternoon as five thousand spectators watched Dublin v. Tipperary football match, Crown forces opened fire on the crowd and in the panic that followed twelve persons were killed, eleven seriously wounded, and fifty-four injured. The official account stated 'the Crown forces were seeking persons concerned in the morning's tragedies and were fired upon when approached'.[17]

Thomas Whelan Execution

Thomas Whelan was born in October 1899 at Faulkeeragh on the Sky Road outside Clifden. His father was a former tenant of Clifden Castle and worked his small holding there. Thomas had nine brothers and three sisters. One of his brothers was a member of the American Army Air Corps and another had fought in the war; his sisters had emigrated to America.

While still young, Thomas worked for a short time for Monsignor McAlpine and was a member of the Clifden Sinn Fein Club. In 1918 he moved to Dublin where he worked for the Midland and Great Western Railway at Broadstone Railway Station. He joined the Volunteers, C. Company Dublin Brigade, shortly after arriving in Dublin and lived in a boarding house at 14 Barrow Street in Ringsend. A handsome young man, he neither drank nor smoked and being deeply religious he was a weekly communicant at Ringsend Parish Church.

Soon after 'Bloody Sunday', Thomas was arrested for the murder of Captain G.T. Baggelly at 119 Lower Baggot Street on the morning of November 21. He pleaded not guilty.

On January 28 1921 four men were charged with Capt. Baggelly's murder; they were J. Boyce, M.J. Tobin, Thomas Whelan and J. McNamara. The case came before a General Court Martial held at City Hall but was adjourned until February 1. On that day the evidence for the prosecution was the statements of two witnesses, one an army officer who lived with his wife in the same house as Capt. Baggelly, and that of a soldier who saw men on the street after hearing shots fired.

The officer when questioned said he was shaving in the bathroom when he

17. Irish Independent, November 22, 1920.

heard footsteps along the hall. The bathroom door was open and two men confronted him and told him to put his hands up. One man covered him with a revolver; this he later identified as Whelan, while another walked in and out of the room; this man he identified as Boyce. A housemaid was pushed into the bathroom along with the officer, but she was never called to give evidence. The officer told the Court he heard shots coming from the direction of Capt. Baggelly's room and he then saw a number of men passing by the open door; these he could not identify. The men in the bathroom then left. The officer went to Capt. Baggelly's room but found he was already dead.

The soldier told the court he was travelling on his motor-cycle along Lower Baggot Street when he heard shots but he did not know where the shots came from. He slowed down and noticed a group of men coming from No. 119. He later identified McNamara as being in this group. He met up again with these men at about Herbert Place where 'they stretched across the road with revolvers'. They told him to leave the bike and go, but then called him back. One of them pointed a revolver at him and he was taken into No. 38 Mount Street. From this group he identified McNamara and Tobin, who was standing away from the main group. He also identified Whelan who he said was attempting to start his motor-cycle. Mr Williamson, acting on behalf of Whelan told the Court that Whelan's defence would be an alibi. Evidence would show that he was not present at the scene and that the 'boy was a weekly communicant and not the class of man that murderers were made of.'
Mr Williamson declared that the reason the officer's maid was not brought forward was that 'she could not corroborate the evidence of the others as regards the identification.'[18]

The case continued on Wednesday 2 February at which Whelan's landlady gave evidence that Whelan came downstairs at 8.40 am on the morning in question and 'asked why she had not called him'. He washed in the pantry and left at 8.55 for 9 o'clock Mass at Ringsend Church which was within five minutes walking distance. He returned at 10 o'clock had his breakfast and retired to his room. She told the Court she did not see him again until dinner at 3 p.m. It would take twenty-five to thirty minutes to reach Baggot Street Hospital from her house, she said.

A young lady living in the same street as Whelan gave evidence that she saw him in the church when she arrived, she saw him approaching the altar rails and receive communion. She too had received communion that morning. Mass lasted forty minutes and she saw the accused leave afterwards. Another witness told the court Whelan passed him on Ringsend Bridge and said good morning, and they spoke for a few minutes. The priest at Ringsend Church said he knew the accused who 'was a weekly communicant for years'; he 'bore a correct and irreproachable character and never took drink'.

Questions were raised by the prosecution as to whether Whelan was a member of the IRA. To this Mr Williamson strongly objected, saying this 'suggestion was not substantiated by evidence but it was an attempt to poison the minds of the Court.'[19]

The prosecution cast doubt on the reliability of the defence witnesses. This,

18. Irish Independent, February 2, 1921.
19. ibid, February 3, 1921.

the defence argued, was 'grossly unfair' to suggest that because 'they belonged to a certain class and might hold certain political opinions' they 'were prepared to come up and perjure themselves on behalf of the prisoner.'

The evidence of the defence witnesses was not to be trusted while the evidence of prosecution witnesses was considered sufficient to have Thomas Whelan hanged.

The trial ended with Tobin, Boyce and McNamara found not guilty. Thomas Whelan was sentenced to death 'subject to revision' but 'had no recommendation of mercy.'[20]

Almost immediately, efforts were made to have the sentence reversed. Monsignor McAlpine declared his own 'firm belief in his innocence.' He encouraged his congregation to pray for the success of all efforts being made for his reprieve. The Monsignor wired the Lord Lieutenant, interceding for Whelan, and 'received a heartening reply'. Rev. Canon O'Connell, the local Rector, also wired the Lord Lieutenant. A memorial from the townspeople was given to Monsignor McAlpine who was going to Dublin to attempt to 'save the life of this unfortunate young fellow.'[21]

Mrs Whelan went to Dublin soon after her son's arrest, and remained until his execution on March 14 1921. The trip was her first experience of a train. During her many visits to Kilmainham and Mountjoy jails to visit Thomas, she spoke of the courtesy of the guards and her son's repeated declaration of his innocence. 'You are not to be worried over me, mother. If I die, I die innocent', he told her.

He solemnly swore that on the morning of November 21 he was not on that street, that instead he 'partook of the Body and Blood of his Redeemer, and that he would consider it a greater crime than murder to do that if he were guilty, and to bring Our Lord Himself to shield him.'[22]

On March 7, the newspapers announced the sentence passed on Thomas Whelan had been confirmed. The date was set for March 14. Five others were also to be executed on that day. 'In connection with the overwhelming evidence which had been given in support of the innocence of Thomas Whelan and Moran', who received the death sentence for a separate killing which took place on the same morning, 'Mr Devlin M.P. had a long interview with Lloyd George and other influential persons, on Friday March 11. Lloyd George promised that the case would be carefully reviewed but would not give any personal assurance 'that his intervention would lead to a reprieve.'[23]

Monsignor McAlpine telegraphed Mr James McMahon, Under Secretary: 'As parish priest to Whelan, the condemned prisoner at Mountjoy, in whose innocence I firmly believe, and for whose reprieve we have memoralised, would you kindly obtain for me permission to see him on next Tuesday. I pledge my honour that I will confine myself to saying a few words of spiritual comfort and consolation and these, if needs be, in the presence of an official'.[24]

It is not known if the Monsignor did visit him on that occasion. All efforts were made for a reprieve up to the evening before the execution. The Lord

20. Irish Independent, February 10, 1921.
21. Conn. Trib., February 26, 1921.
22. ibid, March 12, 1921.
23. Irish Indepentent, March 14, 1921.
24. Conn. Trib., March 12, 1921.

Mayor of Dublin was informed at 6 pm the previous night there was no hope for the condemned men 'as the Government had decided that the law must take its course.'[26]

Just after nine o'clock on Friday 11 March, fifty-six political prisoners were removed from D Wing in Mountjoy jail and taken under heavy guard to Arbour Hill detention barracks. Thomas and five others due to be executed on the same day were then transferred to D wing. Here the condemned cell and execution chamber were situated. The numbers of Auxiliary police and military guarding the jail were increased and machine guns were mounted at 'various points'.

Final Days

The day before the execution, Sunday, saw a huge protest outside the jail. From early that morning, friends and relatives of the condemned men came to visit them and sympathisers gathered at the main entrance. About midday, several hundred women gathered in St Stephen's Green and forming up six deep, they marched to Mountjoy. Prominent members of the American Relief for Ireland watched the procession while another member took photographs outside the jail. Along the route the numbers grew and it was estimated at several thousand when it reached the jail. The rosary was recited in Irish and 'there was a dignity and reverence everywhere which impressed one deeply.'

Friends were allowed to visit the condemned men freely and on leaving were eagerly questioned for news. All were said to be in high spirits, they had attended Mass and received Holy Communion, and the previous nights had sang songs in the cells. 'All were absolutely resigned to their fate'. Many priests visited the men and one, on leaving, commenting on the high spirits of the men, said they had no fear of death. 'Indeed they were like schoolboys preparing for a holiday.'

From four p.m. onwards the crowd increased. They remained outside the prison gates until curfew hour approached, when they dispersed. Mrs Whelan had a long visit with her son on Saturday after which she said, 'You would imagine he was going to a football match, he was in such fine form.' After she had kissed him, he said, 'Mother, if you were all as happy as I am, you would not worry very much. It is well known that I am innocent, and had no knowledge, hand, act or part in the tragedies of the morning of November 21st, and I am reconciled to my fate and prepared to meet my God.' 'He asked to be remembered to his brothers and sisters and father and friends, adding that he would pray for them in the next world'.

On Sunday Mrs Whelan again went to jail, accompanied by two women, one of whom was said to be his 'sweetheart'. He embraced and kissed his mother several times and told her he had given up his hour's recreation in order to sign autographs for friends. Before leaving, Mrs Whelan and the ladies received souvenirs; to his mother and another woman he gave a medal while he gave a keepsake in the shape of a ring to the second woman. This, he told them was 'the happiest day of his life, and he was perfectly prepared to meet his death with a clear conscience. That night, he said, he would sing the old traditional song, 'The Shawl of Galway Grey.'

26. Irish Independent, March 14, 1921.

He embraced his mother and 'bid her a cheery goodbye for the last time at this side of the grave'.

The auxiliary police and wardens declared he was the 'bravest man they had ever met.' A Carmelite priest, Father Devlin, after visiting Thomas said he 'was a magnificent type of young Irishman and a regular attendant and communicant at Whitefriar Street. "I would sooner accuse an infant of murder than Thomas Whelan".' Another priest declared him 'a picture of happiness, bright and jolly, and like a schoolboy about to be relieved from his lessons and start on an enjoyable holiday.'

Mrs Whelan told reporters, 'When all is over I will return to my native Clifden and never see Dublin again. Perhaps it would have been far better if poor Tom had never seen it.' 'It is hard to think that he should have to make the supreme sacrifice for a crime that he had neither knowledge of, hand, act, nor part in, but God's Holy Will be done.'[27]

The Execution

On Monday March 14 1921 the executions were to commence at 6 am. Six men were to be hanged that day, Thomas Whelan (22) and Patrick Moran (27) delcaring their innocence, were to be executed at 6 am. Thomas Bryan (23) and Patrick Doyle (28), both married, were to be executed at seven, and Frank Flood (19) and Bernard Ryan (19) at eight.

A general stoppage of work was called for by the Irish Transport and General Workers Union between the hours of six a.m. and noon. Throughout the morning blinds and shutters were down and business premises kept their doors closed, not only in Dublin but throughout the country, including Clifden. Shortly after five a.m. crowds began to gather outside the prison. As the hour progressed the crowd was estimated to be near forty thousand. The stars were still shining and the air was cold. 'No factory whistle was heard', 'No clang of tram, no roar or rattle of car or motor, no rumble of train — no sound of human activity disturbed the solemn silence that hung heavily over the entire city.'[28]

From every street, great numbers of people moved silently towards the jail. At the gate, statues of the Sacred Heart and Blessed Virgin were placed, surrounded by lights; here Mrs Whelan sat on a chair, protecting herself from the cold morning air with her Connemara shawl. All around her at five-thirty the crowd knelt down on the damp ground and began to recite the rosary in Irish. As six a.m. approached the crowd grew in number and the rosary continued to be recited up to the very last moment. A party of military moved through the kneeling crowd and continued to patrol the area for a considerable time.

Inside the prison, shortly after five a.m., Moran and Whelan attended Mass, celebrated by Canon Waters, prison chaplain, and served by Thomas, the Auxiliary policemen receiving Communion along with their prisoners. After Mass, Ellis the executioner and his assistant approached 'to make the usual preparations before the prisoners would be led to execution.' The men turned to say goodbye to the chaplain, auxiliary policemen and wardens; they then said farewell to one another.

27. Irish Independent, March 14, 1921.
28. ibid, March 15, 1921.

Thomas Whelan, executed March 14, 1921.

*Thomas Whelan, escorted to Court by R.I.C.
and a Black and Tan.*

'They began the procession to the execution chamber, which was situated only a short distance away. Both men walked firmly and fearlessly to the scaffold, where final words of comfort and consolation were uttered by the attendant chaplains.' The executioner attended to the prisoners and both men had their heads covered and 'promptly at 6 o'clock, just as a new dawn was breaking, the bolt was drawn and in the case of Whelan and Moran, the law had taken its course.'

Ryan and Doyle were executed at seven o'clock and Flood and Bryan one hour later. No indication was given to the waiting crowd that the executions were over until eight twenty-five, when the prison gate was opened and a warden nailed a notice on the outside door; the notice read as follows:

'The sentence of the law passed upon
Thomas Whelan and Patrick Moran,
found guilty of murder and
Francis Flood, Patk. Doyle and
Thomas Bryan, Bernard Ryan
found guilty of high treason by levying
war were carried into execution this morning.

By Order.'[29]

The notice was later taken away by a relative of one of the executed men.
At this point Mrs Whelan broke down and gave way to 'heartrending sobs'.

29. ibid.

The crowd again began to pray. Later the relatives left to attend Mass. Masses were celebrated throughout the city for the souls of the six men and tributes and condolences were received from public bodies throughout the country.

In Clifden, Requiem Mass was celebrated by Monsignor McAlpine for the repose of the soul of Thomas Whelan; the church was crowded. Masses were also said in the surrounding districts. Relatives of the men requested their remains be released to them but received no reply.

The remains of the six men were buried the following day, Tuesday at one p.m. within the prison grounds. They were placed as follows: Bryan, Ryan, Whelan, Moran and Doyle. Flood requested his remains be placed next to Kevin Barry's grave. Canon Waters who along with Father McMahon officiated, requested that breast plates bearing the name and RIP be placed on each coffin, but it is not known if this was complied with.

In a letter, written at four-thirty on the morning of his execution, addressed to the Lord Mayor of Dublin and later published in the press, Thomas thanked his lordship for the kindness shown to his mother while in Dublin: 'We were always ready like Irishmen to die for our old cause. I am in the best of spirits now as ever. An Irishman's honour is a great pledge, so like men, we shall meet our doom this morning'. In a statement made by him, he said: 'Give the boys my love. Tell them to follow on and never surrender. Tell them to pray for me, especially "Dev's Own", and I will pray for them. Tell them I am proud to die for Ireland.'[30]

Before leaving for her return journey home, Mrs Whelan wrote to the press, to thank the people of Dublin, particularly those at Ringsend, for their kindness to her during her stay. 'I must say that the military and auxiliaries that I met in Dublin Castle, Kilmainham and Mountjoy were very nice to me, in conveying parcels to and from my boy during his capture'. She went on to thank the Lord Mayor, the Archbishop and Monsignor McAlpine for their efforts to save her son's life. On her last visit to him, her son had requested that she forgive those responsible for taking his life 'as I freely forgive them and all my enemies.' Mrs Whelan declared she was fifty-three years of age and she 'earnestly hoped that before she died she would see Ireland free from such things as courtmartials and English law. She longed to see fulfilled the ideal that Irishmen had long waited and watched for,' 'I hope before many years, not years, but months, not months but weeks, that the sun of freedom will shine on our land.'[31]

However, Mrs Whelan's departure was delayed by the tragic incidents which took place in Clifden following the execution of her son. For her own safety it was thought better that she remain in Dublin, while the town buried its dead and made safe the smouldering remains of fourteen houses, burnt during the sacking of Clifden by the Black and Tans.

30. Irish Independent, March 15, 1921.
31. ibid, March 18, 1921.

CHAPTER IX

'Clifden will remember and so will the RIC'

Shooting of Two R.I.C.

'Two for One'. This was the IRA policy that for every one of their men executed, they would shoot two RIC men.

The shooting of Constable Charles Reynolds and Constable Thomas Sweeney on the streets of Clifden by IRA was seen as retaliation for the execution of Thomas Whelan. The names of the men who carried out the shootings remain to this day a closely guarded secret. However, the events of the night were widely reported in the press and from these reports the following re-construction has been compiled.

On the evening of Wednesday March 16 1921, the RIC strength in Clifden was down to half; a good number were attending the Galway Spring Assizes. That night the evening patrol set our earlier than usual to patrol the streets of the town. At seven thirty four men under the command of Constable Charles Reynolds left the barracks on Main Street. Reynolds was armed with a revolver and ammunition, Constable Thomas Sweeney was armed with a service rifle and fifty rounds of .303 ammunition. The other two Constables were armed with a rifle and shot-gun. The patrol remained together until about nine-forty when they split up into two groups.

Shortly before ten o'clock, two of the constables moved down Main Street and rounded Eddie King's Corner into Market Street; some distance behind followed their colleagues, Reynolds and Sweeney.

As Reynolds and Sweeney neared King's Corner they were approached by three or four men wearing trench-coats. They did not suspect these men but when there was just a few yards distance between them, the approaching men opened fire and both constables fell. Two IRA then came forward and, bending over the bodies, removed their weapons. The other two constables immediately ran to the Market House, opposite King's Corner, to take cover. Three men ran past, firing at them as they did. More fire came from the direction of the Railway Hotel. The constables gave chase almost as far as the Town Hall, but then lost sight of the three men.

They returned to King's Corner to find Constable Reynolds dead and Constable Sweeney badly injured. They immediately went to the barracks for assistance. The Head Constable and his men came into the street and fired several shots; they retrieved the two bodies and returned to the barracks.

Fearing an all-out attack on the barracks, requests for reinforcements were sent to Galway. Telegraph wires were cut but it is believed a message was sent by Marconigram to London and relayed to Galway. Medical assistance was also requested.

A MAP OF CLIFDEN

210

At about ten thirty, Monsignor McAlpine was sent for. On entering the barracks he found 'the two men on the floor. The body of poor Reynolds was still warm and I gave him conditional Absolution, annointing Sweeney.'[1]

Constable Charles Reynolds, aged thirty three, was married with one daughter, just eighteen months old. He had fourteen years service, and was very well liked by the townspeople. A native of Kenagh, County Longford, his remains were transported there for burial on the following Saturday.

Constable Thomas Sweeney was just twenty-four years of age, single and a native of Aughrim, County Galway. He joined the Irish Guards in November 1915 and had an excellent war record but was slightly wounded. After demobilisation he joined the RIC on November 19 1920 and had just arrived in Clifden the January before.

Dr Casey was called and found Constable Sweeney suffering from shock and haemorrhage; he had a wound in the upper part of his left thigh and in his left leg. He was removed to the Workhouse hospital. Constable Sweeney managed to make a statement before becoming unconscious. Later after examination by Dr O'Malley a surgeon from Galway, he was removed to St Bride's Hospital Galway on Thursday afternoon. However, by Friday, gangrene had developed and one leg had to be amputated. Constable Sweeney died of shock and haemorrahge at 7 pm that evening, March 18.

'The Town Ablaze'

In the early hours before dawn on Thursday March 17 1921, St Patrick's Day, Clifden experienced the most horrific night of is history. Never before had blood been shed on the streets, but following the shooting of Constables Reynolds and Sweeney, one civilian was killed, another seriously injured, fourteen houses burnt and several others damaged. The people ran in fear, some to the workhouse, others to the Convent; as their homes blazed and all their personal belongings went up in smoke.

In answer to the call for reinforcements, a special train left Galway for Clifden at twelve-thirty a.m. On board were thirty Black and Tans, with armed men accompanying the driver and the guard. A party of military set out by road. Just before two o'clock, Dr Sandys and Surgeon O'Malley left Galway in Dr Sandys' motor car and arrived at six. Almost immediately after the train bearing the Black and Tans pulled into Clifden Station they set about rousing the citizens. They sought out known associates of Sinn Fein. But as they attempted to gain access to the houses, the men of the house escaped by the rear. In Market Hill Lane (or Up the Arch as it is known locally,) men ran about half dressed or in night attire. The Black and Tans began looting and drinking; as the hours went by they became more and more drunk and began setting fire to the town.

Houses which had been raided several times in the previous months became the targets, but by day-break it became obvious the men were out of control and fears of the whole town catching fire grew.

Among the first to be burnt was a hotel on Main Street owned by Alex McDonnell, but that was not the only loss Mr McDonnell was to suffer that night. At about five fifteen a.m., four or five Black and Tans came around

1. Conn. Trib. March 26, 1921.

Eddie King's Corner into Main Street. What took place in the minutes that followed is not known precisely but according to official statements, made at a military inquiry held in Eglinton Street Police Station on Wednesday March 23 and another held in April: John J. McDonnell left a house on the left of Main Street, he was seen by the group of Tans coming around Eddie King's corner and they called on him to 'halt' but instead he ran down the street. Again they called 'halt' but he continued to run. Two constables then fired, but missed him. John J. then ran across the road towards the smouldering ruins of his father's hotel. As he reached the opposite side a police sergeant and six Black and Tans, in the archway, saw him run past and heard the shouts. They fired, hit him and he fell to the ground. For many hours John J's body lay covered in blood outside Michael Ward's shop — he had been hit in the back of the head — until a doctor passing by saw the body and after examination he had the body removed. The remains were removed to the chapel in the afternoon and buried on Friday at Ardbear. John J. was one of those back from the war; he had served in the Connacht Rangers and was promoted to Sergeant Major in the field. Having come through the horrors of the Great War, after serving King and country, he died on the streets of his home town, shot unnecessarily.

Just before six a.m. Monsignor McAlpine heard knocking at his door, 'For God's sake, Canon, come down — the town is ablaze'. 'I went down to see if I could save anything of poor Clifden. The flames were then far advanced. Willie Clancy's was burning. Alex McDonnell's hotel was reduced to ashes. Crown forces were up and down the street; no one else dared venture abroad. I went round the Square and found that Mr John M. Lyden's and Mr Bartley King's were burning and the forces were engaged in setting fire to Mr M.A. Manning's public house and Mrs Bartley's restaurant.'[2]

At sometime in the night, the home of Thomas Whelan's parents, on the sky road, was searched. They came for his brothers; however they were not to be found and instead their photographs were seized. On finding only the father, grandparents and several children, the Black and Tans refrained from burning the cottage.

The people of the town stayed away until daylight. By then the Auxiliaries arrived and assured them it was safe to return to their homes and that no further interference would take place.

However, day-break did not bring an end to all the horrors of that night. At about eight a.m. while in charge of his brother Patrick's shop on Main Street, Peter Clancy was brutally shot in the head and neck.

A number of Black and Tans came into the public house, which was damaged by an unsuccessful attempt to burn it earlier, and ordered drinks. Then one of them called Peter outside into the yard. Peter later told the courts 'without hesitating I followed him to the yard, on entering which I was struck from behind and knocked against the wall. I then received a bullet, which passed through my throat; this brought me to my hands and knees, and I then received another bullet, which passed through my lower jaw. I fell flat then and received another bullet which chipped some of my teeth. I was then made unconscious.'[3]

When the Black and Tans left, Dr Casey was called for. He found the patient

2. Conn. Trib. March 26, 1921.
3. ibid. October 22, 1921.

collapsed and bleeding heavily. Surgeon O'Malley who was still in the town was sent for and he dressed the wounds and sent him by ambulance to Galway Hospital. Dr O'Malley later described Peter's wounds in court: 'one bullet had passed through the left tonsil and out the right side; another tunnelled through the lower jaw and clipped a bit of the tongue on its way out the opposite side. The third passed through the mouth from side to side, chipping the teeth in its passage.' It was 'nothing short of miraculous that he survived the terrible wounds he received',[4] he said. After a long spell in hospital, Peter did recover but thereafter had great difficulty with speech and eating.

On Friday evening, before news of Constable's Sweeney's death reached the town, after evening Devotions, Monsignor McAlpine spoke of the recent tragedies: 'I never for a moment thought', continued the Monsignor, 'that I would witness such calculated bloodshed or such terrible scenes in Catholic Ireland. My heart goes out in sympathy to the wife of poor Constable Reynolds, who I knew intimately, and who was a splendid type of man.' 'If there was one thing more than another that convinced me that he went before his God, short as was the notice given to him, it is that he was a weekly communicant. The crime by which he lost his life was a pure murder — a dastardly murder — just as was the shooting of poor McDonnell a brutal murder. We have just laid the remains of this innocent boy to rest in Ardbear, nearby the town where no blood has been shed and no violence of this kind known within memory.'

Next day, he told them, the remains of Constable Reynolds would be removed to the mid-day train for burial at his home in Kenagh, County Longford. 'I would take it as a favour and a great tribute of respect to a good man's memory, if the people would attend in large numbers at the funeral.'

'I have known the Clifden people for twenty years and I believe, speaking before God's altar, that I am safe in saying that a Clifden man never had anything to say to these murders, which have brought such suffering and affliction on this peace-loving community.'[5]

Next morning, Saturday, a 'considerable number' of townspeople followed the coffin of Constable Reynolds from St Joseph's Church to the railway station and a large wreath was sent on their behalf. In Galway the coffin of Constable Sweeney, covered with the Union Jack, was brought to the station and the two coffins met. Constable Sweeney was buried at Aughrim, County Galway.

The morning after the burnings slogans appeared on walls. 'Clifden will remember, and so will the RIC' was written across Eddie King's Corner. 'Shoot another member of the RIC and up goes the town'[6] read another. The message was clear. The citizens of the town now began to count costs and a rough estimate was printed in the press.

Compensation

However, it was months before claims came before the courts and even longer before payments received.

In October 1921 Peter Clancy was awarded £2,510.

4. Conn. Trib. October 22 1921.
5. ibid., March 26 1921.
6. ibid.

Mr. John M. Lyden's grocery, bakery and bar £10,250

The house next door owned by Misses King, in which Mr.
Bertie King lives £2,500

Mr. Alec McDonnell's Hotel £6,000

Two houses in Market Hill belonging to Mr. Alec Higgins,
in which his two sisters, the Misses Higgins, school
teachers lived £800

Miss Higgins lost £200

William A. Clancy's licensed house and premises with the
stable adjoining. A horse and two cows were burned to
death in this fire £10,000

Patrick Clancy, his brother, front portion of shop damaged
and goods taken £500

Peter Clancy shot and wounded in the back yard of
Patrick Clancy's House £3,000

Mrs. Bartley's restaurant and the house next door £2,000

Patrick K. Joyce, butcher, house and furniture £2,500

Mrs. M. T. Manning, licensed premises, The Archway £10,250

Bartley King, Draper £7,000

Peter Clancy's licensed premises and grocery,
shop damaged, and goods destroyed £300

Jas. Guilfoyle, a private house about half a mile
west of the town £1,200

Mrs. Matthew Joyce, bootmakers, half a mile
outside the town £1,000

Tom Senior, weaver, a small corrugated iron roofed
house outside the town £300

John Hehir £650

Gerald Stanley £650

Patrick King £110

Mrs. Reynolds and reps. of Const. Sweeney about £7,000

Conn. Trib. March 26 1921.

Mrs Bartley was awarded £375 for personal belongings destroyed.

Patrick King £1,140 for personal belongings.

Bertie King, £1,100 for house and belongings.

Miss Mabel King £240 for personal belongings destroyed.

On January 27 1922 at Oughterard Quarter Sessions the following awards were made:

Mat Joyce £550 for house, livestock and household effects.

Patrick Clancy £660 for shop goods and money taken from the safe. Patrick ran a public house and general store and was in Galway attending the Assizes as a Juror on the night of the 16th. His brother Peter, previously mentioned, was in charge of the premises. 'A considerable quantity of goods were taken away and deliberately destroyed'.[7] Patrick was also an emigrant agent for several lines and produced his emigrant agent's book and bank book to support his claim for £350 cash stolen from his safe.

Another brother William A. Clancy claimed £8,000 compensation for the 'complete destruction of his shop and house, including all the stock and furnishings and livestock consisting of two mares, a foal and two cows which were burned to death. This case was given a long hearing as a list of something like two thousand items of contents was given and scrutinised by the judge. The value of a number of items of furniture was verified by Mr Rutledge an auctioneer. Mr Rutledge had recently gone through William's house and had noticed it was 'over stocked with furniture'. William told the judge he had attended almost all the big auctions in the West, 'his house was more like a furniture shop in Liffey Street than a business shop.'[8] Even his bedroom contained an extra suite of furniture in it.

He also claimed for several old and valuable books in the Irish language to the value of £150. It was explained that he was at one time an Irish teacher in America and a journalist; while there he purchased a number of very expensive books, now out of print. Judgement on this case was reserved until the next Court sitting in Galway.

Alex Higgins, cousin of John J. McDonnell, the murdered man, and brother of the Higgins sisters, well-known schoolteachers at Kingstown school, was awarded £112. Alex was an internee in jail during the time of the burning but his carpentry tools and personal belongings were destroyed with the burning of his uncle's hotel in Main Street.

Several other cases were reserved for the Galway Court. The widow and child of the late Constable Reynolds were awarded £2,434.[9] Mrs Sweeney, mother of Constable Sweeney, was awarded £1,100 and his sister was awarded £100.

P.K. Joyce £1,450 for house and furniture destroyed.

James Guilfoyle, Carpenter, £450 for house on the Sky Road.

Patrick Conroy of Clifden was awarded £320. Patrick's story was pathetic; he had worked for eight years in the mines in England and had come to Clifden on the night of the 16th. He stayed at Mrs Bartley's which was burnt that night and his life savings of £300 together with all his belongings went up in smoke.

Mrs Delia Gallagher, daughter of Mrs Manning, whose house was burnt, was

7. ibid., January 28 1922.
8. Conn. Trib., January 28 1922.
9. Ibid., June 1921

215

awarded £115. Mrs Gallagher's husband was working in England and their savings were burnt in the fire.

John Hehir, saddler, of Clifden, was awarded £625.

Gerald Stanley was awarded £470.

Bartley J. King, Market Square, was awarded £3,524.

It was not until July 1923 that William Clancy's claim was dealt with. He was awarded £3,600 for house, furniture and valuable books.

Kilmilkin Ambush

On Saturday April 23 1921, a patrol of fourteen policemen armed with rifles and bombs, under the command of Detective Inspector Sugrue from Oughterard, left Oughterard at three a.m. They travelled in lorries to Kilmilkin, five miles beyond Maam Cross on the Leenane Road. Their mission was to search the house of Padraic O Maille, M.P. for Galway and Connemara, where it was suspected members of a Flying Column of the IRA were hiding. Padraic O Maille was now an active member of the Connemara Flying Column and his house, Muintireoin, was used as its headquarters.

Near Leenane the patrol left the lorries and continued the journey on bicycles, to escape observation. They cycled in twos, about twenty yards apart. At about five a.m. they turned off the main road and headed towards the house, which was situated about three hundred yards of the main road. As they approached the house, smoke could be seen rising from the chimney; the door opened and closed several times, revealing a light within. Suddenly shots rang out. The men threw themselves off their bikes and tried to take cover wherever possible, most ending up lying up to their waists in a stream which ran along the roadside.

Men poured out of O'Maille's house and took up previously prepared positions on the hills to the rear of the house. 'From here a steady fire was maintained for several hours.' The police later declared the IRA were well armed and equipped with long range rifles and numbered between twenty and thirty. The IRA, however, declared there was just about twenty partially trained and poorly armed volunteers in the house, among them was Padraic O'Maille. The patrol was widely scattered and pinned to the open road with little or no cover, while the IRA were completely concealed in the hills. No retreat was possible. Detective Inspector Sugrue called to his men to reserve ammunition firing only under orders.

The IRA took every precaution to concel their position and even had the elements working for them. As showers of mist and hail rolled down the hillside and concealed its occupants, they opened fire on the road below. One constable told the press:

'Bullets whizzed all around us like hailstones' 'ploughed through the bog and the road, while we lay there inactive except for an occasional opportunity to fire, knowing that if night came without relief we were doomed. When the rain or hailstorm passed, the concentrated fire immediately ceased; not a puff of smoke was to be seen on the hills to indicate the position of our attackers, who then settled down to sniping until another shower or mist came to act as a natural smoke screen on the mountain above our heads.'[10]

10. ibid, April 30, 1921.

Two hours into the ambush, Constable Boylan, who had taken cover behind a low sod fence on the roadside, was hit in the neck and died almost immediately.

Sergeant Hanley received two bullets in the right leg, one below the knee, the other in the thigh. 'So closely was the road watched and so accurate the shooting that the Sergeant's companions were unable to get to him and could only shout words of encouragement and cheer occasionally.' Father Cunningham the curate from Leenane, on hearing there were wounded men on the road secured a car and 'motored into the midst of the fighting.[11] The priest attended to the injured sergeant and tried to get to the body of Constable Boylan but the constant firing prevented him from moving. After several attempts, he was forced to remain crouched behind the car in which he had travelled. At noon a car came along the road, driven by 'Francis Joyce, of Leenane, taking three labouring men to a neighbouring farm for fencing along the road.' Constable Ruttledge, a veteran of the Screeb ambush a fortnight before, lay half immersed in the stream. He crept forward as the car approached and forced the driver at rifle point to stop. He jumped on the running-board as the car bounced forward and commanded the driver to 'Drive like hell'. A hail of bullets came from the hills and firing continued as the car dashed towards Maam. About half a mile from the scene Ruttledge was hit in the left forearm by a long range shot. However, he managed to hold on and at Maam Cross was able to get word to H.Q. in Galway.

R.F. Cruise, the Divisional Commander, mobilised a force of police and auxiliaries and at about one-thirty p.m., seven lorries including an armoured car dashed to the scene. By then the main body of the IRA had retreated into the hills, leaving only a handful of snipers behind. Rapid fire was opened up on the hills from the Vickers and Lewis machine guns the military had brought with them. Soon the snipers too retreated and, when the hills were searched, all the IRA men had vanished.

Behind the house the hills had been well prepared for such an ambush; sod fences were erected with loopholes, ideal for sniper position. They had a clear view of the road while at the same time were entirely concealed.

When the Crown forces entered Mr O'Maille's house they found only Mrs O'Maille, sister-in-law of the M.P., her two young children, an old woman servant and a young girl from a neighbour's house. Mrs O'Maille expressed fears for the safety of her children. After assuring her nothing would happen to them, she was then given enough time to remove some children's clothing and move to a safe distance. Bombs were then placed under the four corners, the roof and flooring of the house and the premises was destroyed. A herd house nearby, from which shots were said to have been fired, was burnt to the ground. Two rifles, two revolvers, a quantity of ammunition, literature and a priest's collar — believed to have been used as a disguise — was said to have been found in the house. Also bedding and beds sufficient to accommodate about forty persons, ample food supplies, including quantities of bacon. Several cattle, horses and sheep were shot during the fighting.

Next day, Sunday, a search of the hills and moors all around revealed nothing; no arrests took place.

11. ibid.

The policemen then returned to Oughterard; they carried with them the remains of Constable Boylan. Aged forty, Constable Boylan, whose wife died just a year before, left behind five children, the oldest just seven years of age. The constable was said to be popular with the people of Oughterard. When his body was taken home that evening, the children came out and the little one, not knowing what had happened, came forward and said 'That is my daddy's bicycle.' 'Where is my daddy?'[12]

Compensation for the children of Constable Boylan was later sought in the courts. They were awarded £600 each, £3,000 in total. His sister May Ellen Boylan was awarded £237.

Constable Ruttledge was awarded £312; this was to include hospital expenses.

Smaller sums were awarded to police who had their bicycles destroyed during the ambush.[13]

An award of £80 was granted to J.B. Walsh of Maamgowna, the owner of the herd house and an award of £95 to John Keane, the herd, for furniture and clothing lost.[14]

As a young boy Padraic O'Maille often heard a legend which told that; among these hills would be fought one of the last battles in a successful struggle for Irish freedom. Padraic recognised this battle fought on April 21 1921 to be the fulfilment of that legend.

The Truce

A truce was called on July 11 1921 and negotiations took place in London between representatives of Dail Eireann and the British Government. On December 6 a Treaty was signed, giving birth to the Irish Free State. The Treaty was brought before the Dail on December 14 but the Dail was deeply divided on its terms, with Arthur Griffith and Michael Collins supporting it and Eamon de Valera and his supporters strongly opposing. Debate and discord spread throughout the country. On January 7 1922 the Dail approved the Treaty by sixty-four votes to fifty seven, with Padraic O'Maille voting in favour. In the months that followed as the British prepared to leave, the Provisional Government set about establishing the Free State.

All workhouses and Union hospitals were ordered to be cleared of inmates. Where possible the inmates were to be transferred to the homes of relatives, taking with them bedding and clothing to the value of £3. Where no bed was available in the home, special permission was sought to allow the inmate take a bed with them.

The Outdoor Relief System was carried on by the District Council until March 31 and the Relieving Officers were maintained until then. On December 8, a stocktake of the contents of the Clifden Workhouse was carried out by Mr Cunningham, Stocktaker for the Executive Committee of the County Council.

By December 9, the majority of the aged inmates, and those not wanted by relatives, were transferred by car to the County Home at Loughrea. These totalled twelve men and three women and were accompanied by the porter, Mr Joyce and Nurse Walsh. Their bedding was sent ahead by rail.

12. Conn. Trib. April 30 1921.
13. ibid., June 25 1921.
14. ibid., January 29 1922.

On that day also, December 9, the IRA took possession of the workhouse together with bedding, clothing, utensils and furniture. The Master, Michael Lavelle, was given leave by the Guardians to vacate his apartments as these were required by the IRA.

By January 21, local press reported the Auxiliaries were expected to move out within a couple of days. In the previous November the Ballyconneely and Carna RIC Barracks were evacuated and their men transferred to Clifden, and a destroyer had to evacuate the Coastguard at Roundstone.

The Connaught Rangers were preparing to move to Dover. 'The regiment have been associated with the Depot at Galway since its establishment and is practically altogether composed of Irishmen who deeply regret this severance of old associations.'[15] The last of the British Forces 'comprising two hundred and sixty men and eighty officers of the RIC evacuated Galway'[16] on Thursday March 9 1922. They left by special train at eleven a.m. and at noon three staff captains of the IRA took over the city's five police stations.

In Clifden, local IRA lined up behind the flag, on the main Galway road and marched into town to take possession of the barracks.

In preparation for the June election, the people began declaring themselves either pro-Treaty or anti-Treaty. In Connemara, very few of the old Flying Column supported the Treaty. Among those who did were Richard (Dick) Joyce, Pat O'Malley and Padraic O'Maille. The rest, along with a large number of Volunteers, supported Eamon de Valera.

In early April, the Derryneed Sean McDermott Sinn Fein Club, Recess, proclaimed their 'desire to place on record our implicit confidence in our representative Padraic O'Maille, that we plight ourselves to give him our fullest and wholehearted support through the forthcoming election, that we approve of his action in supporting the Treaty.'[17]

On Sunday April 9 a pro-Treaty meeting was held in the town, displaying its support for O'Maille and the pro-Treaty side. The meeting was presided over by J.J. Cloherty, County Councillor, and Chairman of Clifden Rural District Council. Mr Cloherty a Roundstone man, told the meeting that if 'he thought the Republic was dead, he would not stand on a Treaty platform, but he believed that the Treaty was the cradle of the Republic.' He went on to say: 'In introducing to them Mr Padraic O'Maille he was introducing to them one of the first Sinn Feiners in Ireland.' Mr O'Maille spoke first in Irish, then in English.

'I am glad that here in Clifden there has been no disturbance of any kind. When I came here from Galway I knew quite well that there would not be interruptions because I know that even though some of my friends of the Flying Column may differ from me, they would not stand for anything in the nature of tyranny. Thank God that in this country at least we are able to keep our heads. There is always room for honest differences of opinion among brother Irishmen but it does not do and the people of Ireland will not put up with it, to have people placing revolvers at the heads of their brothers. We here in Ireland stood against another tyrant, the English Tyrant, we fought the Black and Tan terror and I hope to God that it will never be said of this country at least, that any body of Irishmen will set themselves above the country. You and the

15. Conn. Trib. January 21 1922.
16. ibid., March 11.
17. ibid., April 8.

people of Galway are my masters and the master of my colleague Senator MacNicholls. Before I attended the Dail Eireann meeting I went around and consulted the people and many of my friends in the Volunteers, and the advice I got from them was, support the Treaty, because it was a stopping off ground to reach the final goal'. 'Now my friends, everybody who agrees to have a truce knows in their hearts that we had not power to drive the English enemy out of Ireland, for when the town of Clifden was burnt down twelve months ago, we had only a small force at our command and we were not able to come here and save you from the English enemy; many other towns were burnt down and many a decent Irishman was dragged from his home and shot like a dog on the roadside.' He went on to say: 'they accepted the treaty because they knew it was the best for Ireland and because they knew the position of the Army in Ireland, the economic position, the position of the farmer, shopkeeper and artisan, and every labourer in the country, and they knew that they could not hold out much longer.'

A priest from Saint Jarlath's College, Tuam, Rev. Daniel Corcoran spoke: 'There are constitutional ways of settling differences of opinion; the only means that they obtained in every civilised country and surely they were not going to relapse into savagery and ancient methods, that the people of Ireland would go fighting and killing one another whilst the enemy was laughing behind their backs, and watching an opportunity to march in and wipe them out. Irishmen fighting one with another had led them to slavery to England for the past seven hundred years. The only safe rule was majority rule and he declared that "I tell you that that principle is in danger in Ireland today, because people are setting themselves up against the majority of the people and against the majority of the representatives elected in the last occasion. If the rule of the majority was not allowed to prevail, they had nothing but absolute anarchy. It was for them — the people of Ireland — to vindicate their rights to see that their wishes were accepted."

Henry G. Connolly, Solicitor, then told the meeting: 'by accepting the Treaty they had for the first time in one hundred and twenty years got possession of their country'. With the Treaty, 'they were getting the substance of freedom and it was because they were getting that substance they were accepting the Treaty as the instrument of a better measure of freedom which was bound to come by ordinary evolution of time'.

B.A. Lee, Solicitor, advised the people to 'Take the Treaty if you think it is best in the interest of Parliament and when you have got your arms and ammunition, you can say to England "Clear out — we want you no more".'[18]

Pro-Treaty meetings were held in Roundstone and Cashel at which tributes were paid to the fighting records of men on both sides and 'the good fellowship that prevailed between both parties in County Galway.'[19]

The papers do not report on an anti-Treaty meeting being held in Clifden. However, there was a large meeting held in Oughterard on Sunday April 23. The meeting took place in the Market Square and Mr de Valera was the principal speaker. A large contingent of supporters from Clifden attended. At the conclusion of the meeting, one speaker commented on the peaceful

18. Conn. Trib. April 15 1922.
19. ibid., April 22 1922.

meeting and declared that 'they were all good friends and no matter how things went, they would continue to be good friends'.

But alas this was not to be. With the occupation of the Four Courts in Dublin by the Republicans (anti-Treatyists) on April 13, the rift between the two sides deepened.

In the lead up to the Civil War, the Republicans took action to secure funds and transport. The post offices at Clifden, Ballyconneely and Cleggan were raided on Good Friday 'by undisguised and armed men'. They demanded the proceeds of the dog tax. About £30 was taken from Ballyconneely, but the lady in charge of Clifden 'refused to part with the key of the safe'.[20] However, the men returned next day and obtained the money.

Mr Talbott Clifton, owner of Kylemore House, had his Lancaster car commandeered by Republicans outside his home. While out driving in his Ford car on Thursday April 20, he saw coming towards him his Lancaster, driven by Jack Conneely[a] and occupied by a number of uniformed men. He placed the Ford across the road as a barricade, and armed with a shotgun prepared to ambush the oncoming car. Mr Clifton fired, shooting one of the men, Eugene Gillon in the face and badly wounding him. But the others managed to get away with the car.

Mr Clifton 'left the country after the occurrence.'[21] His house was commandeered. 'It was the first big house I was ever in' Mark O'Malley, veteran Republican and one of its first occupants later recalled. 'There was everything, a bath and blankets, everything that was ever in a house, that man had it.' His only regret was they never unearthed Mr Clifton's guns, which they were sure were hidden somewhere nearby.

The June Election passed off quietly, with about eighty per cent of the people turning out to vote. Padraic O'Maille was re-elected. The year before, in September 1921, he married Eileen Acton of Leegaun, Claddaghduff and upon being made Deputy Speaker of the new Dail, they moved to Dublin.

20. Conn. Trib. April 22 1922.
21. ibid.
    a. Soon after the split Jack Conneely was informed a warrant was issued for his arrest so he joined his companions in the Connemara mountains. He became a Brigadier in the Republican forces. He took part in many battles, among them the Ballinaboy ambush and the re-take of Clifden. Jack rarely spent a night in a bed, preferring to keep on the move, and always carrying a revolver. 'They will never take me alive' he told his young wife Sara. His son Sean was born in 1922, while his father was in the hills. Jack was never captured. After the war he came to live in the town and became a mechanic with Eddie King at the Square.

CHAPTER X

Civil War

The outbreak of Civil War, June 1922, found Connemara in the hands of the Republicans. A number of young men enlisted in the National or Free State Army, while others joined the Republicans, also called Irregulars, in the hills. As previously mentioned, almost all of the Connemara Flying Column went with the anti-Treaty side and from their ranks came the leaders of the 4th Western Division of the Republican Army: Peter McDonnell, O.C., John Kilroy, Vice-O.C., Brigadier Jack Conneely, Commandant Gerald Bartley, Stephen Coyne, Intelligence Officer and Jack Feehan, Quartermaster. The National Headquarters was in Galway city. Former Flying Column members Dick Joyce became a Captain and P. O'Malley became a Commandant. Both men later returned to Clifden and faced their former comrades in battle.

In the early days of the war, life in the town attempted to go on as normal but with the passing of time this proved difficult. The Republicans were tolerated, not supported, by the townspeople but in the sparsely populated hill country they found their home. In the town they occupied the barracks on the Main Street, the workhouse and Sunnybank, a large house situated on a hill north of the town. All petrol was comandeered. Roads were barricaded and trenched, making them impassable. Railway bridges were blown and telegraph lines cut. In an attempt to keep the locals ignorant of the happenings elsewhere in the country, newspapers — particularly the *Irish Independent* — were forbidden. Clifden man James Lee was arrested and detained for a day for possessing a copy of that paper, while Miss Fergus from Roundstone had six copies taken from her and burned; she was warned not to bring such newspapers into the district.

There was an outbreak of fever in the Roundstone area and the local Dispensary Doctor, T. Collins, complained to the Minister for Local Government that he was unable to carry out his duties. 'We are absolutely cut off here, no post or telephone communications, no railway and worst of all, no petrol. I am seriously hindered in the execution of my duties for the want of petrol.'[1] Ambulances attempting to remove patients to Galway Hospital were forced to turn back because of the condition of the roads.

The Republicans demanded all citizens hold permits. This Mongisnor McAlpine flatly refused to comply with. When refused permission to visit a house situated outside the town without a permit, he declared he would 'die by the roadside before he would ask a permit from boys he had baptised.'[2]

As Westport fell to the Free State Army and fears of them pushing on into Connemara grew, the Republicans began burning as they evacuated their barracks. In Oughterard on July 25, the Workhouse and barracks were burnt. That same night the Marconi Station[a] at Derrygimla was set on fire. The Clifden Workhouse was also burned down at this time.

1. Conn. Trib., July 29, 1922.
2. ibid.
a. see Marconi Wireless Station p. 172.

As the Republicans awaited the National Army arrival, there was said to be over twenty barricades of trees and trenches on the main road between Galway and Oughterard, and all by-roads were trenched or barricaded. Communications were poor and the advance of the National Army was not as fast as expected. On August 3, Mr Smith, Captain of the Dun Aengus, arrived in Roundstone with over one hundred sacks of mail. For three weeks now the people had no communication with the outside world and went 'wild with joy'.[3] Two Republicans watched the unloading of the boat but did not interfere; their chief concern was whether the cargo included cigarettes. Richard Berridge of Ballinahinch Castle, arrived and offered to transport two sacks of mail to Toombeola. Captain Barclay arranged for twelve sacks to be taken to the Recess area at his own expense. As the National Army moved further south through Mayo, the number of Republican troops in the town grew. More bridges were blown and more trenches dug. But all this preparation was to no avail; when the National Army did eventually reach Clifden they did not come by road but by sea.

National Army Capture of Clifden

A plan to capture Clifden by sea was devised at Army Headquarters in Galway. Intelligence advised that the Republicans occupied Sunnybank, a dominant position on a hill north of the town and the barracks in the Main Street. Under the command of Colonel-Commandant Austin Brennan, accompanied by Commandant P. O'Malley, one hundred and fifty troops left Galway on Saturday, August 12. The men travelled aboard three large motor trawlers and headed first for Kilronan on the Aran Islands. Strict security was imposed in the city to prevent word reaching the Republicans in Connemara.

The National troops arrived at Kilronan after a stormy passage shortly after seven p.m. and received a warm welcome from the islanders. Here they rested and prepared for the night's journey ahead. One of the 'troopships' was giving trouble and eventually failed. Col-Commandant Brennan enlisted the help of the islanders who agreed to accompany them 'around the dangerous Slyne Head'. By twelve midnight the troops were ready to leave. It was a bitterly cold night and the sea was choppy. They headed north-west and one by one the troops became seasick. Many of them had recently returned from fighting in Limerick and were very experienced men. 'We will make the Charlies pay for this when we get ashore,' they said.

Around Slyne Head it was dark and foggy; the water was coming in over the side of the Aran boat and a little lifeboat which the crew carried was swept away. The experienced islanders voted not to continue so, just fifteen miles from Clifden Quay, they returned to the Aran Islands. They arrived at six a.m. and the men, most of whom had been violently sick, retired to the local hotels. The next day was spent quietly but at two a.m. Monday morning they set sail again.

This time they succeeded in reaching their destination. A column of fifty men under Captain Dundan landed without incident at Mannin Bay, three miles to the south of Clifden. The main body went to Inishturk Island and transferred to boats supplied by local fishermen, 'to whom Col-Commandant Brennan

3. Conn. Trib. July 29 1922.

Commandant Patrick O'Malley.
(1887 — 1971)

Patrick O'Malley was born in 1887 at Attyguidane, outside Cleggan. Educated at the local National School, he joined the R.I.C. and served with them for many years. Horrified by the action of the Black and Tans, he resigned in protest and returned to Cleggan. He immediately joined the Volunteers and became a member of the Connemara Flying Column.

At the outbreak of the Civil War he became a Commandant in the Free State Army. He returned to Connemara as Commander of the garrisons at Clifden and Marconi Station.

After the war, in 1923, Patrick married a Clifden girl Delia Lee, daughter of Bernard Lee* and became a Tax Officer. Patrick and Delia later opened The Magnet Restaurant in Galway city.

* see Lee p.32

Captain Tobias Richard (Dick) Joyce.
(1900 — 1966)

Dick Joyce, a native of Leenane, was a cousin of the politician Padraic O'Maille. At the age of seventeen he joined the Connemara Flying Column, on the same day as his good friend Gerald Bartley.
At the outbreak of the Civil War the friends went their separate ways: Dick became a captain in the Free State Army, Gerald became a commandant in the Republican Army.
   After the war Dick married his cousin, Margaret Joyce*, daughter of James B Joyce. Later they opened a newspaper and tobacconist at the corner of Main Street and Church Hill. Dick died in 1966.

* *see Joyce p.170*

pays a high tribute of praise for their intrepidity and skill.' They were put ashore by the fishermen at Eyrephort, in Kingstown Bay, about five miles north-west of the town at eleven-fifteen p.m. The trek into town in the dark of Monday night/Tuesday morning brought the troops through dangerous hilly ground, ideal for guerilla fighting. The men had been without proper rest now for nights but their 'imperturbability and cheerfulness in the circumstances were marvellous, and they certainly earned the tribute of the Col-Commandant.'

'Captain Fallon was in charge of the advance guard approaching from the North and his men entered Clifden in extended formation at dawn.' To the South, Captain Dundan's mission was to hold some bridges which were known to have been mined, with a guard, to protect the road at the Marconi Station and 'cover the line of possible retreat with a Lewis gun'. Having succeeded in carrying out these, the Captain entered the town simultaneously with the advancing screen from the north. However, word of the attack had reached the Republicans and they began 'to retreat in an easterly and north-easterly direction towards the all-enveloping cover of the Twelve Pins'. Captain Dundan's party encountered some of them crossing the fields, and two were captured with rifles and ammunition.

Captain Fallon opened fire on the town barracks just after six a.m. and continued for twenty minutes in short rapid bursts. 'Then the Captain burst in the barracks door and it was found that the Irregulars had vanished. The place was mined; stores and an ammunition dump, which they apparently had not time to remove, were captured'.

The hill post, Sunnybank, was quickly occupied by Col.-Commandant Brennan and his men 'on whom fire was opened at a range of a thousand yards.' 'This sniper was a plucky soldier for his rifle continued to bark long after the firing elsewhere had ceased, and kept his lone position until the last of the Irregulars had vanished from the scene.'

The fighting trailed away into sniping in the distance and all was over at seven a.m. When the people of the town realised the National troops 'were in their midst' they came out to welcome them and made them breakfast, after which the troops and townspeople attended Mass. During the sermon, Monsignor McAlpine 'bade them a Cead Mile Failte on the part of the long-suffering people'. He told them, 'their hearts were glad, for the National Army — the army of the Irish people — had come to liberate the town from a reign of plunder and arson. He thanked the Irish troops on behalf of the people for what they had done, and on their behalf and on his own, he bade them hearty welcome to the capital of Connemara'.

Col-Commandant Brennan visited the Marconi Station and was assured by the Chief Engineer Mr Matthias, that communications would be restored that evening. (However, this was a vain hope; communications were never restored at the station and it was eventually closed in the 1930's.) Troops garrisoned the station and the town and Commandant O'Malley, Captain Fallon and Lieutenant MacNamara were left in charge.

Republican prisoners, taken during the capture, were held at Clifden and on Thursday removed to Galway under strong military escort. They were: 'Dan Vaughan, Clifden; John Burke, Carna; James Kyne, Goulane, Clifden;

Michael King, Goulane; Patrick Collingham, Derrygimla, Clifden, and John Conroy, Roundstone.[4] John Gavin, one of the Republicans, was said to be seriously wounded but was carried off by his comrades. A number of the National troops were also said to be Connemara men. Col.-Commandant Brennan returned to Galway on Wednesday evening.

The Republicans remained in the hills, returning periodically to snipe at National posts. The mountains of Connemara, the Twelve Bens and Maamturk Mountains, and the Partry mountains of Mayo, were the stronghold of the Republicans. Their leaders had lived here during the Black and Tan war and knew every valley, stream and crevice. In the months that followed, whenever attacks were carried out, snipings or raids, the hills were always a safe sanctuary of retreat. The Republicans made them their home and they became hostile territory for the National troops. Several expeditions were led into the foot of the mountains but these were quickly abandoned when it became obvious that here the Republicans had the upper hand. So instead, garrisons were set up in what were considered key positions along the coast.

The Ballinaboy Ambush

On Wednesday September 13, a patrol on its way to the Marconi Station was ambushed at Ballinaboy Bridge. The patrol, consisting of Commandant O'Malley, Captain Daly, Lieutenant MacNamara and Private McDonagh was delivering a supply of rifles to the garrison there, in a car driven by Lieutenant MacNamara. As they approached Ballinaboy Bridge along a winding dangerous road with high rocks to the left and blind turns on every corner, they motored into a well-planned and carefully laid ambush, said to be the work of

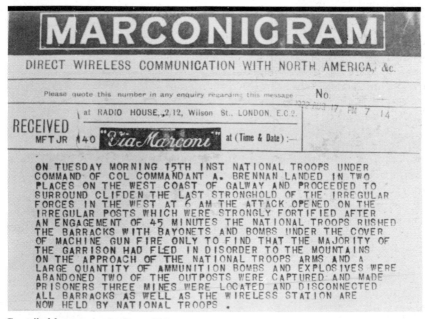

MARCONIGRAM

DIRECT WIRELESS COMMUNICATION WITH NORTH AMERICA, &c.

Please quote this number in any enquiry regarding this message   No.

at RADIO HOUSE, 2,12, Wilson St., LONDON, E.C.2.

RECEIVED
MFT JR 140 Via Marconi at (Time & Date):—

ON TUESDAY MORNING 15TH INST NATIONAL TROOPS UNDER COMMAND OF COL COMMANDANT A. BRENNAN LANDED IN TWO PLACES ON THE WEST COAST OF GALWAY AND PROCEEDED TO SURROUND CLIFDEN THE LAST STRONGHOLD OF THE IRREGULAR FORCES IN THE WEST AT 6 AM THE ATTACK OPENED ON THE IRREGULAR POSTS WHICH WERE STRONGLY FORTIFIED AFTER AN ENGAGEMENT OF 45 MINUTES THE NATIONAL TROOPS RUSHED THE BARRACKS WITH BAYONETS AND BOMBS UNDER THE COVER OF MACHINE GUN FIRE ONLY TO FIND THAT THE MAJORITY OF THE GARRISON HAD FLED IN DISORDER TO THE MOUNTAINS ON THE APPROACH OF THE NATIONAL TROOPS ARMS AND A LARGE QUANTITY OF AMMUNITION BOMBS AND EXPLOSIVES WERE ABANDONED TWO OF THE OUTPOSTS WERE CAPTURED AND MADE PRISONERS THREE MINES WERE LOCATED AND DISCONNECTED ALL BARRACKS AS WELL AS THE WIRELESS STATION ARE NOW HELD BY NATIONAL TROOPS .

4. Compiled from report in Conn. Trib. August 19 1922.

the chief leader of the Republicans in the district, Brigadier Jack Conneely. Nearing the bridge, fire was opened up on them from the rocks above the road by a Thompson machine-gun and rifles. The car slowed down and Commandant O'Malley alighted to take cover. Just then 'a bullet struck his bandolier and cut it in two; it fell upon the footboard, leaving the Commandant with only nine rounds of ammunition in the magazine of his rifle and a few spare rounds in his pocket.' The Commandant took cover on the east side of the road and 'used his ammunition sparingly.'

Meanwhile the car gathered speed and dashed around the corner, coming to a stop behind a gate and some trees. Captain Daley now in charge of the three men, ordered his men to disperse and take cover. Heavy firing followed and after some time the three men managed to get clear and make their way to the Marconi garrison.

Commandant O'Malley, unaware that the three had escaped, was pinned to his position. 'Dominated by about forty riflemen', 'bullets whizzed around his head and cut the turf from his feet'. With only a single round of ammunition left and hope of escape seeming impossible, the Commandant lay still for some time. Presently some Republicans moved forward and as their heads became visible he shot his last cartridge. 'The Commandant now kept vigilant watch with his empty rifle'. Soon, just nine yards off, a head appeared; he saw the Republican leader Brigadier Jack Conneely 'present his rifle take deliberate aim and fire at him.' The bullet went past his head and lodged in the turf. Immediately Commandant O'Malley presented his empty rifle and Brigadier Conneely took cover.

The Republicans then began to surround the Commandant, who attempted to escape. He ran across the road and jumped into the river and 'plunged along for about five yards while bullets cut the leaves.' Again he took to the road and ran in zig-zag fashion, escaping a shower of bullets. At Ardbear he secured a bicycle and 'dashed at full speed to Clifden for reinforcements, breathless, with his empty rifle swung across his shoulder.'[5]

At the barracks the Commandant immediately contacted the Marconi garrison and learned that the three men were safe; Lieutenant MacNamara receiving a slight wound above the right eye. He immediately ordered the officer in charge to extend his men along the south and west of Ballinaboy Bridge. Capt. Dick Joyce with a party of seventeen men set out from Clifden to cover the north-east and eastern districts.

As soon as they left the town, the barracks was shot at by snipers in an attempt to prevent reinforcements reaching the bridge. An immediate comb-out of the hills surrounding Ballinaboy Bridge began. A party of Republicans was seen retreating into the hills. Capt. Joyce followed but the Republicans disappeared into the mountains. An extensive search of the area between Ballinaboy and the main Clifden to Galway road resulted in the capture of four prisoners, some rifles, ammunition and three bombs. The prisoners were: Capt. D. Keane, Roundstone; Lieutenant Salmon, Louisburg, M. Joyce Roundstone, a Quartermaster Lieutenant, and Private W. Conneely, Tollyvoheen, Clifden. The prisoners were held in Clifden and later removed to Galway Jail.

5. Conn. Trib., September 16 1922.

A notice was attached to the church gates throughout Connemara by Republicans, informing the public that from September 30 1922 'All motor cars passing through Connemara, irrespective of who was in them, would be fired on'.[6] The notices were issued by Brigadier Davoren, East Connemara Division.

Sniping attacks on Free State posts continued, as did the blowing up of bridges and trenching of roads. On Friday, October 13, the Recess Hotel, property of the Midland Great Western Railway Company, was burnt to the ground. The staff and guests were given half an hour to evacuate. The hotel was frequented 'principally by the landed gentry as well as English visitors to Ireland.'[7] It had a golf links and excellent fishing facilities.

Glendalough House, situated near Recess Hotel, was also burnt. This had been previously occupied by the Republicans. The burnings were carried out by the Republicans to prevent the National troops billeting there.

On Wednesday, October 18 in the Goulane-Derrylea area, Gerald Bartley and five of his men were captured by National troops from Clifden. Under Commandant O'Malley a search was being made of houses in the area in an effort to track down Commandant Bartley and his men. Commandant Bartley was a 'well-known figure' in the war against the Black and Tans and 'was much sought after' by them. 'He subsequently became a Commander in the Army Executive in the Clifden area and retired from the town with his men upon the entry of the National troops two months ago.'

The two nights previous to the arrest, the garrison at Clifden was attacked by snipers and 'it was suspected, as a result of intelligence received, that Bartley's Flying Column which had been giving the troops some trouble, was in the vicinity'.

On locating Commandant Bartley's whereabouts, the house was surrounded and the Republicans were called upon to surrender. The occupants began to barricade themselves in and prepare for a defence. A Free State description of what happened next went as follows: 'A volley of shots' were fired, 'and becoming convinved of the determination of the troops , Commandant Bartley asked in a loud voice if he surrendered would he be shot outside".

Assured he would not be injured in any way, he emerged 'with his hands above his head, followed by five of his men.'[8] However, in a letter correcting this account, written from Galway Jail on November 6, Commandant Bartley related the following: 'Resistance on my part would have involved the killing of non-combatants whose hospitality we were enjoying. Before I surrendered I stipulated for the safety of the people of the house and also of my comrades. I was assured that they would not be molested.'[9]

Captured with Gerald Bartley[b] were: Captain Paul Conneely, Goulane; Lieutenant John Gavin, Goulane; John King, Omey Island; Thomas Madden, Ballinaboy; Festus Murray, Emlaugh, Cleggan. A Thompson machine-gun was also taken, along with four hundred rounds of ammunition, two rifles and

6. ibid.
7. ibid, October 14, 1922.
8. ibid, October 21, 1922.
9. ibid., November 11, 1922.
b. Gerald's brother Paul was later arrested and both men were held at the Curragh until their release in 1923. Gerald Bartley later represented Galway West in Dail Eireann from 1932 to 1965, holding Cabinet posts in the Ministry for the Gaeltacht and Ministry for Defence.

ammunition, two revolvers with ammunition and some bombs. The prisoners were removed to Galway Jail on Thursday morning and from there were transported to the Curragh, Co. Kildare.

By mid October the National troops had entered Moycullen and Oughterard and every effort was made to restore rail communications throughout the district. By the seventeenth, the first train for three months passed along the line from Galway to Maam Cross. Bridges and torn-up rails were repaired by breakdown gangs. However, the bridges at Recess and Ballinahinch were still wrecked and debris from an overland bridge blocked the track between Maam Cross and Recess.

The advance through Connemara by the Free State suffered a severe set-back at the end of the month when the town was once again taken by the Republicans.

Republicans re-take the town

Clifden stood with roughly one hundred National troops garrisoned in three barracks, number one barracks on Main Street, number two barracks in Sunnybank (situated on a hill north of the town) and a small garrison at the Marconi Station. Although constant sniping attacks were carried out by Republican 'Flying columns' there was nothing to indicate an attack on the scale of the one which took place on Sunday October 29.

The decision to take Clifden was said to have been made just a few days before. The chief reason, it was believed, was to obtain arms and ammunition.

On Saturday night the Republicans, a force of about three hundred and fifty men, approached the town, some by motor but the majority came by sea. The party was made up of men from Kerry, Sligo and Mayo. They brought with them an armoured car, made from engine boiler plates, from a cargo ship captured by the Republicans in Dingle some weeks before. The interior was lined with wool to protect the heads of the occupants. Some local men were used as guides and to guard the outposts, while others took part in the fighting.

The attacking force was said to have 'considerable experience in this class of warfare; they were fine-looking athletic fellows and an officer who had fought all through the European war', said afterwards 'that they were undoubtedly fine soldiers'.[10]

The attack was well planned and organised. On reaching the town, pre-arranged positions were taken up. Houses directly opposite number one barracks were occupied. These were approached from the rear. 'Open up in the name of the Irish Republican Army', they called, knocking on the doors. On gaining entry, they positioned themselves and waited. One of the houses occupied belonged to Michael Lavelle, ex-officer in the Connaught Rangers. During the night, a young Republican told him his name was also Lavelle and that his home was in Mayo. 'My father would go mad if he knew I was here; he is for the other side.' he said.

The Railway Hotel was commandeered, as was the old school building beside Sunnybank, number two barracks. Sniping positions were taken up at vantage points overlooking the barracks; men were positioned even in the belfry of the Catholic Church. The attacks were planned to take place simultaneously at seven a.m.

10. Conn. Trib., December 2, 1922.

View of Railway Station with Sunnybank 'a prominent hill position' in background.
— courtesy National Library.

At six-forty-five a.m. a sergeant of the Guards at Sunnybank went with cans to the water pump situated outside McWilliam's house. He noticed three men standing at the Protestant Church gate and reported the information to his commander on returning. Lieutenant Duffy, in command of twenty-eight men at Sunnybank, dispatched a man to number one barracks to enquire if the three men were from that barracks. Then suddenly 'three Lewis guns were turned on our barracks.'

The firing came from the old school beside them and was joined by rifle fire which opened up all around then. Shots were returned and heavy fire was maintained for some time. At eight o'clock a mine exploded, blowing up the kitchen of the barracks and severely wounding two men. Machine gun fire made it impossible for the men to retreat to safety, so two of their comrades crept on their stomachs into the wreckage and dragged the wounded men clear.

The Republicans now had the advantage; the rubble of the kitchen hid them from the occupants of the barracks.

'The firing of the Republicans continued without a moment's cessation'. One Republican was said to have been hit, a Lewis gunner, but they were well concealed and casualties, if any, were few. At about four p.m. ammunition in the barracks was running low. One Republican, Mark O'Malley, climbed a ladder onto the roof and threw a bomb through the skylight. Suddenly there was a loud explosion and those inside were thrown about as the building began to fall in around them. However, the walls were of the latticed type and there were only minor injuries.

The Republicans then called upon the leader to identify himself. Lieutenant Duffy called back, requesting help for his wounded men. Red Cross men were then sent in to remove the wounded. A Republican leader asked the Lieutenant where the ammunition was; he was led to the kitchen where two

231

hundred rounds were believed to lie in a box under the rubble, but a thorough search revealed nothing. The men were then led off to the school where they were individually searched. The six wounded men were moved to the Railway Hotel from which a red flag flew.

The attack on number one barracks had continued throughout the day. The improvised armoured car arrived almost one hour after the attack began. It moved slowly along the street, passing the barracks. Although intense fire was directed at the slow-moving target, the bullets just hopped off it like hail. The steering appeared to be unsure, and when it reversed it drove into a private house, instead of the barracks as intended. A mine was lowered and the car crept off again. 'A deafening explosion soon followed.' The house was destroyed. The car returned later and blew down the barracks wall.

Three men, Captain Joyce, Corporal Fallon and Private Flaherty rushed from the barracks and threw bombs underneath the car; they returned amid a hail of bullets. Corporal Fallen was wounded in the knee but the others escaped unhurt. The explosion damaged the steering but did little real damage; the crew were unhurt and managed to manoeuvre it up the street and get clear.

All day firing continued, 'the air was filled with the crackling of rifles, the rattle of machine guns, the explosion of mines, the burning of the bombs and the crashing of glass.' Several times the barracks was called upon to surrender but refused. During the afternoon Monsignor McAlpine came onto the street to administer to any in need of his attention.

Following the surrender of number two barracks at four o'clock Corporal Martin, a National soldier, was sent to Commander O'Malley, officer in charge of number one barracks, to ask him to surrender. But the Commandant declared he was 'determined to stick to his post, and if necessary die in the discharge of his duty'.

Under orders of Peter McDonnell, Republican, O.C., Lieutenant Duffy and some of his men then marched, behind a white flag, down the street and in front of the barracks. They called to Commandant O'Malley that Sunnybank had surrendered. They then returned to the schoolhouse. Republicans moved into the house next to the barracks and with pick-axes broke through the adjoining wall. A land mine was thrown in and the building began to burn. Realising the situation was hopeless, Commandant O'Malley surrendered. The time was four-thirty p.m.; the fighting had gone on for nine and a half hours.

The men emerged from the building, covered in grime and almost blinded with smoke. One of the Republican leaders shook the hand of Commandant O'Malley and Captain Dick Joyce as they emerged from the smoking building. The Commandant and the Captain were led away while the remaining soldiers were taken to the schoolhouse on the hill.

While the fighting in the town was at its highest, the garrison at the Marconi station was also under attack. At first the soldiers assumed this was just another sniping attack, and came out to retaliate. They divided into two sections, but quickly realised this was a full scale attack and they were outnumbered.

Fighting continued for several hours, some Republicans were taken prisoner but these had to be released later. A National soldier, Thomas Conneely of Clynagh, Costello, was killed and two others were injured. Two Republicans named Jameson, aged twenty from Ballina, and Morrison, also from Ballina, were killed.

Local people were terror-stricken as the fighting spread into the hills. Two civilians, Conneely and Woods, from Faul, were wounded by stray bullets.

At about five p.m. a party of Republicans accompanied by a National soldier from the town arrived; the soldier called to his comrades to surrender. But a party under Lieutenant Heanue refused and managed to escape with their rifles and made their way to Galway.

In Clifden the Republicans commended the National Army on the 'splendid fight they put up and treated them very kindly.'[11] The Republicans had 'fought a clean fight. The result was inevitable in the circumstances and the National posts gave a good account of themselves.'[12] Later the prisoners were allowed go to different parts of the town and take shelter for the night, all except their former comrades, those two members of the old Flying Column, Commandant P. O'Malley and Capt. Dick Joyce. These men were taken to an island on Killary awaiting transportation to Castlebar. However, it did not take these experienced campaigners long to overpower their guards and escape. Taking their guards with them they made their way through enemy-held country, eventually arriving at their H.Q. in Galway City.

This was the first Sunday in living memory that church services had not taken place. The streets were littered with glass as a result of the explosions; porter and spirits flowed out the doors of Lavelle's pub. Every house in Main Street had its windows and doors shattered. In the houses opposite the barracks not a picture remained on the walls, nor a piece of furniture unscathed. The armoured car was removed and abandoned at Killery. The Republicans did not occupy the town; instead they took up positions in the hills outside and kept watch. Life in the town proceeded normally; for war and occupation were now accepted as normal; telegraph wires were cut, all roads between Oughterard and Clifden were barricaded and no train travelled further than Oughterard. The town was once again cut off from the outside world.

The Republicans visited the town occasionally and acted 'with civility towards the ordinary population'.[13] They took only the food they needed and then in small quantities. It was days before news of the attack reached Galway and weeks before the full account of the fighting was reported in the press.

Following the occupation of Clifden, the National Army in Oughterard strengthened their forces. The newly formed Civil Guards, performed police duty there while the troops patrolled the district.

However the Republicans continued to hold the Connemara mountains and it was felt 'it would take a considerably stronger force than is available to dislodge them.'[14]

Shooting of Padraic O'Maille

In Dublin, the Dail assembled on December 6. The next day General Sean Hales, Speaker of the Dail and Padraic O'Maille, Deputy Speaker, left the Ormond Hotel for the House. They got into a cab and moved off. Almost

11. Compiled from reports in Conn. Trib., November 4 1922.
12. Conn. Trib., December 2 1922.
13. ibid.
14. ibid, November 11, 1922.

immediately gunmen ran out of Capel Street and opened fire. Sean Hales was killed and Padraic O'Maille, struck by ten bullets, was severely wounded; one bullet was lodged close to his spine. Despite his condition however, Padraic was forced to drive the cab to Jervis Street hospital; the cab driver was in a state of shock and unable to proceed. Almost immediately an armed guard was mounted on the hospital.

An all-out assassination campaign against Dail Deputies was feared. Sean Hales was 'a hero of the War for Independence and a staunch Treaty supporter, whose brother Tom was a Irregular leader in Cork.'[15] Padraic O'Maille, because of his strong physique, slowly recovered.

An emergency Cabinet Meeting was called and the decision to execute four imprisoned Republican leaders, Liam Mellowes, Joe McKelvey, Dick Barrett and Rory O'Connor, was reached. On December 8 the four were executed in Mountjoy Jail. The Government declared the executions 'were a reprisal and a solemn warning to those in the conspiracy against public representatives.'[16]

Padraic O'Maille was horrified to hear of the death of his old comrade Liam Mellowes and strongly disapproved of the Government's actions. He wrote to the Mellowes family and received this reply from Mrs Sarah Mellowes and Barney Mellowes, mother and brother of the executed man. 'We know full well that you had neither hand, act or part in planning or being a party to the executions, if so they may be called, of December 8th 1922. We wish that once and for all, idle and slanderous tongues may be stopped and to assure you we feel very sorry that you should have suffered so much.'[17]

The reprisal shooting of the four was regarded by some as an act of vengeance and by others as a demonstration of strong government. Looking at it either way, it appears to have worked in helping to bring about an end to the Civil War.

Some years later Padraic O'Maille[c] met and spoke to one of his attackers. He told the man he felt no animosity towards him and understood he was only carrying out orders.

Republican Round-up

Back in the West, troops were made available for an all-out effort to round up the Republican Western Division in their mountain fastness. A line drawn from Leenane to Maam Cross to Costello divided the opposing forces. East of this line was in the hands of the National Army, west of the line was held by the Republicans. As more and more of the country came under Government control this isolated stronghold of the Republicans became an embarrassment and one which had to be eliminated.

On Monday December 11, Col-Commandant Brennan left Galway for Maam Cross and immediately established a post there. A party of engineers followed in their wake, repairing bridges and roads. By Tuesday evening communications were restored and all through Wednesday night and early

15. J.M. Curran: The Birth of the Irish Free State, 1921-1923. P. 265.
16. Curran p. 266.
17. O'Maille Family Papers.
c. Padraic O'Maille went on to represent Galway in the Dail until 1927. He became a member of the Senate in 1933 until his death on January 19 1946. Padraic's granddaughter Emer Joyce is today a practising solicitor in the town.

Thursday morning reinforcements arrived. Among these were fifty men, 'members of an old Flying Column from County Clare — men who had been through practically every engagement in that county during the Black and Tan regime.' At six a.m. the soldiers 'went forth cheeringly on the big round-up.'

At the same time General Lawlor moved out from Leenane, pushing along to the village of Kilmilken, while another party operated from South Connemara moving northwards. The forces operated in a thin line from North Connemara to South, gradually converging on Clifden. Each section was accompanied by a volunteer guide and without their knowledge of the mountain passes, the streams, lakes and bog, the terrain would have proved impossible to cross.

One of these volunteers, named Joyce, was killed when his group came along the Kilmilken valley in search of food. This, along with attacks on the posts at Moycullen and Oughterard, were the only display of resistance shown by the Republicans throughout the whole operation. As the line moved westwards, and when billets could not be found, the troops spent the night in the open. Food was supplied to the soldiers in the south from Galway daily, the rest lived off supplies supplemented by local communities. At four o'clock on Saturday afternoon, December 16, the Column began converging on Clifden and by two a.m. Sunday morning, they had all arrived.

It was estimated that about fifty to sixty Republicans had left the town just a few hours before their arrival. In their hurry to escape, they dumped their arms and ammunition; in many cases these were hidden to be unearthed later if required. Their leaders advised them to conceal their arms and disperse in ones and twos until this activity had died away. The majority had escaped outside the cordon before it was closed; some escaped by boats, others made for the Partry mountains and other hills in Mayo. A dozen prisoners were captured north of Clifden and about eighteen were picked up in twos and threes in districts to the south. While searching the villages along the coast, a new style in raids was put into effect. Having searched the village, the lorry-load of troops would move off in one direction while another arrived in the opposite direction and began to re-search the village. This system resulted in a number of arrests. General Lawlor and his men doubled back in pursuit of those held up in the Mayo mountains. Not all of the prisoners were named in the press — just the following:

Brigade Adjutant Martin Conneely, Leenane; Val Conneely, Martin Toole, Cleggan, Harry King, Clifden; Michael Ward, Kingstown; John McDonagh, Ardbear, Clifden; Michael Gavin, Goulane; Patrick King, Goulane; J.J. O'Toole, Streamstown. Dispatch Rider; John Reilly, Cleggan; Michael Forde and Michael Staunton, L. Smyth, John Thompson, Peter Kelly, Jas. Kilgalon, Pat Murphy, Thomas Conneely, T. Cavanagh, J. Lynskey, Patrick Murphy.

The people of the town received the National troops with 'general rejoicing'. The armoured car was rescued from Derrynasligaun, at the Killeries, its wheels replaced and driven into town. One officer commented, 'It is of little use to us'. 'But it is safer out of their hands.' The car was now re-named 'The girl we left behind us' and was viewed and examined by the inhabitants with great interest.[18]

18. This description was compiled from reports in the Conn. Trib., December 23 1922.

The troops were billeted in the town and a line of posts were established between the town and Galway. Garrisons were stationed at Recess, Maam Cross, Oughterard and Moycullen. Daily patrols and raiding parties were sent out in all directions and communications re-established. Communications were kept up by lorries mounted with machine-guns. West Connemara was now considered 'free' and was to remain in the hands of the Government troops for the duration of the war. However North Connemara still held a number of Republicans who continued to carry out minor sniping attacks on National posts.

While arrests continued in the South and in the mountains, a number of prisoners were released from Galway Jail on signing the undertaking not to take up arms against the Irish Government. Among those captured in early January 1923 was Maurice Sweeney, Assistant County Surveyor of Galway. Sweeney was captured in Oughterard and it was said that his knowledge as a road surveyor enabled him to make the roads of Connemara effectively impassable; it was under his supervision that the work of obstructing the roads and blowing up the bridges in parts of Connemara was carried out. The condition of the roads was said to be deplorable as, apart from the mining etc., they had not been re-surfaced since before the Black and Tan regime.

Shortly after the Free State take-over of the town, bridges and railway lines were repaired. The first train in seven months arrived in the town. The event created 'mild excitement'. It brought with it a big Christmas mail and a number of people home for the holidays. The station platform was crowded as papers and mail were eagerly snapped up. 'One realised as never before what the cutting off from the outside world meant to the people of Clifden.'[19]

March 10, the press reports fourteen prisoners escaping over the jail wall at Galway. The men, it stated, were principally from the Connemara district. There were at the time in Galway jail, three hundred prisoners guarded by only sixty soldiers.

In April, Civil Guards were taking up positions throughout the country. Their chief occupation appeared to be the seeking out of poteen-makers and the destroying of poteen stills.

May saw local hotels offering attractive rates in an attempt to win back some of its lost custom. May also saw the arrest of the entire Republican 4th Western Divisional Staff; Peter McDonnell, O.C., John Kilroy, Vice-O.C., Stephen Coyne, Intelligence Officer, Jack Feehan, Quartermaster, along with seven others. In a dug-out near where the prisoners were taken, was found one of the largest caches of arms and ammunition yet by troops. This included fifty-six rifles, five hundred bombs, six cwt. of explosives, five hundred shotgun cartridges and large quantities of assorted ammunition, signal rockets, literature and documents. The operation was carried out by troops from Clifden, Recess, Ballinrobe and other centres.[20]

On May 24, Eamon de Valera issued an order telling his men to dump their arms, the fight could no longer go on as there was no possibility of them succeeding. The war was over.

It was many months however before the prisoners were released and

19. Conn. Trib., January 13 1923.
20. ibid, May 26, 1923.

returned home and many years, if yet, before the bitterness and hatred subsided.

Compensation

As always in war, after the smoke has cleared and the dust settled, there comes the day of reckoning. The cost was not only counted in blood, but also in money. The following are some of the awards made by the courts on Tuesday, Wednesday and Thursday, November 6, 7 and 8, 1923. The claims, before Judge Doyle K.G., were for goods and livestock commandeered by the Republicans while in occupation of the town and district, and for property damaged during the many attacks on the town. The number of cases handled on Wednesday was said to be a record, but still more had to be adjourned to the Galway courts, the awards for which are not printed here.

James B. Joyce, Clifden, applied for compensation for eight sheep seized by Republican forces, from his father's lands at Recess, in October 1922 and also for a tin of petrol and a tin of lubrication oil taken in February 1923. The applicant was awarded £16.6.6. P.K. Joyce, Clifden, claimed for meat supplied to the Republicans while in occupation and was awarded £122.2.6d. Bernard Ludden was awarded £11.11.1 for a bicycle taken by armed Republicans. Thomas Connors was awarded £38.0.0d. for sheep taken from his farm near Kylemore. Patrick J. King, Clifden, was awarded £7.0.0d. for shop goods taken. John H. Bourke, Market Street, was awarded £2.10.0d. for goods taken. Patrick McInerney, Clifden, James Sullivan, Mrs Ellen Schley, Clifden, were all awarded compensation for goods taken. Almost every shop in the town was compensated, awards were also made to a good number of shops in Roundstone. Seldom were the amounts claimed queried. Compensation for bicycles taken was also awarded.

Francis H. Taylor, Ballinaboy, Manager of the bar and club at Marconi Station was awarded £32 for cigarettes and other goods taken in August 1922. Burton Torney, Rector of Roundstone on behalf of the Irish Church Mission was awarded £1,150 for the Vicarage, destroyed by fire, on November 8 1922 at Moyrus, Carna. There was a number of claims for sheep taken in the Kylemore district, among them Patrick Conroy, Kylemore Lodge, who was awarded £190 and allowed fifteen shillings expenses for one hundred and twenty sheep. The Republicans had a 'regular butchery'[21] at Kylemore House and delivered the carcasses all over the country.

Towards the end of the year, 1923, the Civil Guard took up residence in the town, using the old R.I.C. barracks. They took over the police duties from the army.

From Famine to Free State

The years from the Famine to the Free State were years of agricultural advancement, expansion of the educational system, commercial awareness and political diversity. They brought many social changes and elevated the participation of the individual in the shaping of his destiny. The 1860's and 70's saw the rise of a well educated middle class. The town produced a number of professional men. These did much to shape the social and political thinking of

21. ibid, November 17, 1923.

Gardai Stationed at Clifden c. 1930

L to R (front): Gardai Kennelly, Morgan, Sergeant Reilly, Gardai Manning and Nolan;
L to R (back): Gardai Sharkey, Carr, An Other, Conway and Gannon.

their day. Just as Alexander Nimmo's roads opened up Connemara in the 1820's, so too, the Galway to Clifden railway assured the continued contribution of foreign influences. However by far the biggest influence on Clifden, in the early part of the twentieth century, was Monsignor McAlpine. Under his direction the town supported the Irish Party. It was branded a pro-British town offering little support to Sinn Fein and the Volunteers. The actions of the Black and Tans; their raids, their lootings and eventual burning of fourteen houses on March 17, 1921, soon changed all that.

In the Civil War the Connemara Flying Column was split. Old comrades, who had once stood back to back to face the enemy, now turned around and aimed their guns at each other. The birth of a Free State opened wounds that would not be healed for generations to come.

West Connemara, which for so long had relied on outside solutions to internal problems, must now display a capacity for self reliance. A change of Government or political attitude could not however, convert the rocks and bogs of Connemara into fertile fields. Here the new state faced the same problem previous Governments had faced; poverty. In October 1923 the local press echoed the comments of the British press down through the generations: 'Stories of distress in the West have become so painfully insistent of late, that one sometimes wonders if they are not exaggerated.'[22]

The following years would teach the people of Connemara that the only solution to this poverty was emigration. The constant drain from the West of its

22. Conn. Trib., October 20, 1923.

young men and women permitted those remaining to subsist with a little less hardship than their forefathers. The remittance from America and the contribution of the old age pension, did much to raise standards in the home. Here there was little employment. For the young girls, it was a choice between shop assistant in the town or domestic service. For the men, it was farm labourer or Council labourer. Millar's tweed mills was the only industry in the town until the 1970's.

Today however, emigration is no longer seen as the only alternative, as more and more young people remain in the district. The rocks and bogs of Connemara have displayed an ability, which may eventually prove to be the salvation of the West: their captivating beauty and broad expanse of colour and charm, have brought the holiday-makers in their thousands. What was once a place of refuge for the wealthy and influential, has today become a haven for European and American alike.

No longer poor, the region has turned to advantage the very objects that once proclaimed it disadvantaged; its landscape. Each small community now works to protect and enhance its uniqueness in an already unique region. Although the homes, guesthouses and hotels are of the highest modern standards, they strive to maintain the Connemara atmosphere of cordiality, comfort and tranquillity.

The efforts put into this industry have not only helped to maintain this region as a place of history and character, but have made the living conditions of the population far superior to those experienced by any previous generation. The benefits are enormous and stretch out, touching almost every home.

However, despite the influx of modern technology, cosmopolitan visitors and the increase in private incomes, the region still produces characters as diverse and interesting as at any previous time. Only time will show if this generation, devoid of a common enemy, is united for the common good or divided for individual gain.

Paul Bartley
1900-1981

Gerald Bartley, T.D.
(1901-1975)

BIBLIOGRAPHY

MAJOR SOURCES.

Andrews, A. The Splendid Pauper. The Story of an Eccentric Victorian Empire Builder, Moreton Frewen. (1968).
Bent, M. A Connemara Family. Unpublished manuscript.
Burkes Landed Gentry of Ireland 1899.
Chief Secetary's Papers. State Papers Office. Dublin Castle.
Curran, J.M. The Birth of the Irish Free State, 1921-1923 (1980).
DeValera, R and Sean O Nuallain. Survey of the Megalithic Tombs of Ireland. (1982).
Finnegan, F. Poverty and Prejudice. A Study of Irish Immigrants in York, 1840-1975.
Galway Archaeological and Historical Society Journal Vol. 2. 1902.
O'Donnell, Rev M. Ecclesiastical and Secular History of Connemara. (1942). Unpublished manuscript.
O'Flaherty, R. A Chorographical Description of West or h-Iar Connaught.
Robinson, The Rt. Hon. Sir Henry. Memories: Wise and Otherwise. (1923).
Ryan, J.H. Paper to Members of the Institute of Engineers of Ireland. May 1. 1901.
Shannon, J.P. Catholic Colonization of the Western Frontier. (1957).
Thornley, D. Isaac Butt and Home Rule.
Thoms Directory.
Villiers-Tuthill, K. History of Clifden 1810-1860. (1981).

Newspapers:
Connaught Champion.
Connaught Telegraph.
Connacht Tribune.
Freeman's Journal.
Galway Express.
Galway Observer.
Galway Vindicator.
Irish Independant.
Irish Times.

OTHER SOURCES

Dalton. History of the Archdiocese of Tuam.
Dangerfield, G. The Damnable Question. A Study of Anglo-Irish Relations.
Lyons, F.S.L. Ireland Since the Famine.
O'Brien, C., Cruise. Parnell and His Party 1880-1922.
O'Hegarty, P.S. A History of Ireland Under the Union 1801-1922.

SPONSORS

Carroll Industries PLC, Dundalk.
Royal Insurance Group, Dublin.
O'Grady's Seafood Restaurant, Clifden.
Gerald Stanley & Son, Clifden.
Hats of Ireland, Castlebar.
The Clifden Bay Hotel, Clifden.
Bank of Ireland, Clifden.
Eamon King Filling Station, Clifden.
Joyce's V.G. Supervalu, Clifden.
Mannion's Victualler, Clifden.
Terrance Sweeney, E. J. King, Clifden.
John J. Ward, Electrical Contractor, Clifden.
Shades Restaurant, Clifden.
Rubber Mountings Ltd., Clifden.
Patrick Pryce, Hardware Merchant, Clifden.
Elizabeth Silcock, Stockbridge, England.
R. J. Connolly & Son, Clifden.

INDEX

E

F

Harris, John, 71.
Harrison, Judge, 42.
Hart, Martin R., 36, 48.
Hazell, Mr, 37, 46.
Hazell, Thomas, 116, 161.
Healy, Archbishop John, D.D., 165.
Healy, Tim, 137.
Heanue, John, 39.
Heanue, Lieut., 233.
Heanue, Thomas, 195.
Heather, Major Dean, 150.
Heather, Edith, 150.
Heather, Eva, 150.
Heather, Rev. George, 150.
Heather, Major George, 150.
Heather, Henrietta (nee Wall), 150.
Heather, Jane, 150.
Heather, Kathleen, 150.
Heather, Medara, 150.
Heather, Walter, 150.
Hehir, John, 214, 216.
Helpson, Mr, 176.
Henry, Mitchell, M.P., 15, 37, 39, 48, 50, 51-
    54, 55, 56, 64-65, 72, 90, 116; opposition to
    Parnell, 61-62; Land Reclamation, 86-88.
Higgins, Alex, 201, 214, 215.
Higgins, Miss, 214.
High Island, 40.
Hill, Mr, 169, 171.
Holberton, Athelstan Leslie, 144, 145.
Holberton, Brian, 144.
Holberton, Evelyn, 141, 144, 145.
Holberton, Frederick, 144, 145.
Holberton, Dr. Henry Nelson, 142.
Holberton, Julia (nee Twining), 140, 141, 142.
Holberton, Nelson, 144.
Holberton, Yves Eric (Nicky), 144, 145.
Holberton, Yvonne, (nee Clementine), 144.
Holleran, Martin, 193.
Homan, Helen Louisa, 131.
Home Rule, 51, 52, 54, 62, 186.
Hussey, Canon, 44-45.

I

Imogene, Gunboat, 62.
Inishturk Island, 223.
Innishannon, 131, 137.
Ireland, Bishop, 79-84.
Irish Church Mission, 43-45, 53, 150, 237.
Irish Party, 51, 152, 159, 167, 168, 171, 186,
    192, 194, 238.
Irish Republican Army, 138, 195, 203, 209,
    216-217, 219, 230.
Irish Republican Brotherhood, 38.
Irish Volunteers see Volunteers.
Irish Volunteers, 186, 195.

Irregulars, 222, 226.
Irwin, Dr., 122n.
Irwin, Rev., 122n.
Irwin, Rev. B.C.B., 122n.

J

Jackson, E.J., 108.
James, Nat, 118.
Jameson, Private, 233.
Jerome, Clara, 134, 135.
Jerome, Jennie, 134.
Jerome, Leonard, 134.
Jerome, Leonie, 134.
Johnston, Mr, 176.
Jones, John C., 39.
Joyce, Emer, 234n.
Joyce family, 35.
Joyce, Francis, 217.
Joyce, Honoria, 23.
Joyce, Honoria, 23, 32.
Joyce, James, 41-42.
Joyce, James B., 130, 167-171, 195, 225, 237.
Joyce, M., 195.
Joyce, M., 228.
Joyce, Mackie & Lougheed, 130, 167.
Joyce, Margaret, 170, 225.
Joyce, Mary, 32, 34.
Joyce, Mrs Mathew, 214.
Joyce, Mattie, 197, 215.
Joyce, Michael (long), 32.
Joyce, Michael (short), 32.
Joyce, Mr, 218.
Joyce (National Soldier), 235.
Joyce, Nora, 32.
Joyce, Pat, 72.
Joyce, Peter, 23, 32.
Joyce, P.K., 167, 195, 214, 215, 237.
Joyce, Redmond, 21.
Joyce, T., 195.
Joyce, Teresa, 24n, 191.
Joyce, Tobias Richard (Dick), 219, 222, 225,
    228, 232, 233.
Joyce, Toby, 167, 171.

K

Keane, John, 153.
Kavanagh, Constable, 69, 71, 75-79.
Keady, Joe, 168n.
Keady, Miss, 193.
Keane, D., 228.
Keane, John, 218.
Keer, Alex S., 39.
Kelly, Michael, 72.
Kelly, Mr, 114.
Kelly, P.J., 163.

Marconi Company, 152, 177, 180, 197.
Marconi, Guglielmo, 172.
Marconi Wireless Station, 35, 148, 172-180, 183, 184, 186, 222, 224, 226, 227, 228, 230, 232, 237.
Marindin, Major, 111.
Martin, Corp., 232.
Martin Estate, 15, 46, 63.
Martin, Richard, 124.
Marwood (executioner), 75.
Mason, Capt., 75.
Mathias, Mr, 180, 226.
Maunfin, 119, 122.
Mellowes, Barney, 234.
Mellowes, Liam, 192, 234.
Mellowes, Sarah, 234.
Mendie, Florrie, 164.
Merlin, Gunboat, 62.
Midland Great Western Railway Company, 92, 93, 94, 96, 98, 99, 102, 105, 202, 229.
Millar's Tweed Mills, 239.
Millard, Mrs Clara, 164, 165.
Millett, Rev., 80.
Minnesota, Connemara Colony in, 79, 81, 82-85.
Mongan, Martin, 195.
Mongan, Mary, 72.
Moran, Patrick, 204, 206, 207, 208.
Morris, Anna Maria (nee Stacy), 148.
Morris, Anthony, 147.
Morris, Anthony, 29, 148.
Morris, Capt. Anthony, 146-147.
Morris, Colonel Anthony, 149.
Morris, Anthony James, 116, 147.
Morris, Catherine, 147.
Morris, Charles, 148.
Morris, Elinor (nee Staunton), 147.
Morris, Elizabeth (nee Hanly), 147.
Morris, James, 146.
Morris, James (Seamus O'Muiris), 148.
Morris, James Anthony, 147.
Morris, James Timothy, 147, 148, 172.
Morris, John, 147.
Morris, Lord, 94.
Morris, Mary, 147.
Morris, William, 147.
Morrison (Republican soldier), 233.
Morrissey, E., 48.
Moumeen, 126.
Moyard, 137, 138.
Moycullen, 99, 101, 108, 114, 230, 235, 236.
Moynihan, Miss, 193.
Moyrus, 46, 237.
Muintireoin, 192, 216.
Muldoon, Dr. P., 32.
Mulkearn, J., 196.
Mullan, John, 77, 78.

Mullarkey, Charles, 48.
Mullarkey, Hubert, 48.
Mullarkey, T., 48.
Munga, 105, 112, 132;
Munga Lodge, 131, 132, 138.
Murphy, H.M.A., 174.
Murphy, James, Q.C., 70-74.
Murphy, Dr. Oliver, 128.
Murphy, Pat, 235.
Murphy, Patrick, 235.
Murphy, Sergeant, 164.
Murray, Festus, 229.
Murray, Henry, 40-42.
Murray, Mr (Moycullen), 114.
Murray, Mr (Oughterard), 114.
Musgrave, Dr. Evelyn (nee Holberton), 141, 144, 145.
Musgrave, Hugh, 123, 145.
Musgrave, Dr John, 145.

N

Nash, Constable, 76, 77.
National Army, 223, 226, 227, 233; take controle, 234-236.
National Volunteers, 186.
Nee, Mr, 199.
Nee, Rev. W., 94.
Nelson, Elizabeth K., 140.
Nicholas, Mr, Solicitor, 196.
Nimmo, Alexander, 11, 86, 238.
Noon, Mrs, 76.
Northcliff, Lord, 184.
Nugent, Rev., 79-80, 81, 84, 85.

O

O'Beirne, Dr., 22.
O'Beirne, Elizabeth (nee Connolly), 22.
O'Brien, Dillon, 81, 83, 84.
O'Brien, Peter, Q.C., 77.
Oceanic, 178.
O'Connell, Rev. W., 156, 168, 204.
O'Connor, Bishop, 79.
O'Connor, Mrs J., 193.
O'Connor, Patrick, 193.
O'Connor, Rory, 234.
O'Farrell, T.D., 70.
O'Flaherty, Donal, 123, 124.
O'Flaherty, Edmond, 124.
O'Flaherty, Margaret, 124.
O'Flaherty, Miss, 180.
O'Flaherty, Morogh, 124.
O'Flaherty, Sir Morogh na Mart, 124.
O'Flaherty, Owen, 124.
O'Flaherty, Thomas, 57.
O'Flaherty, Thomas, 32, 153.

Kathleen Villiers-Tuthill, nee Lavelle, was born and educated in Clifden. A housewife and mother of two sons she now lives with her family in Dublin. Her first book, History of Clifden 1810-1860, was published in 1982.